William Forsythe and the Practice of Choreography

GW00535645

William Forsythe's twenty-year career as director of the Ballett Frankfurt helped to reinvigorate the language of classical ballet. His work today with The Forsythe Company continues to see him lauded as one of the greatest choreographers of the postwar era. He is responsible for challenging fundamental assumptions about choreography and for creating work that draws from such diverse fields as ballet, literature, philosophy, popular culture, higher mathematics, architecture, and cognitive science.

This collection brings together essays from a diverse range of critical voices on ballet and contemporary dance studies, alongside analysis and testament from Forsythe's collaborators and company members, as well as the choreographer himself.

Forsythe's practice is studied in relation to a variety of elements, with essays examining his earlier use of ballet, performance history and development, collaboration, and the uses of music and sound. *William Forsythe and the Practice of Choreography* offers students, scholars, and practitioners of ballet and contemporary dance a fascinating insight into the creative world of this visionary artist.

Steven Spier is Professor and Head of the School of Architecture and Design at the University of Ulster. Previously he was founding president and vice-chancellor of the HafenCity University Hamburg. He is an authority on the work of William Forsythe as well as contemporary European architecture.

William Forsythe and the Practice of Choreography

It Starts From Any Point

Edited by Steven Spier

Routledge
Taylor & Francis Group

LONDON AND NEW YORK

First published 2011
by Routledge
2 Park Square, Milton Park, Abingdon, Oxon OX14 4RN

Simultaneously published in the USA and Canada
by Routledge
270 Madison Avenue, New York, NY 10016

Routledge is an imprint of the Taylor & Francis Group, an informa business

Selection and Editorial Matter © 2011 Steven Spier
Individual Chapters © 2011 the contributors

The right of Steven Spier to be identified as author of the editorial material,
and of the authors for their individual chapters has been asserted, in
accordance with sections 77 and 78 of the Copyright, Designs and Patents
Act 1998.

Typeset in Sabon by
HWA Text and Data Management, London
Printed and bound in Great Britain by
TJ International Ltd, Padstow, Cornwall

All rights reserved. No part of this book may be reprinted or reproduced or
utilised in any form or by any electronic, mechanical, or other means, now
known or hereafter invented, including photocopying and recording, or in
any information storage or retrieval system, without permission in writing
from the publishers.

British Library Cataloguing in Publication Data
A catalogue record for this book is available from the British Library

Library of Congress Cataloging-in-Publication Data
William Forsythe and the practice of choreography / edited by Steven Spier.
        p. cm.
    1. Forsythe, William, 1949–   2. Choreographers–United States
    Biography.   3. Dance teachers–United States–Biography.
    4. Frankfurter Ballett.   I. Spier, Steven.
    GV1785.F66W527 2011
    792.8'2092–dc22   [B] 2010031555

ISBN: 978-0-415-97822-4 (hbk)
ISBN: 978-0-415-97823-1 (pbk)
ISBN: 978-0-203-83223-3 (ebk)

For my parents

Contents

Figures

Contributors

Dana Caspersen is an American artist who has been working in Frankfurt, Germany since 1988, first as a member of the Ballett Frankfurt and now The Forsythe Company. She has contributed to and created numerous works for the stage as a dancer, actress, choreographer, and author. For her work as a performer she was awarded a Bessie for Outstanding Creative Achievement and has been nominated for the Lawrence Olivier Theater Award for Outstanding Achievement in Dance. She is a published poet and essayist, and her written texts have formed the basis for numerous works by William Forsythe.

Senta Driver has been covering Forsythe since 1988, and edited *William Forsythe* in 2000 as vol. 5, number 3 of the journal *Choreography and Dance*. She danced with the Paul Taylor Company from 1967–73, and made dance and other works for her own company, HARRY, from 1975–91. During that time she was a Guggenheim Fellow in 1978, and panelist for numerous public and private funding agencies. She served on the Board and Executive Committee of Dance/USA and spent nine years in the same capacity for the Dance Notation Bureau, finishing in 2006 with a stint as Acting Director of Programs.

William Forsythe is the artistic director of The Forsythe Company, an independent ensemble that he founded in 2004, with the support of the states of Saxony and Hessen, the cities of Dresden and Frankfurt am Main, and private sponsors. The company is based in Dresden and Frankfurt am Main and maintains an extensive international touring schedule. From 1984-2004, Forsythe was director of the Ballett Frankfurt. His most recent works are developed and performed exclusively by The Forsythe Company, while his earlier pieces are prominently featured in the repertoire of virtually every major ballet company in the world. His performance, film, and installation work have been presented in museums and exhibitions worldwide.

Awards received by Forsythe and his ensembles include the New York Dance and Performance Bessie Award (1988, 1998, 2004, and 2007), and

London's Laurence Olivier Award (1992, 1999, and 2009). Forsythe has been conveyed the title of *Commandeur des Arts et Lettres* (1999) by the government of France, and has received the German Distinguished Service Cross (1997), the Wexner Prize (2002), and the Golden Lion at the Venice Dance Biennale (2010). He is an Honorary Fellow at the Laban Centre for Movement and Dance in London and holds an honorary doctorate from the Juilliard School in New York. He was raised in New York.

Mark Franko is Professor of Dance at the University of California, Santa Cruz, and was Valeska Gert Visiting Professor for Dance and Performance at the Institut für Theaterwissenschaft, Freie Universität Berlin in 2008. His publications include: *Excursion for Miracles: Paul Sanasardo, Donya Feuer, and Studio for Dance; The Work of Dance: Labor, Movement, and Identity in the 1930s; Dancing Modernism/Performing Politics* (1996 de la Torre Bueno prize Special Mention); *Dance as Text: Ideologies of the Baroque Body* (Cambridge University Press; Paris: Editions Kargo, 2005; Palermo: L'Epos, 2009); and *The Dancing Body in Renaissance Choreography*. He is editor of *Dance Research Journal*, and edited *Ritual and Event: Interdisciplinary Perspectives*, and co-edited *Acting on the Past: Historical Performance Across the Disciplines*. His choreography has been produced at Lincoln Center Out-of-Doors Festival, the Berlin Werkstatt Festival, The Getty Center, the Montpellier Opera, Toulon Art Museum, and Akademie der Künste (Berlin).

Heidi Gilpin is Chair of European Studies and Associate Professor of performance studies, electronic arts, architectural studies, cultural theory, and multidisciplinary studies in the German Department at Amherst College in Amherst, Massachusetts. Gilpin holds a PhD in Comparative Literature from Harvard University. From 1989–1996 she worked in Frankfurt as *Dramaturg* (conceptual author) for William Forsythe and the Ballett Frankfurt, where they developed strategies of movement research involving architectural principles and interactive technologies. Her book, *Architectures of Disappearance: Movement in Performance, New Media, and Architecture*, and her edited volume of multidisciplinary essays and materials on movement and perception, *The Senses in Motion*, are both forthcoming from the MIT Press.

Chris Salter is an artist, Associate Professor for Computation Arts at Concordia University and researcher at the Hexagram Institute in Montreal. He has collaborated with Peter Sellars, and William Forsythe, and co-founded the collective Sponge, whose works stretched between artistic production, theoretical reflection, and scientific research. Salter's performances, installations, research, and publications have been presented at numerous festivals and conferences around the world, including the Venice Architecture Biennale, Ars Electronica, Exit Festival-

MAC Creteil, V2-Rotterdam, Elektra Festival-Montreal, Dance Theater Workshop, Transmediale, Attakkalari India Biennial and many others. He is the author of *Entangled: Technology and the Transformation of Performance* (MIT Press, 2010).

Gerald Siegmund is Professor for Dance Studies and head of the Master of Arts programme 'Choreography and Performance' at the Justus-Liebig University Giessen. He studied theatre, English, and French literature at the Johann-Wolfgang-Goethe University in Frankfurt/Main. His PhD thesis on *Theatre as Memory* was completed in 1994. In 1998 he joined the staff of the Department of Applied Theatre Studies at the University in Giessen. Between 2005 and 2008 he was professor for Contemporary Theatre at the University of Bern, Switzerland. He is editor of the book *William Forsythe: Denken in Bewegung*, published in 2004 by Henschel Verlag, Berlin. His most recent book *Abwesenheit. Eine performative Ästhetik des Tanzes* was published in 2006.

Steven Spier is a professor and head of the School of Architecture and Design at the University of Ulster in Belfast since 2010. He was the founding president of the HafenCity University Hamburg from 2006–10, and had previously been an academic in universities in Glasgow, London, and Zurich. He is the author of numerous articles in academic journals and magazines in his distinct research areas of choreography as a spatial organisation system; contemporary Swiss architecture (he is the author of *Swiss Made*); and urbanity and culture (he is editor of *Urban Visions*).

Roslyn Sulcas is a dance critic at *The New York Times*, and is currently working on a book about William Forsythe for Farrar, Straus & Giroux. She grew up in Cape Town, South Africa, where she trained as a ballet dancer. After gaining a BA (Hons) and a Masters degree in English literature, she moved to England to study for a PhD. In 1989 she moved to Paris, where she first saw William Forsythe's work, and began to write about dance for *Dance & Dancers* and *Dance Now* in London, *Dance Magazine* in New York, and other publications. In 1996 she moved to New York City, where she still lives.

Freya Vass-Rhee is a doctoral candidate in Dance History and Theory at the University of California, Riverside. Her research interests include cognitive approaches to dance studies, and arts and sciences interdisciplinarity. She is writing her dissertation on the role of perception in the works and working methods of William Forsythe and his ensemble. A former dancer, ballet mistress, teacher, and choreographer in Europe and the USA, she currently works for The Forsythe Company as Dramaturgical and Production Assistant.

Acknowledgements

A book always requires the help and support of many people, but as an architect who writes on Forsythe's work I am more indebted than most authors. David Dunster, also an architect, first suggested that I write about Forsythe's work in 1996, which started me on a journey. I am also indebted to people from dance, who have introduced me to their world and insisted that my insights were worthwhile. These include Bill Forsythe and Dana Caspersen, who have made me feel like family. Senta Driver was hugely encouraging when I was just starting to write about Forsythe's work. Ros Sulcas has been an inspiration for her mastery and insights into Forsythe's work and has become a dear friend. Ann Nugent was prescient about Forsythe's Ballett Frankfurt work. I have enjoyed many discussions, meals and laughs with Kathryn Bennetts, now director of the Royal Ballet of Flanders, whom I met when she was with the Ballett Frankfurt. Dorsey Bushnell, Urs Frey, and Mechthild Ruhl, all once with the Ballett Frankfurt, have been friendly and supportive. I am grateful to be a director of Scottish Ballet, which has been an education in many things. My late education in choreography and ballet was indulged and supported by too many to name but who hopefully know how thankful I am.

I am grateful for two research grants that gave my fledgling work impetus. One was a small grant from the then Arts and Humanities Research Board of the United Kingdom; the second was the surprising support of a Visiting Research Fellowship by the Caledonian Research Fund of the Royal Society of Edinburgh. This allowed me to immerse myself again in my work on Forsythe after completing my book *Swiss Made* by spending six months in Venice at the IUAV. It was there that I became friends with the important dance historian Susy Franco and her husband Shaul Bassi. Lastly I want to thank all the contributors and my editor, Ben Piggott, and Niall Slater for their work and most of all for their patience.

Steven Spier, Glasgow

Credits

'Njinksy's heir: a classical company leads modern dance' was originally published in Senta Driver (ed.), *Choreography and Dance* (Special Issue on William Forsythe), (2000, vol. 5 no. 3: 1–7). It is reprinted with kind permission of Taylor and Francis.

'Aberrations of gravity' by Heidi Gilpin was originally published in *ANY: Architecture New York*, a journal of architecture, philosophy, and cultural criticism, in a special issue on 'Lightness'. John Rajchman and Greg Lynn (eds) *ANY: Architecture New York*, no. 5 (March 1994, pp. 50–5). It is reprinted with kind permission of the author.

'The space of memory: William Forsythe's ballets', was originally published as 'Gedächtnisraum: Die Ballette William Forsythes', in Gabriele Klein and Christa Zipprich (eds), *Tanz Theorie Text, Jahrbuch Tanzforschung 12*, (pp. 397–411, Hamburg: LIT Verlag, 2002). It is reprinted with kind permission of Professor Gabriele Klein. The translation is by the author.

'Choreographic objects' is a slightly modified version of an article of the same title first published in Daniel Birnbaum, William Forsythe and Markus Weisbeck, *Suspense* (Zurich: JRP | Ringier Kunstverlag AG, 2008). It is reprinted with kind permission of the author.

'Inside the knot that two bodies make' was originally published in *Dance Research Journal* (Summer 2007, vol. 39 no. 1: 49–59). It is reprinted with kind permission of the author.

Part one of 'Watching the Ballett Frankfurt, 1988–2009' was originally published as 'Watching from Paris: 1988–1998' in Senta Driver (ed.) *Choreography and Dance* (Special Issue on William Forsythe), (2000, vol. 5 no. 3, pp. 87–101). It is reprinted with kind permission of Taylor and Francis.

Every effort has been made to seek permission to reproduce copyright material before the book went to press. If any proper acknowledgement has not been made, we would invite copyright holders to inform us of the oversight.

Introduction

The practice of choreography

Steven Spier

> [Forsythe and his collaborators] certainly taught me and our production team to be unsentimental about good ideas.
>
> Michael Morris of Artangel on the development of *White Bouncy Castle*

In his 'An Essay on Tolstoy's View of History'[1] (1953) Isaiah Berlin famously quotes the ancient Greek poet Archilochus that, 'The fox knows many things, but the hedgehog knows one big thing', to develop a taxonomy of writers and thinkers. Hedgehogs relate everything to a single central vision or organising principle while foxes are:

> those who pursue many ends, often unrelated and even contradictory, connected, if at all, only in some de facto way … related to no moral or aesthetic principle. These last lead lives, perform acts and entertain ideas that are centrifugal rather than centripetal; their thought is scattered or diffused, moving on many levels, seizing upon the essence of a vast variety of experience and objects.

Admitting that this characterisation is an over-simplification while clearly relishing the parlour game, he argues that it can be a useful starting point for investigation. Incidentally, Shakespeare, Aristotle, Montaigne, Erasmus, Molière, Goethe, Pushkin, Balzac, and Joyce are all foxes.

William Forsythe has been working as a choreographer since he made the duet *Urlicht* (1976) for the Stuttgart Ballet while a dancer with them. In a prolific career he has become one of the most important artists working in any medium today. His career shows an unflinching, almost reckless intellectual curiosity and a genius for making it a catalyst for riveting, challenging, and often entertaining works that are increasingly hard to categorise since they can incorporate speech, film, video, props, music, and dance.

Forsythe's choreographies for the Stuttgart Ballet and other companies over eight years lent him a reputation for pushing hard at the artistic conventions of ballet, including its movement vocabulary, its staging, and its own sanctimonious atmosphere. In 1984 he became artistic director of the then provincial ballet company in Frankfurt, which he would lead for 20 years as the Ballett Frankfurt. Some early critics mistook Forsythe's investigations of ballet, which fascinated him as a system that lends itself to multiple analyses, as an attack. In fact, he saved ballet from itself by demanding it deal with the same influences and issues that every other contemporary art form did. (This could only be considered radical from within the conservative world of ballet.) With access to a huge stage with corresponding technical resources and staff in Frankfurt he systematically interrogated every aspect of ballet, from staging – music, lighting, costumes, and who gets to see what – to authorship, content, and the balletic body itself. His interrogation of the balletic body extended the vocabulary of dance beyond that of ballet and led to a distinctive movement vocabulary. It was thrilling to experience him rejuvenating an art form that had become ossified. Anyone who saw performances at the Frankfurt Opera House could only marvel at how he had engaged a huge, young audience in his quest and their delight in his complex choreographic thinking, artistic daring, and theatrical force.

The world of ballet had never seen such an intellectual in its midst, nor since Balanchine such a radical theatrical language and movement vocabulary. The Ballett Frankfurt was soon sought after by theatres internationally and became a destination for adventurous dancers. Major ballet companies everywhere wanted his work in their repertoire. But the historic, ideological denigration of the body in motion and the conservative nature of the ballet world meant his work was derided as well as embraced. The United States of America especially struggled, curiously seeing the American-born Forsythe as a prodigal son. Other critics, particularly in Europe, realised early on what is now unanimously accepted: that his work revitalised ballet. Drawing on such diverse fields as ballet, music, literature, philosophy, popular culture, geometry, higher mathematics, and cognitive science, amongst others, he opened up possibilities for working that the next generation of choreographers would embrace.

Forsythe's career with the Ballett Frankfurt would alone justify the global accolades and academic attention he has garnered, but after 20 years leading the Ballett Frankfurt he left and founded the much smaller The Forsythe Company. The attempt by the city of Frankfurt to close by far the most daring and innovative ballet company in the world met with international outrage and was seen as an act of vandalism. The city did reopen negotiations but Forsythe decided to leave at the end of his contract. The dance world mourned but Forsythe was suddenly freed from the obligations of running a large, municipal ballet company and so could pursue his work uncompromisingly. While the work of the Forsythe Company certainly does not look like that of the Ballett Frankfurt, it does actually continue Forsythe's investigation of the question of choreography. Or to put it another way, the current work sets Forsythe's earlier operations on ballet in the larger context of his investigations of what choreography is. It is now clear that his body of work has been a continual exploration of choreography itself.

Forsythe's early biography foreshadows the development of work that is physically engaging and intellectually challenging. He was born in New York City in 1949, and grew up in suburban Long Island, where the only classical ballet he encountered was a single lecture-demonstration by the New York City Ballet. He recalls always dancing, at home and in high school, and choreographing musical comedies for his fellow students. Indeed, he has a unique kinetic connection to the world that has clearly influenced his choreography. He entered Jacksonville University in Florida in 1967 declaring a double major in drama and art history. While there he expanded his studies to include his first formal classes in modern dance. At the same time he studied ballet and performed with a regional company under the direction of Nolan Dingman. Forsythe left Jacksonville in 1969 to begin full-time classical training in New York at the Joffrey Ballet School and soon thereafter joined the Joffrey corps. More importantly for his own work he spent most nights watching the New York City Ballet and thus studying Balanchine. He joined the Stuttgart Ballet in 1973 in the last group auditioned by its artistic director John Cranko.

Forsythe's work has been thrillingly diverse. It is a body of research conducted through the practice of choreography investigating the most fundamental questions of art. He has come so far as to ask, 'Is it possible for choreography to generate autonomous expressions of its principals, a choreographic object, without the body?'. Forsythe has thus reached the point of the greatest of the fox-like artists, of fundamentally questioning the supposed precepts of his own medium. In retrospect this seems inevitable. Forsythe has always shown an insatiable and awesome intellectual curiosity and an unsentimentality about good ideas. His work is palpably searching, which helps explain why he is not only renowned in the dance world but also amongst people not necessarily interested in dance or even choreography. He is perhaps, like Berlin's Tolstoy, a hedgehog who acts like a fox.

Note

1 'The Hedgehog and the Fox. An Essay on Tolstoy's View of History' in Henry Hardy and Roger Hausheer (eds.), *The Proper Study of Mankind*, New York: Farrar, Straus and Giroux, 1998 pp. 436–498.

1 Watching the Ballett Frankfurt, 1988–2009

Roslyn Sulcas

Watching from Paris: 1988–1998

I first saw a ballet by William Forsythe in 1988, when the San Francisco Ballet brought *New Sleep,* commissioned a year previously, on its tour to Paris. I can still remember my sensation of mixed shock and excitement as shiny black-clad dancers with slashing arms picked their way on pointe along diagonals of light while Thom Willems's music pounded and wailed. It was certainly ballet. Bravura pas de deux and counterpointed ensemble work flashed before my eyes, but in such a radically new context that I could scarcely believe what I was seeing: ballet without quotation marks around the word, as much a part of the contemporary world as film or architecture or quantum physics.

In fact, Forsythe was scarcely unknown at the time. If I had been in France a few years earlier, I might have seen his *France/Dance,* which Rudolf Nureyev had commissioned for the Paris Opera Ballet in 1983. And just one year previously, his *In the Middle, Somewhat Elevated,* to music by Willems, also choreographed for the Paris company, had made of the American-born choreographer a sudden phenomenon – at least in Europe, where he had been working since 1973. But when I saw *New Sleep,* I didn't know that the Paris critics had hailed Forsythe as a new Balanchine, nor anything else about him. I simply knew that after years of feeling simultaneously bored by, yet still drawn to ballet, I had seen something that made me want to renew my connection to the art.

In many ways, this article is a direct outcome of that first viewing of *New Sleep,* since it was wanting to write about Forsythe's work that led me to a subsequent career as a journalist. Over the decade that has passed since that evening at the Théâtre des Champs-Elysées, I have watched Forsythe's Ballett Frankfurt and his work at every possible opportunity, mostly in Paris, where, serendipitously for me, the company had a second residence at the Théâtre du Châtelet from 1990 to 1998. I have been lucky enough to see almost everything that he has created during this time, as well as having had the opportunity of talking to him frequently about his work. An overview is nonetheless a daunting prospect. Contrary to some critical opinion, Forsythe's work defies ready categorization. It ranges from neo-classical pieces in a recognizable

Balanchinian tradition to wildly theatrical works that incorporate flamboyant mixes of speech, film, video, props, music, dance, and, often, complex technology. All of the work exhibits his genius for lighting. And in addition to the theatrical gifts that are so uniquely his own, Forsythe has extended the vocabulary of dance in a way that goes well beyond the world of ballet, even as he has radically affected the possibilities of that form.

I will touch on a few features of Forsythe's work that appear to me to be central to what he does, rather than provide a chronological overview or discuss a particular aspect in detail. In fact, thinking about how to approach his work made it clear that while there is certainly a choreographic elaboration to be seen over the last ten years, his work shows surprising consistency in many respects: as a choreographer he seems to have been born full-grown, with a distinctive physical style, compositional sense, and theatrical vision at the outset; even if all of these qualities have become ever more articulated as his craft has evolved.

As difficult as it might be to define or describe Forsythe's *oeuvre*, one element nonetheless seems clear to me: that his relationship to ballet is the cornerstone of his work, no matter how far from its precepts he might appear to roam. In earlier works like *Artifact* or *In the Middle, Somewhat Elevated*, the tension between academic forms and those forms pushed to their extremes is explicit. In more recent pieces like *Firstext, Sleepers Guts, Hypothetical Stream II* or *Small Void*, the slippery, dislocated, densely coordinated movement style may initially appear to have little to do with ballet's formal positions and clear lines, but his dancers' classically trained bodies hold that clarity and articulation within the movement, keeping ballet as a shimmering, elusive physical presence reference point to which he constantly returns.

Related to this is a second element that is consistently present in Forsythe's work: a sense of inclusivity. Judging from accounts of his first full-length piece, *Orpheus* (made for the Stuttgart Ballet, of which he was then a member), Forsythe seems always to have believed that when making a ballet anything was possible, both technically and conceptually. This is a simple idea, but an enormous one. It means that nothing – whether in another field like geography or mathematics or mythology, or the history of dance itself, is out of bounds in the creative process and onstage. Antony Rizzi, a dancer and ballet-master with Ballett Frankfurt who has choreographed several works of his own, once put it simply to me: 'The most important thing that Billy taught me', he said, 'is that anything can go with anything'. This is not to do with references or sources of ideas (many of which often appear in company programs, and can engender either delight or hostility because this appears 'intellectual') but to do with the way in which Forsythe refuses to keep the domain of ballet away from other domains. It is a point illustrated in a small way by the incongruously unballetic title of Forsythe's *Herman Schmerman,* a phrase taken from a Steve Martin film which now seems perfect for the ballet's insouciant divertissement charm because the choreographic universe has expanded to incorporate it.

A third element that is clear in Forsythe's choreography is that the way it looks comes, more obviously than is the case with most choreographers, from his own, very specific kinetic connection to the world. In interviews he has talked about 'always dancing' at home, well before he took formal lessons; watching him work, it is clear that he is an instinctively physical person, able to pick up, absorb, and transform movement into a personal idiom, in an uncanny, instinctive, and nearly instantaneous manner. The idiom is fluid, polychromatic, and innately musical, with movement appearing to be generated by the body's own weight and rhythms. Most notably, Forsythe always gives movement marked dimensionality: no step is ever a flat shape in space; it is always a complex volumetric form, existing in its own time.

But what is in fact most notable about the broad configurations for his oeuvre is that theatrical imagination always marks the pure-dance pieces, whether in the unspoken rivalries that underpin the heart-thumping, off-balance extensions of the *In the Middle, Somewhat Elevated*, the friendly, jazzy teammanship of *The Second Detail*, or the heart-wrenching dissolving movement that speaks silently of death in *Quintett*. And choreographic inventiveness always marks the dramatic works; the scrabbling, frantic motions of Part I of *Alien/a(c)tion*; the sweeping grace of *Slingerland*; the buckling, shadowy movement that gives corporeal expression to the hallucinatory dream world of *The Loss of Small Detail*. In all of these, Forsythe shows one of the most important aspects of his art: the ability to create a unified theatrical universe, expressed in part by his choreography, but also through an instinctive capacity to edit, structure, and pace a work. (This is very evident when watching him in the process of making a ballet: on a number of occasions, I have witnessed him change a piece entirely by restructuring and often discarding many of its elements, to immediately greater effect. It always seems like magic, which, like all art at its best, is just what it is.)

This theatrical ability is most apparent in Forsythe's full-length ballets, where structure, rhythm, and an imaginative world have ample space to reveal themselves. Two of the most interesting evening-length works, *Slingerland* and *Limb's Theorem*, were completed in the same year, when I first saw them. *Slingerland,* which I only saw a few times during that season, and which is (to my personal regret) no longer in the repertoire, remains for me one of Forsythe's most poetic and magical ballets, with its post-apocalyptic world of scattered stones, its supernatural fairies of the corps de ballet in tutus that look like crisp, curved potato chips, its Beckettian tramps, and passages in which individuals suspended on harnesses achieve the weightless dream of the dancer, yet float (to mysterious music by Gavin Bryars) in vulnerable limbo, unable to dance without gravity. The brilliant *Limb's Theorem*, on the other hand, offers an architectural black and white world in which the dancers are energy-charged atoms in ever-changing configurations of form and matter, bursting into the space like eruptions from the unconscious, infectiously responsive to the light and sound that shape their world.

In both ballets, however, Forsythe demonstrates how ingeniously he is able to shape a work visually and structurally; both ballets are constructed so that different positions in the theatre offer different content, and almost no seat allows a full vantage point. In *Limb's Theorem* in particular, the full extent of the off-stage is used. Dancers leaping up against the walls, or a man and woman weaving between long propped-up sticks, and then knocking them over, can only be seen from one side of the auditorium. Both ballets, too, feature architectural forms on stage which frame or shape the dance, and which sometimes seem to change or proliferate as objects may in dreams. (The ability to evoke a dream-like universe in which things have their own bizarre logic and reality is one of Forsythe's most compelling talents.) Both ballets are also notable for the way in which they make the lighting, created by Forsythe, as integral to the choreography as are the steps. Exploding and contracting the space, filtering across the stage in uneven and transient shafts, bathing the dancers in a concentrated glare or obscuring them with deepening shadows that intensify the ephemeral beauty of the movement, lighting in Forsythe's hands, in *Limb's Theorem* in particular, is suddenly an explicit, onstage element in the visual composition of the work. (The influence of this on contemporary dance choreographers in France was almost immediately perceptible; it is still odd to me not to see it in the United States of America, even if it can be a relief to be spared the more excessive reflections of Forsythe's work that are sometimes, wrongly, represented as Forsythean style).

All of these elements – theatrical imagination, formal mastery, and lighting as a structural presence – are visible in one of the first ballets that Forsythe made for Ballett Frankfurt after taking up the position of director in 1984. *Artifact*, which is still in the company's repertoire, in many ways remains a paradigmatic work. Forsythe showed that he was not simply working with ballet technique in innovative ways, but was also intensely aware of its history as an art form and its potential to go beyond that history. A four-part, full-evening work to piano music by Eva Crossman-Hecht, J.S. Bach, and a sound collage by Forsythe himself, the ballet is centred around three characters: 'Woman in Historical Costume', 'Person with Megaphone', and a ghostly all-over grey 'Other Person', who move like figures from dreams amidst a large corps de ballet of beautifully symmetrical lines and formations. Using a limited range of word choices (I/You, He/She/They, Always/Never, Remember/Forget; See, Hear, Think, Say, Do; Rocks, Dirt, Sand, Soot, Dust), the woman creates apparently endless narratives, starting and stopping the music and the dance by clapping her hands like a repetiteur, while the man with the megaphone and the ghost attempt to communicate by means of different hand and arm signals that are copied by the other dancers at various points; repetitive ensemble sequences such as variations upon *tendu* with *épaulement*, a recurring motif in Forsythe's work to this day, and the arbitrariness and restrictiveness of the text seem analogous to the combinations of steps performed by the dancers.

Sweeping through an extraordinary range of group and individual formations while the lighting renders the dancers successively present and unreal, *Artifact* sometimes seems like a huge dance processor, chopping up and spitting out bits of Petipa ('More imperial', I once heard Forsythe tell the female dancers in rehearsal as they moved in a paired courtly procession down to the front of the stage), Balanchine, Laban, and Bausch. But the ballet is uniquely Forsythean in demonstrating everything that dance had thought it could do in its short theatrical life, and then more. In the pure-dance, second part of the work, to Bach's Chaconne from Partita No. 2 in D minor for solo violin, two couples surge unexpectedly from the lines of dancers at the sides and back of the stage, performing simultaneous pas de deux of breathtaking beauty which are brutally interrupted several times by the curtain crashing down (and, lined with wooden battens, it really does crash).

It's easy to see this strategy as pure provocation – when you first see the work, it is nerve-wracking. (Has something gone wrong? Is someone hurt? What is the audience supposed to do?) But the uninterrupted flow of the gorgeous, melancholy violin, and the renewed vision, flooded with golden light, that the ballet offers each time the curtain goes back up to reveal the dancers, still moving through another exquisite formation, takes Forsythe's device well beyond the realm of the sensational. And although *Artifact* makes central the way dance works on stage in relation to the other components of theatrical experience and illusion (lighting, framing, the handling of expectations), it has never seemed to me that the ballet is about this in a purely intellectual way. What Part II of the ballet does do, however, is to provide an early and perfect illustration of a duality that Forsythe juggles with through much of his work: the desire for and capacity to attain beauty, and the resistance to settling for beauty.

This tension is also central to another Forsythe ballet that remains emblematic in his repertoire, the hour-long, complex *Die Befragung des Robert Scott*, made two years after *Artifact*. The ambiguities and impossibilities of perfection, or completion, the seeds of dissolution in the dancing body, are contained in a series of solos based on improvisational techniques that Forsythe had been working on with the company. In *Robert Scott*, the movement takes on a new, particularized quality as the dancers focus on making detailed connections between body parts, their ballet-trained limbs stretching and extending in familiar fashion, then mutating into complex, hard-to-read configurations. Perhaps for the first time, Forsythe saw that he could actually develop a physical language of his own. The working idea for *Robert Scott*, he later said, was 'losing your point of orientation', and he did this well enough also to find a new one. The physical explorations in *Robert Scott* that had dancers using their bodies in a newly conceived way to create movement set Forsythe (and his dancers) on a choreographic path that he and they had already begun to explore in other ways. They began spending rehearsal time not just making steps, but also talking, drawing, bringing their lives into the dance; not unusual techniques for many contemporary dance companies, but unheard of for a ballet troupe. What is already visible in *Artifact* – that movement could be question rather than answer, even as it momentarily answers to a longing for perfection – is explicitly articulated in *Robert Scott*.

Die Befragung des Robert Scott, followed by *The Vile Parody of Address*, then *Slingerland* and *Limb's Theorem,* offered the Frankfurt dancers chances to explore the liquid, seamless geometries of movement that they could make by applying new techniques that Forsythe was developing in the course of creating these pieces, while continuing to choreograph more balletic pieces like *In the Middle, Somewhat Elevated, New Sleep,* and *Behind the China Dogs* for other companies. The most important of these techniques was 'reading externally', which Forsythe describes as 'using your perception, your sight, or sense of touch, to read events ... you could look at your finger-prints, or a three-dimensional object, and understand how it functioned as a two-dimensional plan. Then you physically retranslate it back into a three-dimensional event'.[1] But while the details of these techniques are interesting, it is the results and effects they produce that are most important.

Whether or not one knows how the movement was made, the opening moments of *Limb's Theorem* are magical – movement born from nothing and then endlessly elaborated in ever-changing variations on themes. The dancers' bodies appear as polyphonous instruments that can generate movement from any point, rather than taking impetus primarily from the legs or arms around a vertical trunk. A motif of arrangement pervades the dancing: an opening pas de deux has the dancers pulling on another's bodies into balletic shapes, legs stiff and straight, arms held correctly in classical positions, but ignoring the conventional logic that governs the planes and impulses of steps. Any part of the body appears able to determine momentum and direction in an angled, disjointed, slightly scary solo for the central *Enemy* figure in Part II as he makes his way down the diagonal, limbs locking and snapping into position, hands clasping elbows, his white-clad body inscribing convulsive geometrical figures in the air as if caught in a succession of freeze frames. In parallel fashion, the dancing, a constant proliferation and dispersal of pas de deux, solos, trios and group ensembles is decentralized and unpredictably generated; combinations of these forms often taking place simultaneously without any perceptible relation to one another.

Repetition dominates *Limb's Theorem*: the ball that keeps reiterating its rolling trajectory like an uneasy reminder of something just beyond the reach of memory; the lights that keep masking and revealing the dancers' fugitive motions; the large objects that carve and populate the stage; the recurrent leap against the wall; the frozen moments; the music ticking as time seems to expand into space. At the same time, the work is profligate, exuberant, bewildering in its inventiveness. This pairing – repetition and proliferation – is another element fundamental to all of Forsythe's works, even the focused ballets that he has made for other companies. The proliferation also extends, in the larger-scale works, to props, which tend to be few, but to reappear in different contexts and serve different purposes with remarkable economy of means.

Repetition and proliferation are key elements both dramatically and choreographically in the beautiful *The Loss of Small Detail*,[2] which uses *The Second Detail* as an opening section, contrasting its balletic, counterpointed, rhythmic choreography with the boneless, dissolving movement that characterizes Part II. In this section, Forsythe evokes a physical transparency, with movement that seems to have given up all notions of strength to find another kind of internal momentum. Ballet is visible within its shapes, but not dominant, as if the dynamics that generate it have been removed, leaving traces upon the body. For the first time, this way of moving is sustained throughout a whole work, the dance constantly engendered through internal coordinations (a connection between hip and hand, for example) rather than steps as such, creating an impression of a seamless, prodigious proliferation of motion. And the cheerful rehearsal room atmosphere of *The Second Detail* makes way for a blanched universe of myth and symbol, poem and nightmare. Like members of a tribe, the dancers are surrounded by their artifacts, subsumed by forces over which they have no control (Dana Caspersen lifted in slow motion, again and again, away from the table where she is desperately trying to write a message, papers flying into the air; pulled away repeatedly by the same man as she tries to whisper into a microphone; a man desperately shovelling snow into the air as it continues to fall steadily).

This same kind of physical transparency, in which movement seems to be tracing an inner muscular process as it passes through the body, can be seen in *As a Garden in This Setting*, made a year later. Even more pointedly than in *The Loss of Small Detail*, the movement here tends towards dissolution. And disintegration, as the dancers, clothed in bright silk bits and pieces by Issey Miyake move singly or in small groups to a muted score by Willems filled with bucolic noises of insects, birds, and children's voices. Repetitive, sloping, heel-kicking walks by lone dancers form a rhythmic background to long solos and duos in which the dancers' limbs seem to be trembling and buckling at the edges of frailty. In *As a Garden in this Setting* Forsythe appeared to be attempting to let go entirely of controlled movement while retaining an internal form that comes from the dancers' highly detailed renditions. That he was concerned with this in the same year as he made *Herman Schmerman*, a witty exegesis on crisp New York City Ballet style and technique, may seem odd at first, but a close look at *Herman Schmerman*, or any of the ballet ballets, shows the same attention to form and dynamics, simply in a different idiom.

The choreographic developments of the kind to be seen in *The Loss of Small Detail* or *As a Garden in This Setting* have brought with them their own emotive overtones. The sight of the dancers disarmed of balletic certitude, moving without the physical orientation that we are accustomed to seeing on stage can evoke a mixture of fear and tenderness, admiration and curiosity. Perhaps the most explicit articulation of this state and the technique that Forsythe calls disfocus is to be found in *Quintett*, in which the dancers are like King Lear's 'bare, forked man', vulnerable creatures moving with unsteady, uncertain movements that dissolve into and collapse upon each other. As Gavin Bryars's haunting music, *Jesus's Blood Never Failed Me Yet*, gradually becomes audible as a quavering repetition of the titular refrain, they appear to acquire strength in seamless, bewilderingly poignant solos, duos, and ensembles, in which the interwoven partnering, the kinetic reactions, the falling, swooping, skimming movements look so spontaneous that it is hard to conceive of this as choreography.

At the end, a woman stands in the beam of the light-machine/rocket-object on one side of the stage, then drifts backward to fall into an open trap-door, only to be caught and propelled out again as the curtain descends. A moving testament to the need to endure, to resist anomie, to create, *Quintett* is deeply emotional in a way that characterizes few Forsythe works. But emotion is, nonetheless present in all of Forsythe's work, sometimes overwhelmingly so. This is the last element which I would insist upon as fundamental. The emotion is, however, engendered by a complex mix of movement and context, rather than as a specific or desired mood. Forsythe's lack of linear narrative, combined with his prodigious imagination, is often the source of an onstage emotional chaos that can be harrowing because the connections between events feel perceptible yet just beyond conscious grasp. He likes to introduce new elements, obliging the spectator to look again, think again, feel again. The curtains that crash down in *Artifact*, the man who spews forth invective amidst the gorgeous waltz in Part II of *Eidos : Telos*, the sideways scene in Forsythe's brilliant take on musical comedy, *Isabelle's Dance* – all of these are part of the same vision of the world, in which the familiar is continually reconceived, and the unfamiliar repossesses the imagination.

Watching after Paris

In 1996, I left Paris to move to New York, where I still live. Two years later the Ballett Frankfurt's contract with the Châtelet Theatre was not renewed despite the company's popularity with the French public. There were rumours that its director wanted more traditionally balletic work. The company continued to perform in Paris every year, first at the more experimental Théâtre de Bobigny, just outside of the city, and later at the Théâtre de Chaillot, where I continued to watch Forsythe's work on my frequent trips to Europe. But in retrospect, the departure from Châtelet was, in effect, the end of a specific era in Forsythe's work. It also oddly prefigured the events of spring 2002 in Frankfurt.

Towards the end of May 2002, Forsythe was suddenly told that the city had decided not to renew his contract when it would expire in 2004. There was also talk, he was informed, of replacing his company with a troupe that would perform a more conventional classical repertoire. A few days later, a Frankfurt newspaper confirmed that in order to cut costs, the city was about to announce the demise of the Ballett Frankfurt. After thousands of emails, faxes, and letters from the international arts community descended upon the mayoral office, Forsythe was told that his contract renewal was not in danger. But faced with severe budget cuts and an atmosphere of doubt about the tenor of his work, Forsythe decided that he would nonetheless leave at the end of his term. After a great deal of speculation about his future plans, the formation of the Forsythe Company was announced in April 2004. A smaller troupe that would be based in both Frankfurt and Dresden, it would be financed jointly by the cities of Frankfurt and Dresden, and the states of Hesse and Saxony, but independent of opera house bureaucracy.

Looking back, Forsythe's departure from the big, mainstream state opera system to a smaller, more streamlined organization seems inevitable. The civic rumblings about the obscurity of his work were partly fuelled by his growing lack of interest in working in the opera house and creating the proscenium-oriented, big theatrical pieces that he had made during his first decade in Frankfurt. (Presumably the authorities were forgetting – or never knew – how difficult those works had seemed when they were first presented.) And Forsythe himself was increasingly tired of the administrative and bureaucratic demands of his role as an opera house *Intendant*. The move from Châtelet to Bobigny mirrored a parallel move in Frankfurt from the opera house to the Bockenheimer Depot (which then still housed the renowned TAT, or Theater am Turm), a disused tram station that the city had transformed into a theatre. In 1998, Forsythe made his first work there, and from that point on, he began to use its cavernous space with greater frequency to explore different kinds of theatrical environments.

As always, there was no immediately obvious linear structure to this evolution. If anything, his work in the late 1990s was more overtly marked by a series of balletic, abstract pieces (*Firstext*, *Opus 31*, *Quartet*, *workwithinwork*, *Woundwork 1*, *Pas./parts*), although several were made on outside companies. But two different pieces, in 1996 and 1998, were clues to a parallel path of interest that has become increasingly important over the last decade.

The first came about through an invitation from the London-based arts organization Artangel. With Dana Caspersen and Joel Ryan, he created *Tight Roaring Circle* (now renamed *White Bouncy Castle*), a giant version of a child's bouncy castle in the ornate Victorian space of the Roundhouse in Chalk Farm. The audience are also the performers, walking or bouncing on the inflated, curving surfaces, surrounded by Joel Ryan's dissonant, booming soundscape. Losing balance, falling without fear, their physical experience might be seen as a version of the 'disfocus' that Forsythe developed as a choreographic tool while creating *The Loss of Small Detail*. As Forsythe says,

> It was for us an extremely interesting and wonderful thing to be in the castle, in this room of no spectators, only participants, and experience the arising of a choreography which was incapable of being false. It was never false because the parameters of destabilization, unavoidable inclusion in the event, the sheer absurdity and the fact that the castle led you to move in a certain way created a situation where there was

no room for actions that were not connected to the present. This is authentic reaction, something which often gets lost in the rigours of the ballet world, and yet without which ballet is utterly meaningless.[3]

The links drawn between this unchoreographed, destabilized movement by non-dancers and the rigorous control and highly technical specificity of ballet point to the essentially unified nature of Forsythe's approach, however diverse his manifestations of those interests.[4] Three years later, he offered a piece that drew both upon the loose temporal structure of an installation and upon the idea of choreographing the audience. That was *Endless House*, a work that began in the opera house and then – in a way that now seems deeply symbolic – moved for its second section to the Bockenheimer Depot and a more intimate encounter with performance.

Part I, directed by Caspersen, offered Forsythe and his former Stuttgart colleague Ron Thornhill on an initially monochromatic stage, speaking the crazily logical, agonised words of Charles Manson, twitching with tight-muscled, truncated gestures as the sounds of Javanese gamelan music (Kraton Surakarta's 'Sirimpi' ('Provisions for Death')) plays. As they offered their fragmented narrative, waves of glowing colour began to wash across the screens rising and descending behind the men – a visual spectacle of such astounding opulence that it rivalled, then became one with, the sonorous ritualized intensity of the music. Part II entirely remade the frontal concept of the proscenium stage by occupying an extensive rectangle of space, chairs angled towards the stage and mobile screens partitioning the performance space. The audience could move around at will, and because no single spot allowed full vision, a subtle pressure to keep moving prevailed in order to try to comprehend the initially bewildering, diffused action.

Part II of *Endless House* was set to alternately hypnotic and discordant scores (by Ekhart Ehlers and Sebastian Meissner, and by Thom Willems), and it revealed a flamboyant, extravagant, dance-drama that invoked (amongst other things) *Wuthering Heights*, *The Valley of the Dolls*, and Javanese mythology, weaving the dancers into complex patterns and intricate choreographic knots, then changing the focus so that the audience rushed excitedly elsewhere. The need for the rituals of invocation and exorcism suggested by Part 1's music and speech are here given life through driven, hypnotic dances that culminate in a demonic, exhilarating ensemble, then dissipate back to intimate duos – the simmering, continuous life that both precedes and survives the exorcism.

Like a director yoking together a succession of disparate scenes, Forsythe nonetheless shaped the work into a coherent theatrical experience, drawing us into different segments by alternately assembling and disseminating ensemble dances and scenes. At other points, he made several disparate smaller groups (a lyrical pas de deux, a tangled quartet, a man manipulating a woman's face) visually available all at once. These experiments with perception and audience mobility (and the spectator's desire to comprehend all, to see everything) are also related to the experience of watching works like *Slingerland*, and *Limb's Theorem*, which are deliberately designed so that audience members in less-privileged parts of the theatre see facets of the work that are invisible to those sitting in the centre. In that sense, *Endless House* is an extreme version of the more subtle fragmentation of attention that is everywhere in Forsythe's work; it's rare for dancing to take place without an alternative viewpoint happening somewhere else on stage. (Even at the climactic moment of *In the Middle, Somewhat Elevated*, as the central couple lean in dangerously towards one another, a female dancer jumps behind them, claiming our attention just as the lights go down.)

That fragmentation of attention and the panoramic visual mobility of *Endless House* were given more conventional theatrical expression a year later in *Kammer/Kammer*, in which the stage is segmented into modular rooms by similar mobile partitions. These frequently hide the dancers, who are nonetheless seen on large video-projection screens hanging over the stage and the audience. The audience must keep choosing where they will look, what they will watch: 'It's like *Endless House*, but the audience have nice seats', Forsythe quipped.

Although it has several beautiful dance passages, *Kammer/Kammer* could be thought of as a play, filmed in multiple layers before our eyes, and it points to Forsythe's increasing interest in creating work that functions in the context of visual art as well as – or even better than – performance. Like the move from one venue to another in *Endless House*, an early conceit in *Kammer/Kammer* points to a more significant change in direction: before the first performances, the dancers performed a 30-minute ballet to Ferruccio Busoni while the audience (who could hear the music and even catch glimpses of the dancers) waited to be allowed to take their seats. Although this was a kind of joke (as well as a warm-up), setting up expectations for the piece that were then unmatched, it also, in retrospect, seems symbolic of a move away from the abstract, balletic works that Forsythe had made over the previous years. (Two ballet pas de deux in *Kammer/Kammer* were also later replaced by the more intuitive-looking, intricate, knotty movement generated by counter-curvature – both parts of the individual body and groups of dancers moving in opposing, displaced curves.)

In that same year, Forsythe created *One Flat Thing, reproduced*, a stupendously intricate, high-wire act of interlocking systems of reactive movement for 14 dancers under, over, and between 20 tightly packed tables, set to a growling, rumbling score by Thom Willems. It was a further extension of what Forsythe describes as his 'Scott chapter': a series of works that have taken material first created in *LDC* and developed through a number of incarnations, including two versions of *Die Befragung des Robert Scott* and from the second *7 to 10 Passages* and *One Flat Thing, reproduced*.

Forsythe has described *One Flat Thing, reproduced* as a visualization of the phrase, 'a baroque machinery', that he came across in Francis Spufford's cultural history of polar exploration, *I May Be Some Time: Ice and the English*

Imagination. Forsythe's immediate association was with counterpoint, the great musical machinery of the baroque era. By the time the second version of *Die Befragung des Robert Scott* had become *One Flat Thing, reproduced*, he had created a complex contrapuntal system based upon 25 fixed movement themes that are repeated and recombined over the course of the work, and incorporate improvisatory tasks during which dancers translate specific properties of each other's motion into their own variants. These are organized by a cueing system that uses both aural and visual triggers, and the work is organized around the idea of alignments: moments when the dancers' movements echo one another in shape, direction, or dynamic.[5]

> I started thinking, 'What is counterpoint?'. And I came to the solution for that piece, if not for eternity – that it is kinds of alignment in time … *One Flat Thing, reproduced* could be seen an example of a classical organization … (it works perfectly if you set it to Bach). But it doesn't use, or exclude, some of the historical references (pointe shoes, a certain kind of music, a historically specific technique) that would indicate classicism. It is not balletic, but in a sense it is classical. An idea from one domain can exist in another, and thrive just as well, but in a different form. Something as fundamental to ballet and classical music as counterpoint survives in my work in translated form, even if I chose not to use other associated elements.[6]

Alignment is in fact a fundamental principle of Forsythe's work; it is one of the ways that complex – even chaotic – activities on stage are rendered subtly comprehensible. (The interlocking trios and quartets in the third act of *Eidos : Telos* come to mind, but even his straightforwardly balletic pieces demonstrate this principle clearly.) But in *One Flat Thing, reproduced*, he shows a new kind of mastery of this skill; an almost mathematical construction of complexity from the alignment of building blocks of movements as the dancers leap, swerve, jump, duck, and arc between, over, and under the tables. (These white, glossy tables might be ice floes; Thom Willems's rumbling score, their slow movement deep below; the final astonishing cacophony as the tables are dragged forward, a glacier tumbling.)

Forsythe's final major work for the Ballett Frankfurt, *Decreation*, deploys different kinds of organizational principles. Performed at the Bockenheimer Depot it seems firmly to belong to the next era of Forsythe's work – and indeed, it has been performed regularly by The Forsythe Company over the last several years. The piece was inspired by an essay of the same name by the Canadian poet Anne Carson, in which she discusses a kind of unmaking of the personality through love in the lives of Sappho, Simone Weil, and Marguerite Porete, a 14th-century mystic who was burned at the stake. 'Jealousy is a dance in which everyone moves', Carson writes, and the phrase perfectly describes the structure of *Decreation*, in which speech and movement seem to mutate with flickering unpredictability from one person or group to another, flaring into full-blown physicality or operatic sound, simmering into slow, angled physical isolations and silence.

The movement in *Decreation* is both powerful and disturbingly strange – emphatic, extreme propulsions of the body; grotesquely angled, impossible-looking coordinations; faces grimacing as if being pulled by invisible forces. But it is just one part of a greater whole, matched by an equally complex, operatic sound environment. Piano music, composed and played onstage by David Morrow, is a fragmented accompaniment to the action, but so are the voices of the dancers – often electronically distorted into high-pitched squeals or a gravelly horror-movie bass; occasionally soaring into operatic song; frequently forming keening, amplified accompaniment to their movement.

Here the sound is echoed by a musical resonance in the pacing and control of movement; the voice and breath as much generators of movement as they are separate theatrical elements. The idea of a 'breath score' – movement synchronized through the breath – had emerged as early as *Duo*, and later extended in both *N.N.N.N.* and *The Room as it Was*. But it is in *Three Atmospheric Studies*, the first piece made for his company, that Forsythe achieves his most sophisticated use of this idea.

> Dancers are inherently musical because of the nature of movement, and this is an extension of the idea of their musical autonomy. *Three Atmospheric Studies* is rehearsed like a piece of music. Everyone listens to the collective breathing, and the difficulty of learning it is not in the steps but in learning to synchronize your breathing with the group. It's like 'drawing breath', in both senses of the phrase.
>
> William Forsythe, telephone interview with the author,
> 27 April 2010

Three Atmospheric Studies has an important textual component (although it is mostly confined to the second section of the piece), and it is part of the group of full-length works, with *Kammer/Kammer* and *Decreation*, that contain a more overt narrative component than Forsythe's earlier theatrical pieces. The work is quite overtly about war – even more specifically, about the then war in Iraq – and it is perhaps the first time that Forsythe, famously opaque on meaning, has been quite so explicit about content. (Not that other works have lacked social or political commentary: *Love Songs* and *Say Bye Bye* both suggest ideas about gender politics and pop culture; *Artifact* and *Impressing the Czar* are both pieces about social and theatrical hierarchies; *Alien/a(c)tion* contains allusions to the xenophobia that was making headlines in Germany around the time it was created). But it's possible – even probable – that you could look at these ballets without considering those aspects. *Three Atmospheric Studies*, on the other hand, makes its political commentary literally its central point.)

Less obviously, this piece marks the development of a new kind of choreographic structure for Forsythe: a fugal organization. The first act consists almost entirely (in choreographic terms) of a 45-second phrase, performed by two groups in varying forms. At first, each group does the phrase in a straightforward fashion; then, performs it backwards. But as one group begins to reverse the phrase at midpoint while the other keeps going you get, Forsythe says, 'entirely new relationships, new points of interconnectedness between the dancers'. The movement itself, full of sharp, precise angles and voluptuous curving trajectories, has an animal-like, instinctive quality, full of shuddering, stuttering swerves and swoops, yet also shot through with taut balletic lines.

Forsythe continued to explore fugal structures with The Forsythe Company, most notably in *Fivefold*, in which a series of trios offers complex partnered sequences that, here too, retain a balletic extension of line, and a distinctive, characteristic rhythm – surging movement punctuated with tiny arrests that allow the eye to absorb the linkages between the dancers. The search for what he calls 'categories of motion' continues with *Yes We Can't*, in which he uses another structural concept: the idea of unsustainability, whether it be words (like tongue-twisting phrases) or movements that contain contrasting feet and arm patterns too complex to be perpetuated, or physical contact that cannot remain unbroken. In *I don't believe in outer space*, he asked the dancers to memorize the layout of their apartments while blindfolded, and the results became the movement material for the work. In all of these works,

> I was looking for something that didn't have a specific aesthetic, but had specific orientations. It's like the balletic model: you orient yourself towards something, an idea of what you want to do – an arabesque, a pirouette. But now the dancing is more focused towards the dancers' interpretation of an idea than their attempt to accomplish something I want.
>
> William Forsythe, telephone interview with the author,
> 27 April 2010

Yes We Can't and *I don't believe in outer space* are both big, playful theatrical works, apparent continuations of a long line of engagement with dance in evolving relation to other theatrical forms. But in many ways, the second half of this decade – and the shift from the Ballett Frankfurt to The Forsythe Company – was characterized by the prolific non-theatrical installation work that had begun with the Groningen trees and *White Bouncy Castle*. Through *City of Abstracts*, *Scattered Crowd*, *Human Writes*, *You made a monster*, *Nowhere and Everywhere at the Same Time*, *Heterotopia*, *Angloscuro/Camerascura*, *Equivalence* and *The Defenders*, Forsythe has alternated between pieces that use a particular strategy (the balloons of *Scattered Crowd*, the mirrors of *Defenders II*, the need to move slowly in order to perceive the dancer in *Additive Inverse*) to sculpt the audience's movement, and pieces in which it is the dancers whose activity shapes the work.

The installations are also examples of choreography; just under different conditions. As Magritte says, 'An object is not so possessed by its own name that one could not find another or better therefore'. Choreography is not so possessed by theatrical performances with dances that one can't find other examples of choreographic principle. There is obviously a received notion about theatrical performance, but if I contemplate not having access to a theatre, how do I practice what I know without the usual materials? I am not trying to think differently. It's the same idea: Where does choreographic thinking arrive? What are the outer limits of this practice?

William Forsythe, telephone interview with the author,
27 April 2010

This curiosity about limits is perhaps the vital element in Forsythe's work. What are the possibilities of the dancing body? What makes a dance? What is performance? How do you find what you don't know or understand within the category of the known? The constant posing of these questions and a subsequent disregard for the aesthetic and physical norms of any one particular style of movement – or indeed to confine the origins of his choreography to the field of dance – has consistently marked Forsythe's work, from the early Stuttgart ballets to the recent, often hard-to-categorize The Forsythe Company pieces.

For Forsythe, anything – a film sequence, an equation, a linguistic theory – can function as a potential source of movement, an event or object that can be re-envisaged as a three-dimensional, physical outcome. At the same time, his extraordinary theatrical skill makes of each work – even those outside of a theatrical space – a whole world imprinted with Forsythean landmarks. The thrilling arrested moments; the endlessly inventive movement that is both forensically precise and impossibly complex; the brilliant use of light to sculpt both the dancers' bodies and our emotional response to their actions; the way ballet is stretched beyond its recognizable limits, yet glimmers through the contrapuntal forms; the sudden contrasts between chaos and calm, the realm of the unconscious and formal realization – all of these are part of the sum of a Forsythe work. But of course, like any work of art, in the end it eludes definition, like the body itself.

For me, it's [*Finnegan's Wake*] a paradigmatic work: you can't translate it because it is already in many languages, and their coexistence is the whole point – I really admire this sense of the world within language, language as connection machine, bringing apparently different, hermetic ideas together and exploding them into each other. This dissolution of borders between languages is like the dissolution between styles of dancing: what's the difference between ballet and hip-hop? Ballet and tap? Ballet and non-ballet? There is no border, because it is the body.

The body as site of choreographic investigation: choreographic investigation without the body. In the work of the last decade – and most particularly since the formation of his new company – Forsythe has enlarged his explorations from the generation of movement and the questioning of dance's theatrical precepts to an even more ambitious interrogation of the nature of the choreographic act itself. But it's risky to see Forsythe's creative evolution as a linear progression from one kind of work to another. He has always liked to elude definition, to do what is unexpected (or not to do what is expected), to let new creative currents brew slowly amongst apparently stronger current preoccupations. Amidst the prolific installation work of the last years, for example, he quietly created a classical ballet solo, *Two-Part Invention*, for a former Ballett Frankfurt dancer. Does that prefigure a return to the kinds of balletic works that are now the common currency of contemporary ballet repertoires worldwide (and the forebears of a whole genre of ballet choreography we see today)? Forsythe might say that he has never left ballet, or it has never left him, whatever the manifestations of the ideas and principles that formed him as an artist. In the end, *Two-Part Invention* and the tortured, fractured movement of *You made me a monster* or the wild antics of *Flandona Gagnole* are part of the same uncategorizable world – a vision of a perpetual range of possibility, of rich, ever-renewable complexity, and of one particular artist fully inhabiting his world.

Notes

1 Sulcas, Roslyn (1995), 'Kinetic Isometries: William Forsythe on his "continuous rethinking of the ways in which movement can be engendered and composed"', in *Dance International*, pp. 4–9, Summer 1995.

2 Confusingly for chronologers, Forsythe made a different ballet with the same name in 1987.

3 http://www.artangel.org.uk//projects/1997/tight_roaring_circle/statements/dana_caspersen_and_william_forsythe. Accessed May 2010.

4 The genesis of the move towards work that emphasizes choreographic thinking – and, later, creating what he calls 'choreographic objects' – came, Forsythe says, from a 1989 invitation by the architect Daniel Libeskind to be part of a project to mark the 950th anniversary of the Dutch city of Groningen. Forsythe designed 'a rather slow choreography for 50 trees', on the banks of a canal. Each tree was bound by a wire that was anchored to a pillar in the middle of the canal, causing them to bend sideways—'like a corps de ballet'—and to grow in that shape.

5 The elaborate construction of *One Flat Thing, reproduced* can be explored in great detail on an interactive website, called 'Synchronous Objects for *One Flat Thing, reproduced*', (synchronousobjects.osu.edu), created by Forsythe in conjunction with Ohio State University's Advanced Computing Center for the Arts and Design.

6 Roslyn Sulcas, 'Did Forsythe Invent the Modern Ballerina?' http://www.classicaltv.com/the-informer/did-william-forsythe-invent-the-modern-ballerina.

2 Of monsters and puppets

William Forsythe's work after the 'Robert Scott Complex'

Gerald Siegmund

Wear are we going? The Robert Scott Complex

The Bockenheimer Depot is dimly lit. Huge grey felt curtains separate the foyer area from the stage like a permeable wall. The foyer of the old tram depot, which served as an additional performing space for Ballett Frankfurt from 1999 to 2004, is covered in felt, too. Movable cubes in various sizes together with more strips of felt may be individually arranged to form landscapes for seating, lying down, or propping oneself up. On the other side of the threshold the felt interior continues, the stage area an extension of the sculpted space that accommodates audiences and passers-by alike. Sheets of felt are scattered over the stage, which is on the same level as the floor. In its left-hand corner an igloo has been constructed. For a part of the performance it serves as a shelter for the three dancers. Members of Ensemble Modern, a Frankfurt-based orchestra specialising in new music, have taken their seats on the left-hand side of the stage, slightly outside the dancers' range. They play *Opus 1*, a string concerto by the Japanese composer Ryoji Ikeda. Its non-linear sound patterns are interspersed with street noises, spoken words, and static crackle that charge the atmosphere. Towards the front of the stage a huge banner is displayed on the floor that declares '37 years of futility' in huge letters. Yet the writing can only be seen clearly from a vantage point above the stage. Its cry for help seems to be directed skywards.

A figure in a huge afro wig is bopping across the stage. Its knees are bent, its body slightly bent forward. It looks as if it will stumble over its own feet any moment. After a while its wig comes off revealing the dancer Yoko Ando. Two other figures, identified by the programme notes as Ander Zabala and Amancio Gonzales, amble across the stage. They wear huge anoraks and trousers to keep them warm. Their clothes restrict both the range and quality of their movements and warp the contours of their bodies. At one point, one of them lies down on his back and the other tries to bring him back to life. Three people who have lost contact with the outside world. Three people stranded in adverse conditions. If the clothes and the setting are to be trusted, they have ended up somewhere in the Polar region. But during the performance the dancers free themselves from their straitjacket-like clothes and muffled movements. Even the igloo is finally pulled down. They pick up a rope and play around with it, tying each other up and twisting free. With the dancers in short white pants and the igloo collapsing, a change of climate has taken place. A strange and curious new activity sets in that seems to produce movement playfully from the very constrictions of movement.

What I have just described is a small piece by Forsythe, *Wear*, which premiered in Frankfurt 22 January 2004. In the huge repertoire of Ballett Frankfurt, *Wear* is no more than a curious footnote. And yet it is also the penultimate piece that Forsythe choreographed for the company before it was closed by the city of Frankfurt with the end of the 2003/04 season. As such it gains a significance of its own, developing shades of meaning that span the whole of Forsythe's career. '37 years of futility', that plea to heaven, alludes to the very beginning of Forsythe's career as a dancer and choreographer at Jacksonville University, Florida, in 1967. It is a pessimistic summary of his professional life at a point in January 2004 when all the attempts to rescue Ballett Frankfurt, whose director he had been for exactly 20 years from 1984 to 2004, had turned out to be futile. The closure of the institution threatened to jeopardise his whole oeuvre. I shall return to the notion of futility on a more thematic level later on.

The setting of *Wear* makes it clear that Forsythe is revisiting the ghost of Robert Scott, the British naval officer who died returning from his expedition to the Antarctic in 1912, and all the questions Forsythe had asked him since their first encounter in the piece *LDC* in 1985. It is the last in a series of pieces I will call the 'Robert Scott Complex'. This complex leads us into the heart of Forsythe's thinking about ballet and his attempts to rescue it from its *rigor mortis* in the permafrost of tradition. In *LDC* Forsythe sent his company on a working expedition to the South Pole, which served as metaphor for the unknown continent of ballet. This was followed one year later by *Die Befragung des Robert Scott,* [*The Questioning of Robert Scott*], an autopsy of *LDC* in that it reflected on its working methods and means of producing movement. *Scott*, as the self-conscious and self-reflexive 'Lehrstück' of the company was kept in repertoire throughout the 1990s, and in 2000 an evening-length version of it was presented to a Frankfurt audience.

Certain elements from the original production, such as the two tables behind which questioning took place or the man with the bucket over his head circling and crawling around the stage, were kept. Apart from that, the new version bore little resemblance to the earlier one. It contained, however, two shorter pieces that, shortly after the premiere, were extrapolated and have been performed as individual pieces ever since: *7 to 10 Passages* and *One Flat Thing, reproduced.*[1] The two pieces are direct opposites of one another. While the seven to ten dancers making a passage from the back to the front of the stage work with slow internally refracted movements that almost stay inside the body, the dancers in *One Flat Thing, reproduced* literally explode across 20 tables neatly arranged in five rows. The tables are moved constantly and resemble shifting ice floes that turn the necessary repositioning of the dancers towards one another and the tables into extremely hard and dangerous work.

Viewed from this perspective the title *Wear* does not only refer to the strange costumes of the dancers. It also plays on the homonym 'where', thus re-opening the question of where ballet's place is in contemporary society. What is the relation of its coded language to the individual bodies of the dancers? How do they relate to it? How do they find their place in its structure?

What Forsythe takes with him after his friendly, but long overdue departure from Robert Scott's ghost in the Bockenheimer Depot, is the figure of the monster. The monster raised its head for the first time when Robert Scott froze to death in the eternal ice. It has accompanied Forsythe ever since in the disfigured, elongated, warped, twisted, and highly complex shapes of his dancers. In *Wear* Forsythe finally buried ballet as his starting point for creating movement. It is the coda of a lifetime spent working on its mechanisms and possibilities. But it is also the timid and, in this particular piece, sketchy attempt to move on, a farewell and a hello.

In the following pages I will deal with this period of transition from the Ballett Frankfurt 2003/04 to the new company Forsythe set up at the start of 2005, The Forsythe Company. I will begin by providing some information about The Forsythe Company and how it came about. I shall then come back to the figure of the monster and spell out its implications for Forsythe's aesthetics. After a brief return to the questions Robert Scott's ghost raised in connection with the monster, I will apply its concept to Forsythe's more recent pieces, such as *Decreation* and, to some extent, *we live here*, the very last piece for Ballett Frankfurt in April 2004. The last sections are dedicated to Forsythe's new stage work for The Forsythe Company, *Three Atmospheric Studies* and *Clouds after Cranach*. Forsythe here weaves current social and political issues into the theatre situation in a way that is best described as processes of translation.

Changing institutions

At the beginning of 2005 Forsythe's new company took up work. It was formed after the city of Frankfurt decided to close its municipal ballet company, the Ballett Frankfurt, which had been headed by Forsythe for 20 years. The decision in spring 2002 was made for financial and, surprisingly, artistic reasons, and provoked international protests. The city hall was flooded with e-mails, faxes, and letters from all over the world underlining the absurdity of such an act. Why close down a successful company that had brought the city of Frankfurt international attention? Why stop a unique artistic trajectory that had revolutionised the way we think about ballet? Initially the protests were successful. In 2003, the decision was reversed and negotiations with Forsythe begun. These ultimately failed and the city indeed closed its ballet company at the end of the 2003–4 season. Difficult demands on the side of the city as well as a certain weariness on Forsythe's part with continuing after the mutual trust and respect had been destroyed may well have played their parts as well.

At the initiative of lawyers, public relations agencies, and other Frankfurt businesses, however, a model was devised that would keep Forsythe and a company as creative engines in Frankfurt. In contrast to the Ballett Frankfurt, which was a municipal company, The Forsythe Company became a private one. It was made possible by a public–private partnership, rare in Germany, which included the states of Hesse and Saxony, the cities of Frankfurt and Dresden, as well as corporate sponsors that are responsible for a quarter of the company's budget. About a quarter of the required budget the company raises from ticket sales and by extensive touring. The contracts ran for five years and were renewed. It now has two home bases: one in Frankfurt, and from September 2006 onwards the Festspielhaus in Dresden-Hellerau. (The latter played a crucial role in the development of modernism in dance. It was there that Emile Jacques Dalcroze and Adolphe Appia experimented with rhythmical movement and stage lighting. It was the place where dancers such as Mary Wigman and Marie Rambert were trained at the start of their careers.)

Although it was highly unlikely that after the end of the Ballett Frankfurt Forsythe would not be gainfully employed, it was feared that the artistic experiment that he and his dancers had been engaged in for almost 20 years would come to an end. The Forsythe Company did permit a continuation of this experiment in both movement research and its framing in theatrical or everyday situations, independent of the whims and constraints of politics. Forsythe's development as an artist has always been related to questions of the institution, which he in turn questioned. His appointment as artistic director of the Frankfurt Opera Ballet, as it was then called, in 1984 enabled him to work with a body of dancers on a permanent basis, which made his exploration of the parameters of ballet possible. As artistic and from 1990 also administrative director of the Ballett Frankfurt, it became financially independent of the opera's and the theatre's budgets, a financial autonomy that would help lead to an even greater artistic one.

In 1999 the Ballett Frankfurt was given the Bockenheimer Depot, an old tram depot that was redesigned to become the home of the TAT theatre, as an additional performing space. Together with the architect Nikolaus Hirsch, Forsythe sculpted the interior into a contiguous social space to that outside the theatre. Using primarily felt, they transformed the space into one where things might happen, but where the transformation into another space, a stage, had not yet taken place. Although work for the huge opera stage continued to be produced, the major evening-length ballets were now developed for the renovated Bockenheimer Depot with its flexible outlines and multiple possibilities of changing the relation between audience and stage. Significantly, the smaller pieces choreographed for the opera stage like

The Room As it Was or *N.N.N.N.*, often denied this traditional space. They take place on a small strip of stage right in front of the audience, before a backdrop that shields the depths of the stage.

What continues to be a driving force in Forsythe's own company is the idea of a laboratory for research into dance. His pieces develop and incorporate knowledge about dance. They bring systems of thought to the world of dance that influence the quality of movement and the way it is perceived and conceptualised. His pieces are, as he once said in a conversation, hypotheses about ballet and dance; his work is an ongoing process of self-reflection and questioning, a process that establishes a field where things can happen without stipulating an outcome. In order to understand to what extent Forsythe's work had taken on a new direction in the transitional phase between the two companies, let me return to what I have called the 'Robert Scott Complex'.

Ballet spawned a monster

In the 'Robert Scott Complex' Forsythe connects the race to the South Pole in 1911–12 with the choreographer's quest for ideal forms, perfection, and new steps. The South Pole serves as an image of ballet, the unknown continent, while the scientists and explorers eager to discover new territory are transformations of the choreographer and his ballet company researching their craft.[2] As a third component, the dancer's body is brought together with the idea of the monster in Mary Shelley's gothic novel of 1818, *Frankenstein*. While searching for the source of life, Victor Frankenstein creates a monster out of body parts stolen from a mortuary. Whilst craving love, the monster only ever provokes horror and disgust. In the end the monster chases its creator across Europe, until Frankenstein loses it in the eternal ice of the North Pole, the equivalent of the limits of the world in the early nineteenth century. For Forsythe the body of the monster serves as a metaphor for the body of the ballet dancer. Both are artificially created, put together to create an ideal body that nonetheless ultimately fails to meet the demands of its creator. Yet who exactly the monster is in Mary Shelley's novel remains unclear. It is obviously Frankenstein's creature, a creation out of fragments of dead bodies brought to life. But the term monster also applies to Frankenstein himself, an ambitious individual breaking the laws of nature and society by assuming the role of a god-like creator.

Let us briefly consider what a monster is and does. According to Michel Foucault the human monster came into being at the end of the eighteenth century. Until that point, a monster was primarily considered to be a hybrid of animal and human, an anomaly of nature that mixes what by rights should remain separate; two individuals or two sexes in one body, for instance. For Foucault, the human monster is a category that refers to the field of law in the broadest sense, including the laws of nature. The human monster as it was conceived of at the close of the eighteenth century is a breach of the law that cannot be accommodated and answered by the law itself. It is a singular appearance exposing the limits of established knowledge, an aperture into the unknown.

> It is the limit, it is the moment the law turns around, it is at the same time the exception which only occurs in extreme situations. Let us say the monster is that which combines the impossible with the forbidden.
>
> (Foucault 2003: 77)

Combining the impossible and the forbidden, the monster generates a different field of knowledge. It opens up a new area of investigation that tries to explain its anomaly. The monster generates discourse from its vantage point at the limits of established discourse.

During the nineteenth century the discourse created by the monster was that of psychiatry. This new science took the monster as a paradigm for a whole new species of individuals; abnormals were created by psychiatry as its very own area of investigation and production of knowledge. Psychiatric discourse gives the abnormals a criminal nature and character. Their crime is not simply a deed any more. It is always inherent in their monstrous character that, even if a crime is not committed, equates the individual with its potential deeds.[3]

The monster is therefore a self-referential figure. By overstepping natural laws it brings those laws into focus. But by being a self-referential figure it also retroactively alters its parameters by producing other forms of discourse that open up established ones. The etymology of the word monster has two Latin roots: *monere*, to warn or to admonish, and *monstrare*, to show or to put on display. In its visibility the monster is more than visible because it always demonstrates something. It points towards itself and towards the laws it oversteps.

What does the monster have to do with ballet in general and with Forsythe's idea of ballet in particular? Interestingly, at the time of the emergence of the human monster, ballet was undergoing a revolution too. With the writings of Charles Blasis a new pedagogy established itself from 1820 onwards, which would change the nature and look of ballet. Susan Leigh Foster sums up this development brilliantly: nineteenth-century pedagogical practice removed the spatial geometry of the stage to the body's interiority. There it erected not a grid, but a central core/line with appendages. This schemata of head, torso, arms, and legs underlay the graceful shapes and metered movements that each body performed, changing its geometric configuration with every motion the body made (Foster 1996: 257–8). As a consequence of this newly developed interior geometry exhibited 'through straight or curved shapes' (Foster 1996: 258) of the body, both the nature of the steps and their sequencing changed, thereby giving rise to what we now call romantic or, by extension, classical ballet.

If Forsythe considers this newly devised body of the ballet dancer to be a Frankenstein's monster, he does so by showing that it is an entirely artificially assembled body. The balletic body is made up of isolated limbs, lines and their proportional relation that are reassembled to create an ideal body, larger than life and nature, yet articulating its rational principles. This body does not look monstrous to us from today's vantage point. But at the time the figure of the arabesque that Blasis claimed to have invented was precisely the new and strange figure that pushed the dancing body to its limits. From its monstrous point at the limits of the system was established the new language of ballet, the code of Terpsichore. While being monstrous, ballet's break with the laws of nature was eclipsed by another figure that covers up the monster inherent in ballet's law. This second figure is the puppet, which with the monster form a pair. They are inseparable and yet one is the undoing and the truth of the other.

In his famous essay 'Puppet Theatre' Heinrich von Kleist argues 'that there could be more grace in a mechanical doll than in the structure of the human body' (Kleist 1983 [1810]: 181–2). The puppet, if it is constructed correctly, is more graceful in its movements than any dancer because its movements defy gravity. The *vis motrix*, the moving force, that sets the puppet in motion, is the soul. This moving force, however, resides outside the puppet, thus turning it into an extension of the puppet player. In order for the marionette to move gracefully, the player has to place himself in line and harmony with the puppet's point of gravity, turning himself into a mere extension of the puppet. If the correspondence is established, he may ultimately be replaced by a mechanical device altogether. The soul always resides in the centre of movement, which corresponds to the puppet's centre point, thus making the appendages of the limbs follow its movements naturally and with ease. The puppet and its player form a unit that achieves the most perfect movements when they are at their most mechanical, i.e. when they are executed without consciousness.

Writing at the time of monster mania in both literature (the gothic novel) and, according to Foucault, science, Kleist's extremely complex text from 1810[4] develops the ideal of the new dancer with its central core line in terms of the ideal of the puppet. Dance and ballet in particular (this argument is put forward by Mr. C, first dancer at the opera of the town) are articulations of a higher, divine ideal. The means to express this is the notion of grace, which can, however, only be achieved unconsciously. Grace transforms the flesh of the fallen body into a soulful and harmonious one. Ultimately it is not the body that dances, but the soul. The text thus reveals something of the religious subtext underlying the early nineteenth-century construction of the ballet dancer, who becomes a mere medium lifting the body upwards to face God (Legendre 2000).

What does the monster have to do with this? Kleist's text provides examples of what happens when this union of soul and movement fails.

> 'Just watch P.,' he went on, 'when she is playing Daphne, and looks back at Apollo who is pursuing her; her soul is in her vertebral column,

and she bends as if she were going to break in two, like a naiad of the Bernini school. Or look at the young F., as Paris, standing among the three goddesses and handing the apple to Venus; his soul – it is really horrible to see – is in his elbow.'

(Kleist 1983[1810]: 181)

In these examples both soul and the centre of movement do not originate in the body's centre of gravity. The monster raises its head, which is 'fearful to behold', when the ideal of the puppet breaks down. Its body emerges at the limit of the puppet when it shifts within its form centres of gravity that defy the presumably natural and graceful lines and curves that a centred movement would produce.

What Kleist's ballet dancer denounces as a lack of talent and inadequacy on the dancer's part has, however, implications for a new way of moving. What happens if the soul as the moving force indeed settles in the elbow, which in turn becomes the centre of gravity? What happens if this new centre resonates with other regions of the body that pick up the movement and form other centres? Viewed from the perspective of the ideal puppet, those dancing bodies deviating from it are monsters. They are self-referential figures in that they operate within the field of ballet, yet push its rules to their extreme limits. In this sense, William Forsythe's project of 'building within ballet' (Siegmund 1999: 36) has spawned monsters of ballet, monstrous dancing bodies that point towards ballet's rules, while pushing their possibilities and meanings into the open.

The puppet as Kleist conceives it, however, makes a more radical point. The text also posits that if a dancer wants to become the incarnation of idealness, he or she has to overcome consciousness and, by implication, decision-making. To be identical with the ideal therefore means to be a puppet, i.e. no longer human, but a thing. The soul as a moving force, when it has returned to itself, thus ultimately turns into a thing. This implies that the dancer is only human when there is a rift between itself and the symbolic order in which it operates. This distance between our bodies, desires, and the symbolic order (the steps, figures, and syntactical rules of ballet) is precisely the reason why we are human beings and not puppets. This insight has further implications for Forsythe's universe. He works with this gap. His dancers are their own instruments, constantly making decisions within choreographic structures. They work with the rules rather than being ruled by them let alone being identical with them.

Let us return to the discussion of 'The Robert Scott Complex' to link this idea with Forsythe's ideal of ballet. What brings the ideas of the South Pole, a ballet company at work, and Frankenstein's monster together is the idea of failure or, as mentioned above, futility. Robert Scott lost the race to the South Pole against the Norwegian Roald Amundsen because he was using motor sleighs that broke down in adverse weather conditions. What was considered to be the most advanced technology of its day proved to be a failure – with deadly consequences. Technology did not get him to his destination, and neither will technique, as such, get the ballet dancer to his. Technique enables him or her to meet the demands of complex figures, balances, and step sequences. But it will never enable him or her to fulfil ballet's ideal construction. It is precisely this structural failure inherent in the ideology and practice of ballet that spawns the monster. Why? Another analogy between the South Pole and ballet may explain this.

In geographic terms, the South Pole is an abstraction, a mobile geography that changes position according to the perspective of the viewer. The position of the Pole, or any other object for that matter, is entirely dependent on the angle from which it is viewed. Its exact position can therefore only ever be located by taking the *difference* between the various perspectives towards it into account. This phenomenon is called parallax, a term Forsythe used as the title of a triple bill in 1989, which included what was to become the first part of the ballet *Slingerland* one year later. Ballet, for Forsythe, is a similar abstraction or idea.

If the South Pole is only a perspectival construction that keeps changing position with every step you take in its direction, then the traveller, like the dancer, can only fail its ideal. The dancer can only ever go through the idealness of ballet's figures without being able to inhabit, express, or hold them. In an interview with Roslyn Sulcas, Forsythe stated: 'You cannot do arabesque – arabesque exists as an idea. You can approach arabesque, and move through arabesque, and sustain yourself there for a greater or lesser time. You can try to do arabesque, which is a lot of fun, and we spent a great deal of time trying' (Sulcas 1995: 8).

Ballet is like a Platonic idea, an *eidos*. It is an abstraction that can never be translated into an actual performance without losing its perfection and clarity. Art in Plato's universe is always already two steps removed from the original idea. One: the idea is represented in the actual world we live in. Two: art imitates these imitations of forms and figures, thereby removing them one step further from their original perfection. In the past, ballet dancers have tried to embody the idea of ballet by striving for perfection, giving rise to a whole system by which to judge it: this ballerina does arabesque better or more perfectly than that ballerina, for example. For Forsythe arabesque is an idea that has no equivalent in the real world, which means that every dancer who tries it must inevitably fail because his or her individual body gives it slants and imperfections that stand between the idea and its realisation. If, however, you consider arabesque or any other figure or step from the ballet code to be a performative act that only comes into being when being performed, then any approach to arabesque is equally valuable, creating a different potential for meaning, feeling, or association. If arabesque as such does not exist, then the dancers can only move through it.

Dancers quote arabesque, but by iteration they also change it. They can approach it from various angles before they move on. It only exists when moving, which shifts it to a different place every time you think you have moved there. The specific flow of movement of Forsythe's pieces results from this: no going from point A to point B and climaxing at each point, but going through the points, transforming them into something else before moving on again. Each arabesque is a singular performative act that inevitably draws on other acts before it. Not least of all, it draws on the dancer's bodily memory established in years of training and dancing. This links the notion of performativity with the idea of the monster as an equally singular appearance. It is an occurrence within the laws of ballet that transforms these laws.

Decreation

One salient feature of Foucault's definition of the monster is that at the limits of a particular discourse it produces knowledge that causes this discourse to change its founding parameters. The monster is an anomaly that gives rise to new disciplines of knowledge. Having finally torn down 'The Robert Scott Complex' in *Wear*, Forsythe has also left the whereabouts of ballet. While the dancers of his company are still an anomaly in the world of ballet at large, their monstrous shapes during the last year of Ballett Frankfurt's existence have relocated positions and changed territory. His last piece for Ballett Frankfurt, *we live here*, may be read as an allegory of this. If *Robert Scott* served as the blueprint for over a decade's work on ballet's principles, *Decreation* serves as a model for a new area of investigation. It seems as if Forsythe's prime interest is no longer sequencing steps in time and space and devising choreographic structures that the dancers then have to fill themselves, but exploring physical states, states the body is brought into by specific methods of movement production. I will first consider *Decreation* before I spell out the allegories in *we live here*.

Decreation was premiered on 27 April 2003 at the Bockenheimer Depot in Frankfurt. In the first scene a woman catches the lower half of a female dancer somewhere in space with her camera and projects it onto a screen at the back of the broad and deep stage. Dana Caspersen enters this stage and positions herself behind it, her body now becoming a montage of two images that do not match. With a grotesquely distorted mouth she talks about a liar and a traitor and accuses her imaginary listener of leading a double life, while she simultaneously pulls at her top with pointed fingers. Suddenly she disappears and Georg Reischl, who as an interpreter delivers most of Anne Carson's text together with Caspersen and two other dancers, jumps out from behind the screen like a jack-in-the-box.

The title *Decreation* refers to Carson's eponymous opera in which the Canadian writer uses three interspersed stories to talk about love, jealousy, and the journey of the soul towards God. Carson confronts the mythological story of Mars, Venus, and the betrayal of her husband Hephaistos with a text by Marguerite Porète, a thirteenth-century mystic who explores her love of God by using the ideal of courtly love as her foil. The third strand is provided by the author's meditations on the French philosopher Simone

Weil's relation to God as a means of working through the separation from her husband. From these love triangles Carson derives *Decreation* as a process of self-interrogation, a productive undermining of the self leading to the creation of a space for something new.

As usual with Forsythe these stories are not represented on stage by characters who act out love, betrayal, jealousy, or hope. Instead, he derives a structural principle from them, namely the indirectness of movement and emotions, the bouncing off of each other, the making of detours before one reaches one's goal. Caspersen describes the movement principle thus discovered as shearing:

> It is a state that the body enters into where no approach, neither vocally nor physically, is ever made directly. For example, as we approach a microphone, or a person, our thoughts might move in that direction, but our bodies ricochet backward, off of the thought, in a series of oblique refractions. The body becomes a proliferation of angular currents, a state of complex, fragmented reaction.
>
> (Caspersen 2004: 114)

During the rehearsal process the company experimented with all kinds of undirected action, like tying themselves up with ropes or drawing with charcoal on sheets of paper (Boenisch 2004: 60). Towards the end of the piece a round table that had been resting next to the screen is pushed forward. The dancers fetch their chairs and sit down around its coal-dust-covered surface. Roberta Mosca, a burning cigarette between her toes, rolls herself across it until the black soot covers her entire body. Suddenly the dancers break off this ritualistic scene by dragging their chairs to the back of the stage and dispersing across the space.

The movement thus produced is useless in the literal sense of the word, namely free from intentions and therefore potentially free from depicting anything in particular. The company tried to create movement from the impossibility of creating movement. The result is not a choreography of steps. The piece is structured according to theatrical principles such as contrasting proximity and distance of actions in space, or the dynamics of scenes and music. *Decreation* creates bodies that are inhabited by conflicting forces not taking them anywhere in particular. The piece highlights a certain physical sensibility that far exceeds the boundaries of ballet. They are bodies undone because they are plural bodies in one body .The dancers are monsters precisely because they divest themselves of any kind of form or identity. They dance neither roles, characters nor according to any kind of dance technique. Theirs is a unique sensibility of responding to movements surrounding them, picking them up almost by osmosis in order to turn themselves into alien bodies. How this communication works has raised the interest of neurobiologists, communication designers and philosophers. This is precisely the function of the monster. Forsythe's monsters have left the discourse of ballet to enter other areas of research that might respond to them.[5]

we live here

'Oh dear, oh dear. There is something going on here'. Dancer Reischl bends down to speak the sentence into a microphone that is set at the height of a child. Electronically distorted, his high-pitched voice sounds immensely sweet and funny. Oh dear, oh dear. There is something going on here, indeed. He is later joined by Amancio Gonzales, who has undergone a similar transformation, and the two princes – or princesses, as the case may be, because they cannot really make up their minds – look for help. An evil magician wants to chase them from their village that is the stage of the Frankfurt Opera House. But while in *Sleeping Beauty* a lilac fairy comes to the rescue, in Forsythe's *we live here*, we have a green and a black fairy, the latter of whom initially stipulates the prince to just say 'yes' to whatever the evil magician suggests.

For Frankfurt audiences it was obvious who was whom in this act of defiance. The evil magician Rothbart is Frankfurt's culture secretary, who sacrificed the ballet to please his colleagues from the Social Democratic Party, thereby saving his own political career. The black (the colour of the conservative party) fairy is Frankfurt's conservative mayor Petra Roth, who initially didn't care if the ballet lived or died. And the green fairy is the cultural spokeswoman of the Green Party who, an avid defender of the ballet, is reduced to complaining all the time without much effect.

In 1983, Forsythe was the one who blew the fairies of classical ballet off the stage of the Frankfurt Opera House. Until his arrival in Frankfurt with his seminal backstage ballet *Gänge*, Ballett Frankfurt had been a traditional company with only moderate inclinations to bend and twist its dancers' bodies into new directions. Over the following 20 years neither the fairies, nor the princes and princesses, returned to their original abode. That he brought them back for the premiere of *we live here* on 16 April 2004, the last piece for and of Ballett Frankfurt, was another allegory: an allegory on his own past and history. In the political quarrels that led to the magistrate's decision to close down Ballett Frankfurt at the end of that season, one argument was rumoured to have been used repeatedly: the city's ballet did not fulfil its representational function by staging the classics. Ballet, if it is to be subsidised by the city, should represent an ideal order. Forsythe brought the fairies back, but he did it in such a way that must have felt like a slap in the face of those who wanted the old order re-established. The 17 dancers act and dance in a pseudo *Star Search* manner, grinning inanely into the audience and depicting a world of entertainment that has become increasingly superficial and free of both attitude and content. One dancer mimes the rock star thanking us profusely for being with him tonight, while the face of another looms large on the video screen above the stage staring bleary-eyed into the void. Another character walks amongst the formations of dancers urging them to relax, while trying to hypnotise both them and the audience into quiescence. Like a business consultant and spin doctor he pleads with them to turn their frustrations into positive thinking. Thom Willems's score of lopsided loops is peppered with chords from Yma Sumac's 'Mambo', which almost get the dancers going in a formation. But before they can step out, the music changes.

Ballet as mindless entertainment – whether this was the direction that leading Frankfurt politicians wanted the ballet to take remains open to speculation. As far as movement is concerned *we live here* followed the lead of *Decreation*, creating a new, hybrid genre for which there is no name yet. Apart from moving, the dancers also have to act, sing, mime, and draw, which they do with increasing self-confidence. Dancers press their bodies against the back wall, a piece of black chalk in their hands, leaving marks whenever they move. Slowly the phrase 'Reason is Content' appears, before the wall is pulled backstage. *we live here* is neither ballet nor – and despite the use of spoken words – *Tanztheater*. It is neither a play nor a musical in the West End sense of the word. The promise of the evening lies in this undecidability.

Translation processes

In the first year of its existence The Forsythe Company launched several projects. The performance *You made me a monster*, premiered at the Venice Biennale on 28 May 2005, pays homage to the monster as a structural figure in Forsythe's discourse by putting it in the title. In an autobiographical text projected onto a large video screen Forsythe links the illness of his wife, the ballerina Tracy Kai Meier, who died of cancer in 1994, to the idea of the monster. The cancerous growth turned her into a monster, forcing her to walk with her torso bent forward, breaking a wonderful dancer in two. It made her an alien in her own body, which stopped functioning according to the rules of biology. In 1992, at the time the disease was discovered, Ballett Frankfurt was working on a piece called *Alien/a(c)tion*. It was inspired by the wave of xenophobia that swept across Germany at the time, hatred directed towards Turkish families and other immigrants. They, too, were vilified as monsters disrupting the presumed identity of the German state and its citizens. Monsters, it seems, question identities: of individuals, bodies, states, discourses, and art forms such as ballet.

In an open-space situation the audience in *You made me a monster* may assemble human skeletons from cut-out pieces made of cardboard and attach them on to metal poles sticking out of eleven tables spread across the room. What may have started as a truthful rendition of the human anatomy soon turns into a wild and uncontrolled growth of limbs, bones, and structures balanced precariously. Suddenly three dancers attract attention by their distorted and quick movements. Their live voices are turned into cries and groans by computer programmes.

To generate movement the dancers use these grotesque paper skeletons of monstrous growth to isolate lines and their connections. They study them intensely before copying them on sheets of paper provided on the tables, thus visualising them before turning them into movement. The monsters, whom we, the normals, cannot accommodate, are the dancers dancing among us, next to us, picking up forms und figures the audience itself has produced to translate them into a highly disturbing physicality.

On 23 October 2005 the installation performance *Human Writes* was premiered at the Schiffbau Theatre in Zurich, Switzerland. For this piece Forsythe returns to improvisation methodologies he had developed for *Decreation*. The difficulty of producing movement under adverse conditions is here translated into a political statement. Advised by Professor Kendall Thomas from Columbia University's School of Law, Forsythe makes the Universal Declaration of Human Rights of 1948 his topic. *Human Writes*, a pun on human rights, is a physical enactment of the difficulties that prevent the realisation of universal human rights. For their work Forsythe and Thomas chose three articles from the declaration: number 19 granting everyone 'the right to freedom of opinion and expression'; number 22 guaranteeing everyone access to the cultural life of a community; and number 26 safeguarding everyone's right to education.

Sixty tables are evenly distributed throughout the brightly lit room. Excerpts from the three chosen articles are written in pencil on huge sheets of paper covering the tables. The task the dancers have to perform together with the audience is to bring those thin and barely visible lines into existence. Pieces of charcoal and ropes may be used to spell out the letters. But nobody is allowed to do it directly. A set of rules stipulates that contact with the paper can only be indirect. The coal is thrown at the tables to mark the letters with dots. It is tied to a rope held by two people across the table and, once the partners have developed a common rhythm, bounced up and down. Dancers stand with their backs to the tables, while the tables are moved by members of the audience as if they were the writing instrument. The noise in the room soon resembles that of working in a coal mine. The piece is an archaeological endeavour to excavate what seems to have been long forgotten. The realisation of human rights is a precarious endeavour always threatening to undo what it is trying to bring about. It meets resistance and may have to contend itself with small steps and major detours, but it can only succeed if everyone cooperates.

Atmospheres

On 21 April 2005 the Forsythe Company presented its first stage work at the Bockenheimer Depot in Frankfurt: *Three Atmospheric Studies,* which incidentally consisted of only two parts. After the premiere Forsythe experimented with new parts and sections until, towards the end of the year, the piece found its definitive form. It now includes another of Forsythe's new pieces, *Clouds After Cranach*. The first two acts of *Three Atmospheric Studies* now consist of the two *Cranach* sections, whereas the third act picks up the second part of the original, dropping the original first act altogether.

Atmospheres are related to monsters. They are, as the German philosopher Gernot Böhme phrases it, 'spaces in as much as they are "tinged" by the presence of things, of human beings, or environmental constellations, i.e. by their ecstasies' (Böhme 1995: 33). Atmospheres are created when things step out of themselves, transcending their status as things, and connect with the subjects they confront. Atmospheres are the ways in which objects or other human beings affect us even before they communicate their meaning by turning into signs. The theatre is a space where objects, things and human beings always make their presence felt in a singular way. Since they appear out of context, having thus suspended their functional meaning, they first of all draw attention to themselves as singular occurrences. Everything that happens on stage is therefore more than visible. Everything is monstrous, creating an atmosphere precisely because of its monstrosity, which is the way in which it makes its presence felt as an atmosphere. And yet the atmosphere of *Three Atmospheric Studies* depends just as much on the subjects and formations presented as on the things not seen, heard, or enacted. Atmospheres also point towards the absence of connections, to what is missing, the gaps in the fabric of things that affect us. They are spaces where the missing things turn towards us to question our identity uncannily.

Clouds After Cranach takes its cue from a painting by Lucas Cranach: 'Klage unter dem Kreuz' ['Lament beneath the Cross'] from 1503. The first part is a pure dance piece. What is striking in the context of a Forsythe piece is that the six female and six male dancers fall into poses forming smaller groups. Full of fear they direct their gazes upwards or to their partners before they start to move again, pushing, pulling, sliding, twisting and turning, arms and legs jarred out of centre. Composition One, dancer Jone San Martin, declares at the very beginning of the piece: 'My son was arrested'. She points towards another dancer whose body is bent over backwards with an expression on his face as if invisible hands are strangling him. After this short introduction she leaves the stage and the dancing begins. After about half an hour the audience has to turn around. This turn not only means that it now faces the other side of the hall. It also implies a change of perspective, at the same time linking and separating the first two parts of the piece. What happens now retroactively gives meaning to the abstract dance of the first section without explaining everything. Martin, now in a pink dress, sits on a chair and starts telling the story of her son, who was arrested because he wanted to help her daughter and her two friends, whose life was in danger after a bomb attack on a house. Slowly she spells out the story word by word, sentence by sentence, as if she herself wants to come to terms with the unspeakable that has happened. She is clearly engaged in an exercise of understanding what cannot be understood and integrated into the normal way of things. Another dancer sits in front of a full clothes rack taken from the store rooms of the theatre. Matter-of-factly, Amancio Gonzales translates her words into Arabic, always changing her words slightly, subtly correcting her, so that what she says is not what he makes of it. What we hear are versions of what has happened, versions that make what has really happened impenetrable.[6] With his hands a third dancer describes small details from five compositions. Although he regularly announces their numbers, we never get to see them, having to deduce the content from the pantomime he uses. He moves in what looks like a spider's web of small ropes, which might just as well be the lines of perspective from the paintings made visible on stage.

The solution comes towards the end of Act 2 when the audience leave the auditorium for the intermission. Two pictures are hung on a black wall. One is a reproduction of Cranach's painting. The other is an enlarged press photo. Four men can be seen dragging a man away from a house that is ablaze with fire. His body is bent backwards, his face distorted in pain. In the upper right hand corner of Cranach's painting an ominous dark formation of clouds can be seen. In the same spot on the press photo, smoke curls up into the air. Five centuries later, the clouds of Cranach have become signs of destruction caused by bomb explosions.

Dance, theatre, and visual arts, movement, spoken word, gesture, and image, Forsythe works with various genres of art and their specific means. He separates them in time, giving each its own space to communicate. And yet the three sections of the piece meet in the space that separates them from each other, in the absence opening up between them. In this absence violence, pain, loss, and suffering are not represented, but atmospherically suggested to us, because ultimately they are unrepresentable. They are that monstrous thing that we cannot accommodate. The insistence during the performance that everything we see or hear is a translation and thus not the thing itself, which is forever lost in the process of translation, prevents the piece from taking on a cynical or patronising attitude towards the victims of bombings, floods, or earthquakes to which the third Act of *Three Atmospheric Studies* alludes. Once again, catastrophes are not enacted on stage. They are not mimetically reproduced by character and plot, pretending that it were possible to understand them by acting as if the pain were real. The translation process within *Three Atmospheric Studies/Clouds After Cranach* is primarily a process of self-reflection. It lays open the working methods of Forsythe, the artist. But by reflecting on its own means it oversteps its boundaries, thereby also opening up perspectives on social processes.

The gap that separates the arts as systems of representation from the unrepresentable is also a physical space inhabited by two bodies. One is the body of the audience, the other is the body of a dancer, here Martin. The audience literally sits on the rift that separates part one and part two of the piece. It bridges the gap which can never be bridged, because by turning around, the scene behind their backs may suddenly produce things that go unseen. Members of the audience must try to integrate the various sections by themselves. The body of the dancer clearly shows how difficult that is. From a woman willing to learn and understand, she becomes more and more desperate and obstinate. Her body, which is stiff with tension, bends out of shape, as if it were impossible for it to integrate the tensions of our time into a harmonious image. The days of the puppet, is seems, are clearly over.

After Forsythe's departure from 'The Robert Scott Complex' in *Wear*, the dancers in his company are no longer monsters of ballet, the limits of its ideal puppet. They are monsters carving out spaces and undergoing experiences that cannot be accommodated into any functioning symbolic system of representation. They create atmospheres of nervous disquiet and the unknown. This new function of the monster has evolved during the last year of Ballett Frankfurt's existence. It now continues to develop in the work of The Forsythe Company.

Notes

1 On 1 May 2002, a new version including *7 to 10 Passages, One Flat Thing, reproduced* plus *Break, Intermission, Before and After,* a work by Mårten Spångberg, was shown. The evening was called The Scott Work/2002.
2 For this whole section see also Siegmund (2004).
3 Cf. especially Foucault's lecture of 22 January 1975, in Foucault, *Die Anormalen*: 76–107.
4 Kleist's text is, in fact, extremely complex and contradictory. It makes use of embedded narratives and dialogues, thus blurring logic, references, and points of view to the point of illegibility, as some critics have argued.
5 See, for instance, Hagendoorn, (2004).
6 This is the same procedure Forsythe used for *The Loss of Small Detail* in 1991.

References

Boenisch, Peter M. (2004) 'Ent-Körpern, Ent-Schreiben, Ent-Schöpfen. Wie sich die Tanztheorie von William Forsythes *Decreation* zur Dekonstruktion der Diskurse über das Ballett verleiten ließ', in *Forsythe. Bill's Universe. Ballettanz das Jahrbuch*, Berlin: Friedrich Verlag.

Böhme, Gernot (1995) *Atmosphäre*, Frankfurt am Main: Suhrkamp (translation by the author).

Caspersen, Dana (2004) 'Der Körper denkt: Form, Sehen, Disziplin und Tanzen', in Gerald Siegmund (ed.), *William Forsythe – Denken in Bewegung*, Berlin: Henschel Verlag.

Foster, Susan Leigh (1996) *Choreography and Narrative: Ballet's Staging of Story and Desire*, Bloomington, IN: Indiapolis University Press.

Foucault, Michel (2003) *Die Anormalen*, Frankfurt am Main: Suhrkamp (translation by the author).

Hagendoorn, Ivar (2004) 'Towards a neurocritique of dance', in *Forsythe. Bill's Universe. Ballettanz das Jahrbuch*, Berlin: Friedrich Verlag.

von Kleist, Heinrich (1983 [1810]) 'Puppet Theatre', in Roger Copeland/Marshall Cohen (ed.) *What is Dance?*, Oxford: Oxford University Press.

Legendre, Pierre (2000) *La passion d'être un autre. Étude pour la danse*, Paris: Seuil.

Siegmund, Gerald (1999) 'Amerika wird in Frankfurt weitergetrieben: William Forsythe', in *Ballet International/ Tanz Aktuell*, 4.

Siegmund, Gerald (2004) 'Räume eröffnen, in denen sich das Denken ereignen kann' in Gerald Siegmund (ed.) (2004) *William Forsythe – Denken in Bewegung*, Berlin: Henschel Verlag, pp. 34–37.

Sulcas, Roslyn (1995) 'Kinetic Isometries', in *Dance International 2*, p. 4.

3   Splintered encounters

The critical reception to William Forsythe in the United States, 1979–1989

Mark Franko

> The intellect is properly our means of acquiring ideas that lie out of the ordinary.
>
> (Bonnot de Condillac 2001: 69)

Prior to the formation of Ballett Frankfurt in 1984, Forsythe's choreography was performed in the United States by the Stuttgart Ballet, the Netherlands Ballet, the Joffrey Ballet, the Paris Opera Ballet, the Lyon Opera Ballet, the New York City Ballet, and the San Francisco Ballet. Ballett Frankfurt had its U.S. debut in 1987 at Purchase, NY, and its New York City debut in 1988 at the City Center. Finally, Ballett Frankfurt toured nationally in 1989, after which it did not return to the United States of America for ten years.[1] The journalistic critical response in New York during this decade was, with a few exceptions, hostile, and the hiatus in US appearances until 1999 may have been dictated in part by this response. Anna Kisselgoff, chief dance critic of *The New York Times*, was practically Forsythe's sole supporter. Despite occasional misgivings, Kisselgoff recognized the importance and originality of Forsythe's work in a way that no critic writing in America until Roslyn Sulcas was willing, or able, to do.[2]

At first glance, the hostility of the critics seems due to Forsythe's iconoclastic, historically, and critically informed relationship to the classical ballet tradition. This relationship is widely recognized and intelligently dealt with in German criticism. Gerald Siegmund (Siegmund 2002) has spoken of an *Auseinandersetzung* – a sustained and productive argument with the classical tradition – and Sabine Hushka (Hushka 2001) has noted the *Selbstbezüglickkeit* (self-referentiality) of Forsythe's movement vocabulary in the context of that tradition. Choreography that takes a re-writing of the ballet tradition as its subject matter was not received in the United States, however, as a productive and creative form of engagement with tradition; rather, it was taken to be nihilistic and an outright threat to the art form. Critics reproached Forsythe for betraying or undermining ballet as a discipline.

Critical reception, however, as Forsythe himself proposed to me, cannot be restricted to journalism, but must also encompass the reactions of the general public and of artists.[3] In a 1990 interview Forsythe put the status of the dance expert in the United States into question: 'A lot of people from different disciplines, strangely enough, seem to understand what I am doing and that I am definitely concerned with ballet' (*Ballet Review* 1990: 86). The clear implication is that those assigned to comment from within the discipline did not properly grasp what he was up to. On the other hand, Forsythe has described the response to his work from other dance artists in the US as frequently close to 'amorous'. There is also ample evidence of audience response in the reviews themselves. Kisselgoff reported 'the resounding cheers – continuing after the house lights went on' at a 1987 performance of *New Sleep* in San Francisco (1987a). In 1988 she remarked: 'The following he has picked up locally [in New York] in the last 10 years was delirious with enthusiasm' (1988). These are just two among numerous examples.

The wider journalistic response remained nonetheless tinged with skepticism and incomprehension. The dance critical establishment resisted Forsythe's critical engagement with ballet, and resisted the enthusiastic audience response to that engagement.[4] Some critics even wrote their own resistance into their review. Alistair Macaulay, not an American critic at the time though reviewing *France/Dance* in 1988 for *The New Yorker,* wrote: [T]he piece is an exercise in pointlessness, so organized that the audience is excited' (1988: 79). The choreography is seen as some kind of evil ruse placing the audience under its spell.

Siegmund asked Forsythe about his possibly conflicted relationship with America on the occasion of Ballett Frankfurt's return to New York in 1999 with performances of *Eidos : Telos* (Siegmund 1999).[5] My analysis here shall not focus unduly on attitudes toward expatriation: part of the journalistic game was to set Forsythe up as controversial and polarizing – 'Audiences will love him or loathe him' (Thorpe 1989: 81).[6] Presumably, the loathing is motivated by the qualities in his work that can be perceived by American audiences as European.[7] It approaches xenophobia. I want to focus instead on the intellectual content of critical responses, and on the rhetorical strategies used to frame these responses keeping in mind that Forsythe's work, starting with *Artifact* in 1984, distinguished itself by a critical exploration of ballet as a choreographic and theatrical idiom.

In Forsythe's own context, not that imposed upon him by the media, I believe the word deconstruction is justified, if we reject the media's co-optation of this term as a vague synonym for a sort of dissection, but in the proper sense Jacques Derrida intended in a 1972 interview:

> To "deconstruct" philosophy, thus, would be to think – in the most faithful, interior way – the structural genealogy of philosophical concepts, but at the same time to determine – from a certain exterior

that is unqualifiable or unnamable by philosophy – what this history has been able to dissimulate or forbid.

(Derrida 1981: 6)

Just as the understanding of structure as armature was always erroneous when applied to structuralism (I will return to the structuralist label), so deconstruction is not a dismantling or pulling apart. Deconstruction leaves its object intact yet changed through the lifting of the object's self-imposed interdictions. It acts, as Derrida specifies, from a certain inside and from a certain outside: the inside is faithful to the tradition; the outside is implicit in but unavowed by the very same tradition. Despite the reputation for nihilism that deconstruction garners in some quarters, its key critical concept, *différance* – a neologism in French, which by exchanging an 'e' for an 'a' combines the sense of differing with that of deferring or delaying – provided a theoretical and conceptual framework since the 1960s for the study of differences of all kinds. Forsythe himself has understandably rejected the deconstructive label. Yet, having been influenced by Derrida, deconstruction is part of the intellectual tradition he draws upon.

Ballet and intellect

Forsythe's relationship with the American critical establishment during the 1980s was, indeed, complex, if not vexed. I attribute it to the rejection of intellect in dance, and most particularly to the rejection of intellect in ballet. The pervasive use of language Forsythe's work deploys at multiple levels, and the inspiration he drew, and spoke about quite publicly during this period, from the work of Roland Barthes and Michel Foucault, engage concepts of representation with conceptual dimensions of ballet that are iconoclastic from a social and political perspective. Kisselgoff perceived the link between the social and political context of Forsythe's interests, and his complex connection to questions of language:

> Social protest or at least social critique was usually at the heart of Mr. Forsythe's earlier works. Even today, the linguistic structures he transposes to his choreography to create analogies between dance idioms and spoken language are often at the service of social commentary.
>
> ('Three Premieres' 1987)

The 1980s, it is also worth noting, saw the emergence of Dance Studies in the USA, and Forsythe's interest in some of the same critical sources that would motivate a different vision of dance history and theory among young dance scholars links him to what, at that time, was a particularly American tendency in one sector of the dance world.

I do not want to overemphasize this comparison because early Dance Studies was not particularly concerned with ballet. I do want to point out, however, that Forsythe was moved by some of the same intellectual sources that influenced the first wave of Dance Studies, notably Barthes and Foucault. By calling upon modes of critical theory that have since gained recognition as poststructuralist, Forsythe asked the audience to become critically aware of how dance functions like a language – or, rather, a code – that could be re-engineered as an agent of its own theoretical interpretation rather than simply displaying itself as an aesthetic object for the consumption of the connoisseur. This approach is evident as of 1984 with *Artifact*, which I believe is a highly analytic piece concerning the space of the stage and the historically determined conditions of reception for dance.[8]

The injection of critical theory into ballet and the formal innovations conducted at both the technical and choreographic levels form a remarkably complex conjunction, and call for a highly developed critical practice to match it. Instead the critics almost uniformly labelled Forsythe's work 'intellectual' (by this was meant: 'not thought because thought cannot take place in dance'), or 'spectacular' (as in: 'not art because too engaged with theatricality'), or both, as conjoined most recently by Jennifer Dunning when she recalled the 'would-be intellectual dance spectacles' of the 1980s (2007: B12). There was virtually no recognition that Forsythe's use and abuse of spectacle was a means with which to examine how ballet achieves its effects. One problem for the critical establishment was the migration of the critical faculty itself from the critic to the choreographer. Forsythe's choreography was inducing thought that undermined the very (fragile) premises of North American criticism.

But there is more. Forsythe spoke back to the critics, thus evincing his own critical exigency. His comments often advocate a more intellectually informed level of critical discourse; his work is intended to provoke such a discourse. At his most caustic, he called American dance criticism 'semi-serious' and 'pseudo-historical'.[9] These comments hit hard because the critical establishment assumed the role of protector of the dance field – and most particularly of the ballet field – from the inopportune incursion of intellect. Hence, the encounter between Forsythe and the critics – perhaps this is a more relevant term than reception since in actuality very little was received – took place across a splintered terrain: within the choreography of ballet and its public reception, within the critical discourse that would account for this choreography and reception, and within a counter-discourse that challenged the basic critical tenets of journalistic writing on dance. This counter-discourse was staged in programme notes, post-performance commentary such as letters to the editor, and in interviews.

The subject, then, is not the intellectualizing of dance – a damning term in most art criticism – but the role of intellect in the creation of choreography and the role of intellect in the discussion and critique of ballet performance. It was precisely the intellectual function that American criticism would deny to ballet. 'Don't think: dance!' was the message. Forsythe, however, addressed and continues to address how dancers do think, and the instrumentality of thinking to dancing.

Anti-intellectualism

The journalistic response to Forsythe, and Forsythe's critical reaction to that response, reveal the dirty little secret of 'anti-intellectualism' in American dance criticism. For the concept of anti-intellectualism I rely on Richard Hofstadter, *Anti-Intellectualism in American Life*: The common strain that binds together the attitudes and ideas which I call anti-intellectual is a resentment and suspicion of the life of the mind and of those who are considered to represent it; and a disposition constantly to minimize the value of that life.

(Hofstadter 1962: 7)

Hofstadter reviews evidence since the eighteenth century for a tradition of American anti-intellectualism in religion, politics, business, and educational practices and philosophies.

Yet, anti-intellectualism in ballet criticism cannot be based, as it is in American life according to Hofstadter, on 'arrant populism', and 'the mindless obsession with "practicality"' (1962: 407). After all, ballet is, or was in the 1980s, a highbrow art form to whose staid public Forsythe's young enthusiastic audience of the time might themselves be considered rabble-rousers. It can also not be fully explained by what Roslyn Sulcas has called the 'inherent conservatism' of a codified technique evoking 'a conservatism of response' (1991: 7) since Forsythe appears in a post-Balanchine landscape. The public that appreciates Forsythe was branded as an assemblage of arrant sensationalists, bored and masochistic, even self-destructive, thrill seekers. One critic wrote:

Forsythe's star rises at an opportune moment. Many ballet goers now are impatient with entertainment, musical continuity, directness of tone, and other traditional goals and values. They want to be shaken up. And Forsythe may be the man to give their fantasies the kick in the head they crave.

(Aloff 1988: 77)

The engagement of the audience with ballet is, on this account, sado-masochistic. The choreographer is pictured as assaulting the audience with a 'kick in the head', which also signifies the latter's pleasure in seeing how the art of ballet can be abused, brutalized, and humiliated.

Kisselgoff implicitly acknowledged the association of the intellectual in American life with what Hofstadter has called 'the idea of political and moral protest' (Hofstadter 1962: 38) while also defending the commercial viability of intellect in ballet: 'Mr. Forsythe is a breath of fresh air. He is different and it is understandable why he cannot work in the safe precincts of American ballet'. But she goes on to say: 'There is room for dissonance in all art – even art with a box-office sensibility' (1982: H8). One perceives the hint of a shared interest between conservative modernism, and box office profits. Kisselgoff swims against the tide, as she juxtaposes 'cannot work' with 'There is room'. Business, in Hofstadter's account of American culture, tends to be anti-intellectual, and ballet is related to business through its historical relation to popular entertainment.[10]

I evoke Hofstadter here also for the way he characterizes the so-called abstract qualities of intellect:

> The case against intellect is founded upon a set of fictional and wholly abstract antagonisms. Intellect is pitted against feeling on the ground that it is somehow inconsistent with warm emotion. It is pitted against character, because it is widely believed that intellect stands for mere cleverness, which transmutes easily into the sly or the diabolical. It is pitted against practicality, since theory is held to be opposed to practice.
>
> (Hofstadter 1962: 45–6)

When he labels Forsythe 'a thoughtful rather than imaginative choreographer', Clive Barnes (1987: 26) encapsulates this complex of codes with which to damn the intellectual. This particular review shows how tortuous the line of argumentation must become once audience enthusiasm and anti-intellectualism converge in the dark inner world of the ballet critic. 'And as for bringing down the house', wrote Barnes of *Artifact* in 1987,

> Forsythe's many admirers can take heart, just as his many detractors must take note, that audiences love, but really love, him. And whatever I may personally think as a critic, I never forget the storming cheers of a genuine audience. *I just ignore them.*
>
> (Barnes 1987: 26, my emphasis)

The danger of Barnes's disregard of the public is to posit a popular enthusiasm for the most traditionally unpopular of traits: intellect.[11] Rather than allow this apparent contradiction between the critical resentment and the popular approval of intellect to stand, however, Barnes assailed the choreographer's ability to infuse intellect into dance by accusing him of being 'provocatively *pseudo*-intellectual' (1987: 26). The apparent popularity of intellectualism on stage calls forth the corresponding charge of pseudo-intellectualism, begging the question of what authentic intellectualism in dance actually looks like. Barnes sees the audience wax enthusiastic about false intellect; with this rhetorical sleight of hand he reasserts the traditionally anti-intellectual character of the American public, which could only be enthusiastic about intellect in/as spectacle by misrecognizing it. Far from being sado-masochistic, the public is painted as being irrevocably confused.

The northeast of the United States in general and New York in particular, are paradoxical sites for anti-intellectualism in the arts, a phenomenon usually considered to emanate from Middle America. If it seems unrealistic to posit such a thing as a dance critical establishment responsible for this brand of anti-intellectualism – most critics take exception to any account of their own power – I would respond that it is precisely this attitude in the 1980s toward the impossibility of ballet as a postmodern phenomenon with a poststructuralist orientation that lends a certain common identity to critics, such that one might characterize them as members of the critical establishment. Anti-intellectualism arose in ballet criticism as poststructuralist panic.

The ideological cards are almost too transparently on the table in a 1985 *Wall Street Journal* review that acknowledges Forsythe's 'fashionable' and 'trendy' status. We find once again the theme of the inappropriateness of language, but also the inappropriateness of theatre *tout court* when apprehended in its 'visual – as opposed to kinetic – means'; that is, the inappropriateness of 'speech, sound, lighting and even stage machinery as equal partners to dancers' bodies'. The potentially problematic qualities of intellectualism that language brings to the ballet stage, primarily in Kisselgoff's discussions, are displaced in this review by the more threatening loss of the disciplinary (modernist) status of ballet itself as 'an autonomously communicative medium'. 'If, as it seems more than likely, he [Forsythe] is going to play an increasingly important role in American ballet, can there be any future for the art as we have hitherto known it? The answer, alas, must be no' (Harris 1985). For this critic, the choreographer's European credentials work against him because the critic claims Central Europeans never did grasp disciplinary closure. '[H]is output exemplifies a characteristically Central European mistrust of dance as an autonomously communicative medium' (Harris 1985). The problem is that 'the crux of a Forsythe ballet is its concept' rather than 'the rich possibilities available through the rich vocabulary of classical ballet' (Harris 1985). If we want to speak of Central Europeans, Adorno comes to mind as the great defender of modernism against kitsch: yet, in the *The Wall Street Journal*, modernism is cast as the saviour of kitsch.

Kisselgoff, on the other hand, apparently welcomed Forsythe's theorizations of his approach to movement. In a long tangent to her review of *Say Bye Bye* she asks: 'What has Mr. Forsythe been reading?' And she quotes him: '"I'm reading Barthes on the origins of narrative. It's difficult to avoid it. Audiences tend to project narrative on your work. We don't have to be afraid of it, but we have to find out how to restructure it"' (1983: H8). Her willingness to engage with the role reading played in the genesis of Forsythe's choreography was, and still is, admirable.

Things got a little more complicated, however, around issues of form and content, the use of language, and what it means to restructure the audience's projection of narrative onto dance, issues that Kisselgoff returned to periodically in her reviews. The invasion of dance making by language games might lead to interesting structural results, but the spoken word on the ballet stage did substantially more. Journalists identified no tradition, such as the baroque – highly appropriate in the case of *Artifact* – whose value is to allow for a self-referential or reflective analysis to be performed by the choreography itself from an interdisciplinary perspective that would justify language. Language and literature tended instead to suggest issues of content and form, and the choreographic result was critiqued as content-weak. 'Mr. Forsythe', wrote Kisselgoff of *Square Deal*, 'has jarred us by transposing ideas from literary theory and literature. There is a sense that he is trying to break up form in order to create content' (1983: H8). The form Kisselgoff is discussing is the narrative form of ballet: 'Mr. Forsythe's premise is that ballet can attempt to create narrative without overtly appearing to do so. A parallel concern has preoccupied modernist literature since the end of the nineteenth century, and yet remains startling to a ballet audience' (1983: H8).[12] Here, Forsythe is not countering ballet aesthetics as much as countering the audience's tendency to read narrative into movement.

If one assumes that Forsythe's interest in Robbe-Grillet's *nouveau roman* leads him to attempt to reconfigure narrative, one would then have to assume that the whole history of avant-garde film in opposition to Hollywood narrative is likewise an attempt to reconfigure narrative. It may be more accurate to say that it attempts to obliterate narrative. Consider feminist film criticism and feminist avant-garde cinematic practice, Yvonne Rainer comes to mind, where narrative is thought to purvey severe ideological gender bias. The assumption that there is no way out of narrative goes hand in hand with the misapprehension of Barthes and Foucault as structuralists: 'Structures in language as applied to culture', writes Kisselgoff, 'make for Structuralism. This is what Mr. Forsythe is telling us sub rosa in his ballets' (1987b: n.p.).

In his opposition to 'total history' in *The Archaeology of Knowledge* Foucault focuses on synchronic rather than diachronic sequences of the past. He studies the emergence of the statement (as opposed to the document) in relation to other statements in a synchronous historical moment. This appears to be a structuralist manoeuvre, but Foucault distinguishes his own work, which could only very marginally be characterized as literary theory, from structuralism (Foucault 1972: 15–16). Foucault has stated: 'I have never been a Freudian, I have never been a Marxist, and I have never been a structuralist' (Foucault 1998: 437). In the conclusion to *The Archaeology of Knowledge* he frames his entire scholarly project as anti-structuralist. He also dismisses the polemic with structuralism at that time (1969) as out of date (Foucault 1972: 199–201). Kisselgoff's sense that Forsythe takes a structuralist orientation from Foucault and that Foucault is involved with modern literature forestalls the awareness of Forsythe's poststructuralist orientation. The difference between these two orientations is significant, and one might almost say it led to a major misunderstanding.

Structuralism is dedicated to the analysis of how signs create meaning and work to support ideologically stable and immutable structures like narrative; poststructuralism, on the other hand, examines how signs migrate outside ideological closure. Structuralism is reductive; poststructuralism is anti-institutional.[13] Barthes, Foucault, and Derrida radically question the premises of literature, history, and philosophy, respectively, as institutions. Barthes transforms literature's style/content into *écriture*, Foucault transforms history's cause/effect into genealogy, and Derrida transforms philosophy's *logos* into grammatology. These methodological transformations do not lay waste to literature, history, or philosophy per se, but they do reconceptualize what these disciplines can accomplish once emancipated from their own self-imposed restrictions. They assail disciplinarity. While Kisselgoff sees the interconnectedness of Forsythe's politics and his formalism – and, not surprisingly, associates his formalism with structuralism – she does not fully articulate his iconoclastic purpose.

Foucault's critique of the document, frequently cited by Forsythe at this time, holds the key. The ballet tradition itself acquires the instability, the discontinuity, of the historical document that is part of a 'discursive formation' without historical inevitability or, in other terms, open to reinterpretation. One tier of Forsythe's interest in Foucault's critique of the document in the historical discipline reveals the (dis)continuity of the subject as a central concern of his choreography.[14] Forsythe combats the audience tendency to read movement as narrative because the discontinuity of the dancer with him or her self leaves no place for narrative.

In 1987, Kisselgoff wrote two reviews of *Artifact* that assailed Forsythe's references to Foucault, not because the ideas themselves were inappropriate to ballet, but because they materialized in discursive form on stage. One of these two reviews explicitly recognizes Forsythe's procedures for the first and only time in American criticism to be poststructuralist, rather than structuralist. This reckoning with Forsythe's use of language, neither as narrative nor as metaphor for movement alphabet in the choreographic process, but simply as words uttered on stage, constitutes in my view a critical awakening and a consequent crisis of reception. Why do they talk in *Artifact*, asks Kisselgoff of a ballet she had seen and reviewed before? Because, 'Mr. Forsythe is obviously exploring his earlier interest in the writings of French poststructuralist literary theorists' (Kisselgoff 1987). Not only do the dancers talk, but also, during a violent altercation, they yell. Kisselgoff concludes with a plea for 'less screaming, more dancing'. Yelling becomes the symptom of an anti-institutional rather than reductive formalist procedure. 'The difficulty in *Artifact*', continues Kisselgoff, ' ... is the proportion of spoken text in relation to the danced passages. Mr. Forsythe is at his best when he simply choreographs' (1987c: H4). While an analysis of *Artifact* to counterbalance this claim adequately is beyond the scope of this paper, this review conflates, as do many others, spectacle and theatricality with the jargon of continental theory. Speech is to yelling as structuralism is to poststructuralism.

In a published letter that I have been unable to relocate, but that I do remember reading, Forsythe retorted that Kisselgoff had probably never read Foucault. Perhaps more important than this tit-for-tat is the fact that Kisselgoff, despite her admiration for Forsythe, saw the dance, or at least the ballet in this instance, as an exclusive act, one that should in good conscience forgo the incursions of the voice. Yet, poststructuralist theory might be conceived here to play a positive rather than a nihilistic role: 'I think that Derrida and Foucault', remarked Forsythe in a 1990 interview, 'opened me up to be inclusive – to see that dancing is not an exclusive act'.[15] The increasingly interdisciplinary directions of his work since then suggest as much, and render moot the anxiety over the future of ballet. Forsythe's work of the 1980s demonstrates a profound respect for the differences that ballet can evidence with, by, and through itself. But, his differential, if not to say healthily deconstructive, view of ballet – one that allowed the outside in and turned the inside out – challenged some dance reviewers in the USA at that time to see more than they were able. Their defensiveness and the resultant leap to judgment is what put the status of the dance review itself as document into question.

Acknowledgements

This chapter could not have been completed without the generous assistance of William Forsythe, Freya Vass-Rhee, Mechthild Grossman, Eleanor Skimin, Roslyn Sulcas, Steven Spier, and Suzi Winson. Its conclusions and errors, however, are entirely my own.

Notes

1   The hiatus was interrupted initially by performances of *Eidos : Telos* at BAM in 1999. Forsythe works such as *Behind the China Dogs* and *Herman Schmerman* were nonetheless seen in New York during the 1990s.
2   Roslyn Sulcas began reviewing Forsythe in Paris in 1988, and in New York after 1996.
3   Personal conversation with the author, 2 August 2007, New York City.
4   Senta Driver discusses this resistance (Driver 1990) and immediately acknowledges 'the most unaccountable' attitude of critical reception (p. 86).
5   This invites comparison with the German reception of Forsythe and the way his national identity is situated in German discourse.
6   Perhaps the most perverse twist given Forsythe's identity as an American working in Europe comes from Joan Acocella's review of *Behind the China Dogs*: 'Forsythe is one of the foremost purveyors of European apocalyptic ballet, and perhaps because he is not European but American, his work stands out from the rest as being the most cleanly unsentimentally brutal and the least sincere. Béjart, Bausch – you feel as though they may actually see the world that way. Forsythe, it looks like a good sales angle'. Joan Acocella, 'Forsythe Unleashed at the American Musical Festival. Dogfight', in *7 Days*, 25 May 1988, 48. Acocella, like many of her colleagues, feels obliged to confront audience response: 'Why, then, did all that clapping seem loud not just with pleasure but also with endorsement, validation?' Her answer: it is the backlash of the public against ballet: 'this "elitist" art, with its straight backs and fine manners – it too is getting a kick in the pants … We get to piss on the palace stairs'.
7   The prominence of European contemporary dance in New York during the 1980s was largely due to the BAM Next Wave Festival, regularly lamented in

dance columns of *The New Yorker*. In a special issue of *The New Criterion* on 'New York in the Eighties', Arlene Croce dismissed BAM as follows: 'New York does possess the best in dance; it is also hospitable to the worst in dance. I cite as an example the parade of mediocrities from abroad sponsored in recent seasons by the Brooklyn Academy of Music'. Arlene Croce, 'Arlene Croce' in *The New Criterion*, Summer 1986, 16.

8 And it should be remembered that Forsythe was simultaneously innovating in the ballet vocabulary, notably around the extension of Rudolf von Laban's theory of the kinesphere. (Spier 1988). For an extended analysis of *Artifact* see Franko, Nitra, Slovakia: *Constantine the Philosopher*, University Press, 2010: 84–101.

9 'I see the people who chronicle the art much less as people who exercise critique than as pseudo-historians. There is a wonderful introduction to *The Archaeology of Knowledge*, by Michel Foucault, in which he discusses the dilemma of the verity of the document ... In terms of these kinds of people that are writing it's so sad that they are saying, "I am a critic". We're talking about the theory of dance; these people are talking about the theory of critique. Dealing with *The New Yorker* is like dance on a level of Dance Masters of America. It's semiserious.' Forsythe quoted in Thorpe (1989: 83). The opening of *The Archaeology of Knowledge* contains the passage on the document that was posted on the Ballett Frankfurt website. One indication of the low tolerance in the critical establishment for any such dialogue with the artist is to be found in Arlene Croce's infamous thought piece on Bill T. Jones's *Still/Here*: 'Jones's message, like Forsythe's, was clear: No back talk! Anything you say not only will be held against you but may be converted into grist for further paranoid accusation' (Croce 2000: 713). For more on the *Still/Here* controversy, see Franko, Mark (2009), 'From Croce's Critical Condition to the Choreographic Public Sphere' in *Dance – Movement – Mobility*. Proceedings of the 9th International NOFOD Conference (Nordic Forum for Dance Research) Tampere, Finland: Department of Music Anthropology: 27–40.

10 See Franko 2002: 108–13.

11 See Hoftstadter's development of the difference between intelligence and intellect in Chapter Two, 'On the Unpopularity of Intellect' in *Anti-Intellectualism*: 24–51.

12 In a 1998 Paris interview with Rosyln Sulcas, Forsythe said: 'I don't narrate. I can't. I think that I'm missing a narrative gene! ... The "elements" are just there, and I can't explain why, although in the logic of the piece they are absolutely necessary. Of course, you can come up with explanations afterwards, but that's after the fact. There tends to be a universal desire to project narration into dancing ...!' This interview was posted on the Ballett Frankfurt website.

13 In post-structuralism, the sign itself is then no longer as important as the sign's movement. Hence, we are no longer properly in the domain of the sign at all, but in the domain of the trace; not in the field of ideological closure, but in that of differ(a)nce. 'An allegiance to difference conforms to a respect for alterity and the other. Politically, the translation occurs immediately in the regions of feminism, racism, and international politics, and locally in reading cultural texts in light of the others they exploit, exclude, or represent' (Jay 1987–8: 195–6).

14 Foucault writes: 'Continuous history is the indispensable correlative of the founding function of the subject: the guarantee that everything that has eluded him may be restored to him; the certainty that time will disperse nothing without restoring it in a reconstituted unity; the promise that one day the subject – in the form of historical consciousness – will once again be able to appropriate, to bring back under his sway, all those things that are kept at a distance by difference, and find in them what might be called his abode' (1972: 12). On the

apparent synchrony of discursive formations, see Chapter 5 of *The Archaeology of Knowledge,* 'Change and Transformations': 166–177. See Franko 2010.
15   Roslyn Sulcas, unpublished interview with William Forsythe, Paris, 30 October 1990. Typescript in William Forsythe clippings file, Dance Collection, New York Public Library for the Performing Arts at Lincoln Center.

References

Aloff, Mindy (1988) 'Review', *Dance Magazine* LXII(1): 77–9.

Barnes, Clive (1987) 'Frankfurt's Forsythe saga' in *The New York Post* (15 July), p. 26.

Bonnot de Condillac, Etienne (2001) *Essay on the Origin of Human Knowledge,* trans. Hans Aarsleff, Cambridge: Cambridge University Press.

Croce, Arlene (2000), 'Discussing the Undiscussable' in *Writing in the Dark: Dancing in the New Yorker,* New York: Farrar, Straus & Giroux.

Derrida, Jacques (1981) *Positions,* trans. Alan Bass, Chicago, IL: University of Chicago Press.

Driver, Senta (1990) 'A Conversation with William Forsythe', *Ballet Review* 18(1) (Spring), 86–97.

Dunning, Jennifer (2007) 'Deconstructing the Costs, and Emotions, of Warfare', *The New York Times*, March 2, B12.

Foucault, Michel (1969, 1972) *The Archaeology of Knowledge*, trans. A.M. Sheridan Smith, New York: Pantheon.

Foucault, Michel (1998) 'Structuralism and Poststructuralism' in *Essential Works of Foucault, 1954–1984*, volume 2: *Aesthetics, Method, and Epistemology*, ed. James D. Faubion, trans. Robert Hurley and others, New York: The New Press.

Franko, Mark (2002) *The Work of Dance: Labor, Movement, and Identity in the 1930s*, Middletown: Wesleyan University Press.

Franko, Mark (2010) 'Archaeological Choreographic Practices: Foucault and Forsythe', forthcoming in *History of Human Sciences* ('Foucault Across the Disciplines') (2010).

Franko, Mark (forthcoming) 'Body-Language and Language-Body in Louis Marin, Michel Foucault, and William Forsythe', in a special issue of *Ars Aeterna* 'Unfolding the Baroque: Cultures and Concepts', Catherine M. Soussloff and Alena Smieskova (eds), Slovakia: Constantine the Philosopher University Press.

Harris, Dale (1985) 'Dance: William Forsythe's Frankfurt Ballet', *The Wall Street Journal*, 21 June, n.p.

Hofstadter, Richard (1962) *Anti-Intellectualism in American Life*, New York: Vintage Books.

Hushka, Sabine (2001) 'Der Tanz als Inschrift. Die Bewegungsästhetik von William Forsythe', *Tanzdrama* 61(6): 26–61.

Jay, Gregory S. (1987–8), 'Values and Deconstructions: Derrida, Saussure, Marx', in *Cultural Critique* 8 (Winter 1987–88).

Kisselgoff, Anna (1982) 'Forsythe's "Say bye-bye" Startles and Excites', *The New York Times*, 1 August, H8.

Kisselgoff, Anna (1983) 'Forsythe Transposes Literary Theories to the Stage', *The New York Time*, 20 November, H8.

Kisselgoff, Anna (1987a) 'Dance: Two Premieres by San Francisco Ballet', *The New York Times*, 3 February, n.p.

Kisselgoff, Anna (1987b) 'Dance: Three Premieres by the Frankfurt Ballet', *The New York Times,* 18 July, n.p.

Kisselgoff, Anna (1987c) 'The Sound and the Flurry of William Forsythe', *The New York Times,* 19 July, H4.

Kisselgoff, Anna (1988) 'Dance: Vibrant Frenetics From Frankfurt, a la Forsythe', *The New York Times,* 15 June, C24.

Macaulay, Alistair (1988) 'Acid Rain', *The New Yorker,* 25 July, 79.

New York Times (1985) 'Dance: Three Premieres by the Frankfurt Ballet', *New York Times*, 18 July.

Siegmund, Gerald (1999) 'In Frankfurt, America is Alive and Kicking' in *Ballet International* 4 (April): 34–7.

Siegmund, Gerald (2002) 'Echos und Schatten. William Forsythe's Ballette' in *Tanzdrama* (62)1: 62–71

Spier, Steven (1988) 'Engendering and composing movement: William Forsythe and the Ballet Frankfurt', *The Journal of Architecture* 3 (Summer): 135–146.

Sulcas, Roslyn (1991) 'William Forsythe: the poetry of disappearance and the great tradition', *Dance Theatre Journal, p. 4,* 9(1, Summer).

Thorpe, Wist (1989) 'Forsythe to the Fore' *Interview* (June).

4 Nijinsky's heir

A classical company leads modern dance

Senta Driver

I first heard it from Paul Taylor: the suggestion that the real founder of modern dance was Vaslav Nijinsky. The notion comes, in fact, from Lincoln Kirstein. It rests on an appreciation of the choreographer Nijinsky's profound innovations in movement design and group structure. Perhaps it also reflects that the Russian dancer was committed to a personal vision rather than to the primacy of the classical materials he inherited.

What made us think Nijinsky was a ballet choreographer at all? The answer is probably his context, the Diaghilev company, and his training more than his actual product. Consider the choreographic material of his fully completed works. They could all be taken for radical modern dance, but they were performed by ballet dancers, and presented by a company with an otherwise classical repertory. The elements of the Russian ballet tradition were being used to forge an utterly original direction. What made us think George Balanchine ran what was essentially a modern dance company, compared to other ballet companies of his era? One usually cited his departure from the classic repertory and school of steps and his commitment to a single, progressive artistic vision and a distinctive movement vocabulary. Ballet is defined, like all arts, by its makers, and by the dancers and choreographers who accept influences that they find persuasive, and build upon them.

When an artist with a thoroughly classical background is denounced on the grounds that he 'destroys ballet', either the work is weak or ballet has developed dangerously reactionary thinking. Those who do not make work are periodically moved to lock down its definitions: this was ineffective in 1912 when Nijinsky created his first full professional work, and it will continue to be so. We can celebrate a profound advance into new thinking when a choreographer spends his artistic life inside the classical school, shows veneration for the *ballet d'école*, informed respect for Balanchine and ballet history, and regular reliance on the pointe shoe, but makes work with unorthodox expansions of the vocabulary, fractured yet theatrically astute structure, and constant sympathies with the work of major modern dance innovators.

William Forsythe has given his field a daring new direction and scope. His work is frequently begun in notions about light rather than music. Like the finest artists, he teaches the dance audience new skills for looking at things. For his sake we have developed a capacity to see in extremely low levels of light, even as his dancers have learned to be able to move freely, in groups, through a blackout. We can follow the logic of a known classical step through long new permutations. A *penché* may plunge in extraordinary directions, or a *fouetté* be created by picking up the dancer and hurling her manually around 360° as she executes the legwork—and we still recognise the source. As Forsythe has often stated, he treats the premises of classical technique as a usable language capable of new meaning, rather than as a collection of phrases and traditionally linked steps that retain traditional rules, shapes, and content subject only to rearrangement. Aside from his enrichment of the *ballet d'école*, his approach greatly strengthens the dancers who use it. This is apparent physically as well as in their intellectual development, and it shows up in a look of knowledgeability and engagement on stage. Most dancers in outside companies who are cast in Forsythe pieces look like different artists in his work. They visibly know what a depth of information lies behind their movement.

Forsythe has taught classical dancers to generate their own material by applying structural devices to their familiar techniques. Drawing upon the theories of Rudolf von Laban, which Forsythe has carried forward in what he calls Improvisation Technologies, he vitally expands the movement vocabulary. His style has developed over the 14 years in Frankfurt from a forceful, weighted and athletic one using the pointe shoe as a pole vaulter might, into a much warmer and more fluid realm. He has a permanent affection for pointework, and never abandons it for long, but recent works are sometimes danced in socks, soft slippers or even bare feet, and an increasing use of silence and tenderness is apparent. The dancers examine each other, touch and handle and interfere with each other in intricate assignments, and work extensively with and close to the floor. The structure of the pieces can seem confusing, but they are assembled with astute theatricality. They are carefully built to pace the evening well, and they progress with their own logic. His approach and movement thinking resonate with the methods of the great modern dance innovators such as Merce Cunningham, Trisha Brown, and Twyla Tharp. Both his artists and the dancers of other companies who have worked with him demonstrate a range of new virtuosities. These days one rarely sees as much original material for the body in a whole season of modern dance as Forsythe offers at Ballett Frankfurt.

The range of Forsythe's thinking is illustrated by the various plans he made for a new work at the Roundhouse, a former railway turntable shed in London. He has described three successive concepts: transformation of the building into a huge *camera obscura* with the image projected into the cellar onto a field of tightly packed narcissus; video on the skylight atop the building; and, finally, (the actual project) raising the 'world's largest bouncy castle', an inflated structure with a trampoline floor in which the audience created all the movement. The piece, (now called *White Bouncy Castle)*, is known to him and Dana Caspersen, who made it with him, as the *John Cage Memorial Choreographic Cube.*

Ballet tells us where ballet is going. Not even the most ardent devotees of what used to be can do that.

We had half expected to see moderns, with their alleged superiority of imagination, take over the classical field. The stream of new choreographers making work on and off pointe for ballet companies suggested to some that the future of ballet lay outside its fold. Are we now looking at the opposite, a classically-based artist who emerges as a profound leader of modern dance? Certainly in addition to his rich physicality, there is more adventure, more risk-taking in topic and visual design and structure in an evening at Ballett Frankfurt than one finds in most contemporary dance. There is also more aesthetic daring. Many modern dance artists have widened their reach into popular culture and its resources, but no one has managed a surreal parody of a Broadway musical, expertly sung Ethel Merman-style by an entire ballet company, quite on the level of *Isabelle's Dance.* Forsythe is, more simply, a profound leader of all dance, going in directions once reserved for moderns by means of a classical vehicle. He observed in the program of his April 1998 season at Theater Basel, 'I use ballet, because I use ballet dancers, and I use the knowledge in their bodies. I think ballet is a very, very good idea that often gets pooh-poohed.' He trusts the tradition. He believes it is his, and that it is fertile. What does his work say about the old dichotomy, now that he has opened ballet's physical vocabulary, without losing its classical base, by the use of modern dance gambits?

To be comprehensive about his achievement, including his pursuit of intellectual theory, irreverence, architectural theory, humour, the advantages of computer technology, and the role of children's perspective in the art of adults, requires a book-length treatment. The illuminating factor in his process is his huge curiosity about everything around him, how it works and what happens if something is knocked awry. This and his simple, candid respect for other artists are the elements that stand out.

Forsythe has profoundly enriched our art form in his 22 years of working, taking the utmost care to evade the centre of attention. He has a remarkable capacity, such as I have only seen before in the great teacher Helen Alkire, for keeping his mind open and at work on new challenges.

He has forged a new kind of beauty in dancing.

5 Timbral architectures, aurality's force

Sound and music

Chris Salter

A single sound is heard in the theatre. It resembles, at least in the first moments, a stringed instrument playing an out-of-tune, pentatonic scale. As the sound continues, it has difficulty completing its phrase, as if something were prohibiting its resolution. The sound comes apart, decelerating and simultaneously continuing its search for an end. Other sounds gradually enter this strange aural field to which we somehow cannot rapidly enough adjust our perception: percussive glissandos and longer, legato lines that start and suddenly fade. There is a feeling of suspension that some great storm of force is about to erupt in the theatre.

A wild torrent of noise is unleashed. The existing tonal lines grow denser to compete against a sampled amalgamation of slowed-down percussion, screeching fragments of an Evan Parker saxophone solo, a swarm of insects, whistling and shattering glass, *shukuhachi* and *taiko* drum blasts, the piercing whine of a Tokyo convenience store at midnight. The sound grows denser and louder. Elements enter and exit in random bursts. The musicians in the pit pound away at the electronics. There are unique moments, however, when no one steers the aural monster except the room. Waves of feedback grow like solitons, some dying in the instant while others are re-sampled, played on top of and enfolded back into each other, travelling across the space in constant acceleration. At times, the room injects its own frequencies into the downpour of music. The sound moves in and out of control, having its own mad internal sense of order and chaos, intensity, velocity, and flow. The mix is a swarm of sound, which Forsythe describes as 'so dense that I can't even listen that fast' (Salter 1997: 96).

Over the past three decades William Forsythe's deep interest in sound as theatrical and choreographic material in itself has resulted in work where the acoustic becomes almost inseparable from the visual and corporeal on stage. If, as Goethe famously stated, 'architecture is frozen music', then music and sound in Forsythe's *Weltanschauung* is melting architecture – a transmutating flow of timbres, dynamics, and rhythms akin to what the Polish mathematician and philosopher Hoëne (Joseph) Wronsky labelled 'the corporealization of the intelligence that is in sound' (Cox and Warner 2004: 19–20). The acoustic universe that Forsythe's work incorporates is body and event simultaneously; forces whose colours, lines, shapes, and textures colonize space, reconfigure time, and rupture perception.

From his earliest radical ballets through to his epic-scaled *Gesamtkunstwerke* of the mid to late 1990s, Forsythe's deployment of stage languages like sound, lighting, video, and scenography have developed in parallel with his relentless questioning of the perceptual-political frameworks by which we come to experience the dancing body as a medium of expression and way of knowing the world. He has generated works that 'function both as theoretical models and as entertainment' (Papadakis and Libeskind 1995: 96).

The position of music in Forsythe's *oeuvre* radically departs not only from its traditional subservience to dance in the ballet scores of the seventeenth century, but also from its narrative underpinnings in the works of pioneers like Lully and Tchaikovsky, and in the twentieth-century modern dance of Isadora Duncan, Ted Shawn, and Jacques Dalcroze. Even if music for dance does not completely escape its narrative chains with the moderns, its radical transformation in relation to the choreographic event does commence in the same epoch as the savage rhythms and pagan violence conjured up by Stravinsky's 1913 score to Nijinsky's *Rite of Spring* as well as the Futurists', Edgard Varèse's, and later, John Cage's collapsing of the long-standing distinctions between music and noise. Like Varèse, who could only dream of having at his disposal the technological means to harness 'the entire universe of sound', and Cage, for whom composition was simply the organization of any sound in time and space, Forsythe's artistic practice also aims for a dissolution of sensory boundaries between the ear, eye, and skin. This fusion is brought on partially by the manipulation of a sonic *nous* fluctuating between tonal order and noisy disorder.

In the mid-1930s in his self-described theatre of cruelty, the French theatre actor and theorist Antonin Artaud articulated music and sound's critical position as stage elements that could 'act directly and profoundly upon the sensibility through the sense organs' (Artaud 1976: 247). Around the same time, Varèse was theorizing a new kind of acoustic space in which music would no longer be wedded to the linearity of Johann Fux's counterpoint but instead be constituted by 'sound masses, of shifting planes', setting forth the phenomena of 'penetration and repulsion' (Cox and Warner 2004: 17). 'Music', as Gilles Deleuze wrote in 1981 trying to get beyond the assumed figural concepts of representation exemplified in the work of painter Francis Bacon, is 'not a matter of reproducing or inventing forms but of capturing forces-rendering sonorous forces that are not themselves sonorous' (Deleuze 2003: 49).

In Forsythe's choreography, music and sound are no longer relegated to the background of a dance but instead run independently in parallel to the organizing of bodies. It is difficult to understand the phenomenological impact of his work without also grasping the sonorities that assist us in experiencing the intricate architectures of time, space, and movement emerging on the stage. Furthermore, although many a critic and writer have done so, it is equally problematic to speak of Forsythe's artistic journey without acknowledging his musical partnerships, most importantly his 26-year collaboration with Dutch composer Thom Willems. Although Forsythe has worked with a variety of musical artists during his career, from English minimalist Gavin Bryars to Max/MSP software developer Leslie Stuck and house accompanist David Morrow, it is Willems's mainly electronically produced scores and sonic environments that have elevated music and sound to the level of dramatic character and force in Forsythe's work with the Ballett Frankfurt and later The Forsythe Company.

A classically trained student of Louis Andriessen and Jan Boerman at the Royal Conservatory in The Hague, Willems integrates pop as well as the twentieth-century classical avant-garde influences of Berio, Stravinsky, Xenakis, and others while pushing the extremes of the frequency spectrum for the spectator/listener. His electronic scores embody Forsythe's differentiated compositional strategies and his sonic contribution has indeed been one of the chief determinants for the powerful affect of Forsythe's dances, a point astutely made by one of his long time commentators, the German critic Eva-Elisabeth Fischer: 'William Forsythe wanted to collaborate with Thom Willems because his music made images appear and revealed structures.'[1] Moving from early minimalist meditations (*LDC*) and the hard, disco-influenced rhythmic lines of 1980s works like *Limbs Theorem* to the disconcerting passages of noise and silence that constitute the musical landscapes of *As a Garden in This Setting*, *The Loss of Small Detail*, and *Eidos : Telos*, Willems's sometimes brash and other times barely audible, multi-layered sonic contexts create 'a space to cradle the dance'; a space that 'gives the dancers a foundation, a plateau and a stage where they can react on multiple levels' (Bayerischer Staatsoper 2004: 14).

Extensively playing with, while departing from, the Western musical canon's vocabulary and regimens, Willems blurs sound and music, improvisation and structure, and live interaction and playback, inventing ways for sound to occupy and transform the choreographic event spatially and temporally. In using the expression timbral architecture I want to suggest that music and sound not only have a melodic or rhythmic function (as assumed in most dance scores) built up from what Trevor Wishart calls 'the myth of the primacy of pitch' (Wishart 1996: 23), but also a fundamental acoustic-architectural one, both in form (morphology) and in the merger between temporal and spatial structure (Wishart 1966: 11–43).

While I will discuss some examples from Willems's numerous tape-based pieces composed for Forsythe, this chapter focuses in particular on the increased interest in techniques of live, computer-based processing with acoustic and software instruments or human voices. This interest was a central aspect of the sono-choreographic body of work starting with *Eidos : Telos* and continuing with *Sleepers Guts* and *Three Atmospheric Studies* that utilized techniques of live, computer-based processing with acoustic and software instruments or human voices. Indeed, it is in such 'DSP productions', as Forsythe recently referred to the use of digital signal processing techniques, to 'generate a world' (*Eidos*) or 'turn the dancers into their own instrument' (*You made me a monster*), that the future role for music and sound in dance is being conceptualized and invented.[2] In this sense, Forsythe and Willems's understanding of music's aesthetic-technological scaffolding parallels the work of another well-known choreographer/composer duo: Merce Cunningham and John Cage. Famous for exploring the indeterminate relationships between movement and music (something that differs markedly from Forsythe and Willems's process), Cage and fellow musicians such as David Tudor, Gordon Mumma, and David Behrman were also early pioneers in the real-time transformation of sound by way of electronic and computational techniques used in Cunningham's choreographies starting in the late 1950s.

The use of techno-scientific processes to transform sound or to generate never-before-heard synthetic sonorities has, however, a far greater conceptual and corporeal impact than just the extension of sonic possibilities through digital tools. The work that Willems and computer musician Joel Ryan undertook on *Eidos : Telos*, in particular, re-conceives, through technical systems, the role of music composition in dance from purely score-based playback to that of a dynamic instrument and environment, or what I have termed elsewhere audio scenography: the replacement of visual scenography with a continually transforming audio landscape (Salter *et al*. 2007). In response to a typical musically uninformed critic who described Willems's scores as 'very hard, very percussive, and very industrial – call it what you want', Forsythe replied, 'I don't think that's fair. Thom Willems gives you acoustic space to dance … He makes acoustic environments. We have done away with the sets. We have acoustic environments' (Forsythe 2003).[3]

To understand how Forsythe and his musical collaborators work to reconceive and transform the position of music and sound in relation to dancing bodies, we will first explore Forsythe's interest in the affect of sound on the spectator/listener and, in particular, sound's ability to go beyond narrative and representation and be rendered into intensities and forces. This strategy is based in the experimental, modernist performance and composition practices of Artaud, Varèse, and Xenakis. We shall see how Artaud's challenge to develop new sonic stage languages and techniques parallels Forsythe and Willems's interest in using new technological processes to yield unknown experiences in the spectator.

Taking the example of *Eidos : Telos*, one of the productions on which I collaborated with Forsythe and Willems on sound and interaction design and which featured live signal processing of acoustic instruments, we will explore the move away from the conception of composition as notation or description represented in a score and towards its reconception in the creation of new kinds of instruments, where a dramaturgical coupling takes place between techno-scientific/engineering processes and dramatic forms.

Finally, I will examine the shifting of dance music composition in Forsythe's work towards the design of total acoustic environments. I will argue that the concrete techniques of diffusion and spatialization that make up the acoustic environments developed by Forsythe's musical collaborators directly embody his conception of the movement of bodies on stage, creating complementary relationships between trace forms of moving, three-dimensional sound, and the dynamic architectures produced by such dancing bodies. The different materialities at play in Forsythe's choreographies span between human bodies and technological systems and result in a transformation of each through the other.

Intensities and forces

Forsythe has repeatedly stated that the composition, amplification, and diffusion of Willems's music are the most important elements in the panoply of theatrical devices at work in his dances. The ways in which Forsythe understands and positions music within the context of dance, and its affects on the perception of that dance to a spectator, stray from conventions, particularly balletic ones. Whereas historically music has been primarily used in classical ballet to illustrate aurally and accompany the on-stage narrative, Forsythe's pronounced aversion to narrative and representational modes of movement in general logically frees sound for other purposes, namely to generate powerful psycho-physical results. 'Going through every kind of acoustical dimension', Willems's sonic spaces forge an extremely complex, contrapuntal timbral and spatio-temporal relationship to other events taking place on stage, sometimes directly aligning with the dancers' movements while at other times operating independently on their own trajectories.

For example, in what is usually defined as the colour of a sound or its timbre, the spectral relationship of frequencies and the varying strengths of their amplitudes, Willems's work has always behaved in qualitative extremes, moving from melodically recognizable lines that are barely audible to sudden, full frequency densities that for many an audience member (and critic) approach the realm of noise due to the listener's inability to detect any proper ratios of harmonic relationships.[4] The timbral manipulation and control afforded by technologies of computer synthesis and sampling, where individual frequencies can be precisely shaped and built up into dense sonic layers, suggests a radically different way of listening to music within the context of dance, from an element which directly illustrates a movement to an enunciation of different quanta of densities, colours, and shapes.

Beginning with Arnold Schoenberg's dodecaphonic transformation of harmony, which removed the narrative reliance on a tonal centre and the tempered variations thereof, the concept of music as a dynamic field of changing forms and densities rather than a linear, point-to-point harmonically driven narrative refers back to early twentieth century shifts brought on by machine age technologies. Demanding an end to music's reliance on melody and harmony, and instead celebrating the incorporation of previously unheard machine sonorities, Luigi Russolo's (in)famous 1910 Futurist treatise 'The Art of Noises' suggested the dissolution between noise and sound. 'As it grows ever more complicated today, musical art seeks out combinations more dissonant, stranger and harsher for the ear. Thus, it comes ever closer to the noise-sound' (Cox and Warner 2004: 12). Employing new machineries of noise-making, what he termed *intorumori*, Russolo sought to harness the new sonorities arriving from 'the throbbing of valves' and 'the muttering of motors' by musically regulating and tuning such 'movements and vibrations of time and intensity' through emerging technologies.

A similar language describing music as 'zones of intensities' of 'various timbres or colours and different loudnesses', appears in the writings of Varèse. Perhaps more than any other early modernist twentieth-century composer, Varèse heard the possibilities that new 'sound producing machines' could yield. Through technological means, sound could facilitate physical and emotional sensations in the listener by changing timbre from 'something incidental, anecdotal, sensual or picturesque' to 'an agent of delineation' (Cox and Warner 2004: 18–21).

Another essential modernist influence is the dense, dramatic aural landscapes of the Greek-born composer Xenakis. Known for his development of 'stochastic music', in which probability and other statistical/computational procedures were used to generate complex 'movements of thought', Xenakis's interest lay in the entropic macro- and micro- 'sonic entities' that behave like the phenomena of hailstorms or a sudden political riot in a city street. The unexpected, violent shifts of scale, density, articulation, and motion inherent in such events 'made out of thousands of isolated sounds' epitomized, for Xenakis, the age old tension between 'chance, disorder and disorganization' versus reason, order, and organization – a theme strongly resonant with Forsythe and Willems's own artistic interest in challenging the viewer/listener's orientation of order and disorder.

From alteration through the disappearance of perceivable harmonic relationships or the use of socio-technically wrought machines (as Félix Guattari would label them) such as statistical models and advanced mathematics to generate wiggling paths between order and disorder, what such modernist approaches have in common is a move away from music as a representational medium and towards the sensation of its physical, vibratory qualities – an impact, that Deleuze, paraphrasing Artaud, writes 'is none other than the action of forces upon the body or sensation' (Deleuze 2003: 40). While not necessarily employing the advanced mathematical systems that Xenakis sought out to create a music that would go beyond linear polyphony to one through which 'densities, durations, registers, speeds, can be subjected to the law of large numbers with the necessary approximations', Willems's compositions go beyond the 'lattice system of pitch' (Wishart 1996) in order to evoke a space of vibratory and clangorous forces; one that engulfs the listener in its micro- and macro-sonic structure and its frenetic and simultaneously, glacial movement in time (Xenakis, 1992: 16).

Willems's electronic tonalities demand a technical apparatus, an instrument capable of producing, articulating, and reproducing such elaborate sonorities. Part of Forsythe's on-stage technical rehearsals when assembling works have thus focused on the best possible acoustic rendering and shaping of sound relative to the specific performance space, with devices such as real-time spectral analyzers and equalization hardware playing a critical role. Peppering the air with statements like 'we need a bit more at ten kHz in order to vibrate the air', and 'let the subwoofers come in ten milliseconds later', Willems and the technicians design, tune, and tweak analyzer and equalizer settings in order to achieve precise frequency balances, amplifying and attenuating the complex timbral shapes that evolve over time and shift the air.

Composition, sound design, and engineering fuse into what Gordon Mumma labelled the 'total configuration' of 'sound sources, electronic modification circuitry, control or logic circuitry, playback apparatus (power amplifiers, loudspeakers, and the auditorium), and even social conditions beyond the confines of technology' (Mumma 1976). The act of composition thus relies as much on the accuracy of machines and their exchanges with the particular characteristics of the performance space's acoustics as with traditional pitch lattice techniques. In this sense, Willems's music betrays its electronic-technical roots. Although notated through software, the extremely precise use of particular frequencies, densities, speeds, and textures in his acoustic environments transcends their ultimate representation and storage in pure notation/inscription and instead relies on a tangled technological infrastructure to assault, disorient, and defamiliarize the act of listening and, consequently, seeing, during Forsythe's works.

Instruments

Artaud's call for 'research, from the point of view of sound, into quantities and vibrations of sounds to which we are absolutely unaccustomed', also suggests the production of technical instruments for the rendering of extreme acoustic sensations (Artaud 1976: 247). In delving into acoustic methods to metamorphose the spectator from passive listener to active participant, Artaud grasped the potential of modern technology to construct new instruments leveraging sound's vibratory, almost magical, abilities in order to go beyond illustration and towards something purely physical. Further, a desire for the unheard would transcend what he felt were the sonic limitations of traditional musical instruments, re-evaluating ancient and forgotten instruments or creating new ones. In a remarkably similar manner, Willems moves towards fulfilling Artaud's dictate to develop new sonic languages for the stage by way of new instrumentalities, not only through his multiple scores produced with the complexities of a studio apparatus (famously labelled its own instrument by Brian Eno) but also in his two central Ballet Frankfurt collaborations with real-time computer musician/ instrument builder Joel Ryan: *Eidos : Telos* and *Sleepers Guts*.

It is difficult to generalize how Forsythe and Willems work together since their process is specific to each project. Forsythe states that Willems 'can come in at any stage. He can walk in two days before the premiere or he can hand me a piece four months before. It varies every time' (Forsythe 2003). Up until the mid-1990s, much of Willems's output for the Ballett Frankfurt took the form of elaborately crafted, multi-track and multi-channel studio-based recordings using exclusively electronic instruments, namely synthesizers and samplers. Yet Forsythe's epic *Eidos : Telos* acts as a turning point for their collaboration – the first major production to depart from Willems's earlier tape-based studio compositions to work with live, real-time signal processing of acoustic instruments in close collaboration with Ryan. Faced with both the cost of studio time and Willems's and Forsythe's desire to work with live musicians, the two engaged Ryan to develop computer-based musical instruments that could help alter the tonalities of acoustic ones. A former student of Herbert Marcuse at the University of California at San Diego in the mid-1960s, the polymath Ryan also studied physics at Pomona, music with Ravi Shankar and finally, computer-generated sound, first at Stanford and subsequently at Mills College in California in 1976 under the direction of composer and electronics whiz David Behrman and composer Robert Ashley.

Through Behrman, who, along with David Tudor and Mumma was one of the leading pioneers in the development of live electronics in musical performance, Ryan was introduced to and soon became part of the legendary hacker scene at Mills in which technology-savvy graduate students in electronic music were beginning to take advantage of the San Francisco Bay area's artistic-techno-scientific culture.[5] Exploiting the increased availability of inexpensive, user-programmable microcomputers, Ryan began writing custom programs using digital signal processing techniques in order to extend the possibilities of acoustic instruments and to invent new ones.

While historically the use of computers in music (much like the dodecaphonic structural techniques formulated by the serialists) has focused on the production of formal abstractions to be used in the compositional process, real-time electronics are much more intimately linked with the physical, embodied act of musical performance itself. Here, the descriptor real-time in computer sound generation has a specific meaning, denoting procedures where the processing of input (sound via a microphone) takes place at approximately the same time as output (sound in an acoustic environment), in contrast to the early days of computer music in which sound synthesis took hours, if not days, to compute.

In his seminal article 'Effort and Expression', Ryan describes the framework of real time as one of 'hands on performance which forces the composer to confront the abstractness of the computer head on'. The computer could aid the immediacy of the performance situation,

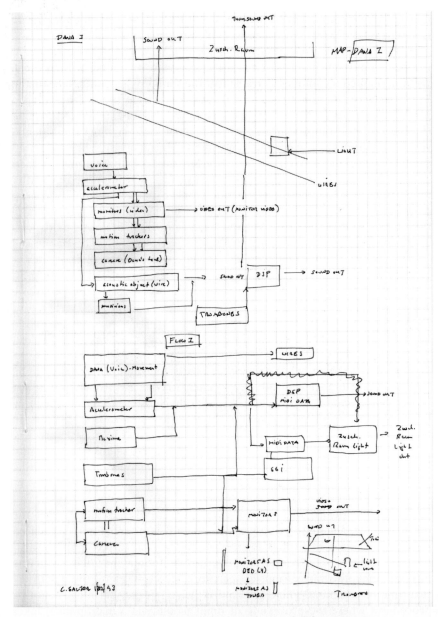

Figure 5.1 Author's notes for *Eidos : Telos* (Permission of Chris Salter)

'putting physical handles on phantom models' where the 'physicality of the performance *interface* [my emphasis] gives definition to the modeling process itself' (Ryan 1992). In fact, it is this connection between the abstract formalism of computational processes and the real world, embodied act of playing through the construction of a new performance interface/instrument that Ryan has exploited in his own artistic work, and which subsequently has had a noted impact on Forsythe and Willems's approach to sound.

In 1992 while working as scientific advisor at the Amsterdam-based Studio for Electro-Instrumental Muziek (STEIM) on sensor-augmented instruments, Ryan developed techniques to transform the sound of a stainless-steel piano wire with custom digital signal processing algorithms written in assembly language. Treating the wire itself as a sound producing source, Ryan amplified the metal with a contact piezo pickup and used a nylon-strung *saranghi* bow in order to excite the material, all the while changing processes like filters and delays to achieve different sonic alterations.

This process could be seen as similar to how an acoustic musician produces different timbres and dynamics by continually varying the physical playing techniques of the instrument. In his solo projects that sonically mutate constructed materials (i.e. the wire) as well as in collaborations with musicians like saxophonist Parker, cellist Francis Marie Uitti, trombonist George Lewis or violinist Malcolm Goldstein, Ryan's practice bears strong similarity to Mumma's previously discussed 'total configuration of sound'. The notion of instrument extends from the physical material of the acoustic sound-making body (violin, cello, or wire) and its sonic excitation via

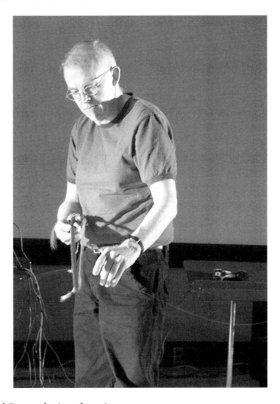

Figure 5.2 Joel Ryan playing the wire

human gesture (bowing or reed blowing) to electronic and computational components (microphone pickups, the hardware and software of computers and loudspeakers) and even the acoustic space through which the sound is ultimately transmitted.

It is this concept of instrument that becomes a central element in the overall sonic-dramaturgical framework of *Eidos : Telos*, a choreography devoted to exploring the political and perceptual shift between order and disorder. Divided into three parts and scored for acoustic (one violin and three trombones) as well as software-based computer instruments, *Eidos : Telos*'s core musical motif that spans across all three acts is Willems's quoting and manipulation of the central cadenza of Stravinsky's *Apollon Musagète*. In the first act entitled 'Self Meant to Govern', individual phrases of Stravinsky's score notated and altered by Willems are increasingly fragmented by Maxime Franke, the live violinist on stage, as well as picked up by the ensemble of trombones located in the wings and subsequently transformed by Ryan's DSP instruments.

These motifs and methods reemerge in the work's highly theatrical second act, a kind of solo enactment of the Greek Persephone and Ariadne myths where the sound design no longer illustrates but wholly becomes the environment. Drifting through a densely layered acoustic Hades constructed of pre-recorded sampled sounds and live acoustic violin processing, dancer Dana Caspersen is surrounded by a scenographic landscape of projected anatomical maps and a net of stretched steel cables criss-crossing the stage like a colossal spider's web. These massive cables, which are amplified by contact microphones, become a large-scale sonic instrument when the dancer plucks them. Featuring further altered fragments of the Stravinsky piece, Willems's tonal environment is increasingly twisted and masked by the sonic chaos unleashed by Ryan's direct amplification and digital transfiguration of violinist Franke, who once again appears on stage, as well as the dancer's voice and percussive contact with the cables.

After building to an aural climax punctuated by a series of short ostinatos generated by Ryan's input through a multi-tap digital delay line of the trombones' singular, pulse-like notes, the act concludes with a starkly reduced melodic line from Monteverdi's madrigal 'Amor, dov'è la fe'' from *Lamento della Ninfa*, performed by Franke against accents provided by the processed trombones.[6] Finally, in the work's almost apocalyptic third part, only the trombones reprise themes and patterns already heard throughout the course of the evening, culminating in a fiery further extension of the ostinato structure from the second act's climax.

Here Willems and Ryan push *Eidos : Telos*'s sonic evolution to its (ironically) ultimate *telos*, building up thundering waves of sound based on the same multi-tap delay technique of mutating individual notes played by the trombones into drone-like lines and layering these drones into a wall of sound that has the sonic force of a tidal wave. (Additionally in the third act of *Eidos : Telos*, Ryan, in an homage to his own wire piece, processes the amplified sounds of the mass of steel cables that criss-cross the stage.)

I have described the compositional framework of *Eidos : Telos* in detail to illustrate both the creation and extension of new instrumental sonorities by way of technology as a fundamental compositional strategy and how such technical processes help in directly structuring the piece's dramaturgical evolution. Indeed, acoustic technologies built from abstract, formal engineering and mathematical principles permeate and organize many moments of *Eidos : Telos*'s thematic canvas of absence, disappearance, haunting, the body as subject and site for memory, and the experience of recollection itself. Moreover, the embodied interaction, or co-production taking place among the human players, acoustic instruments and computational systems that Ryan so well articulates in 'Effort and Expression' also directly influence the mechanics of the piece's creation and production.

This co-production of human, machine, and material is made even more explicit when examining *Eidos : Telos*'s development and rehearsal process – one that owes more to the composer's interest in extending the improvisational possibilities of musicians together with new computer-based sonorities than to the construction of a fixed object-score, whether acoustic or electronic. During the three-and-a-half-week rehearsal period when the work was created, Willems, Ryan and I closely worked with Franke and the three conservatory-student trombone players to develop extended playing techniques such as plucking, pressure bowing, bow scraping for the violin, tongue fluttering, mouthpiece and slide disassembly, use of mutes, and other devices for the trombone that would stretch the respective instruments' sonic vocabularies. Indeed, my notes taken during these early sessions confirm the fluid working process of composition subscribed to by Willems and Ryan and partially enabled by the improvisation between human players and machines.

Figure 5.3 From Part Three of *Eidos : Telos* (Permission of Dominik Mentzos)

The nature of the music's composition in these early stages stems from Franke trying out a series of recombinant possibilities with various playing styles of the violin. We continually shifted patches and parameters on the Eventide DSP 4000 Harmonizer, this being the main signal processing equipment, trying out how different violin playing styles reacted to certain parameter shifts while recording and notating interesting effects derived from the real-time interaction. Ryan built playable algorithms in the MIDI (musical instrument digital interface) based, real-time object language MAX in order to control the harmonizer from software; a playable instrument that is assembled out of hardware and software (Salter 1997). The writing and development of the score consisted of sessions which generated a fluid vocabulary of improvisational techniques and associated computer instruments in hardware and software that could be recalled in performance by keeping a comprehensive archive of these sessions on digital audio tape (DAT).

Much of the dramaturgical foundation of the pivotal second act was structured not only by the dancer's acting choices, but also from the computer instruments built by Ryan and Willems. The extent of this collaboration between dramaturgical choices and music-technology techniques is patently evident in an earlier, sensor-driven 'interactive' conception for the scene where Forsythe describes the dancing body and sound mutually playing each other in order to lead to a total theatrical event. Within this event, music and sound would become dramatic partners with the stage action through the utilization of movement sensing technologies; technologies which were subsequently cut from the scene due to technical complications.[7]

In the interest of translating the normal, visually dominated concept of scenography into the acoustic realm, Forsythe, Willems and their sonic collaborators extended the larger sonic context of dance itself by turning both dancers and their surroundings into a sounding body. Although this strategy is most obvious in *Eidos : Telos* through the amplification and processing of acoustic instruments and the scenery itself (the web of steel cables), it is certainly not unique to this particular work. Richly layered acoustic spaces inhabited by amplified and live-processed performers' voices and objects are an artistic strategy used in many of Forsythe's dances, most notably in *As a Garden in This Setting* where wireless contact microphones transform ovular wooden sculptures resembling Marcel Duchamp's chocolate grinders into acoustic forms that are 'broken, stripped of relations, of objects unknown and terrifying' (Barthes 1967) when physically rolled onto their sides by the performers. Among countless works using the miked voices of dancers, *The Loss of Small Detail* is paradigmatic for live vocal processing/harmonizing serving part of a larger strategy to use technical systems to defamiliarize the meanings we derive from the sound of the human voice.

The layering of both human voices and the sonic behaviour of the environment as an instrument are taken to their extreme in *You made me a monster*, a piece combining dance, vocal concert, and sonic environment.

Its sound design is generated strictly by the behaviour of the dancers' voices and bodies converted into howling, thudding instruments by live DSP techniques used first by Ryan but now designed by Andreas Breitscheid and IRCAM-based Max/MSP developer Manuel Poletti.[8] Capturing the cries, moans, shrieks, and physical falls of three dancers who wear microphones, *You made me a monster* continues Forsythe's, Willems's and Ryan's earlier strategies in *Eidos : Telos* to convert the 'dancer into their own instrument'. In making the performer the sound source itself and then using the stage as the site of distortion and transformation of such sounds, a total acoustic world is composed that shifts dance into a realm where physical and acoustic bodies blur and merge with each other.

Environments

With its ultimate metamorphosis of dancing body to an acoustic medium, *You made me a monster* certainly could be seen as the apotheosis of Forsythe and Willems's move towards the creation of all-enveloping, total acoustic scenographies. But this shift is also fundamentally rooted in another discipline outside of music and sound, namely both artists' fascination with the dynamics of architecture and more specifically, how trajectories, flows, textures, surfaces, and lines are made both visually and aurally manifest through the dancing body's encounter with and production of space. Forsythe has long been enamoured by architects and vice versa. *Limb's Theorem*, for example, was in many ways a paean to architect Daniel Libeskind, and featured gigantic, cut-out objects inspired by the jagged forms of his *Micro-Mega* drawings. Architects ranging from Mark Goulthorpe, Tadao Ando, Paul Virilio, Nikolaus Hirsch and Steven Spier have had close associations with Forsythe, either through collaboration or by their critical and theoretical observations about spatiality, structure, and the body. Forsythe's interest in spatial dynamics goes far beyond mere visual inspiration or representation and intersects with Willems's similar interest in the aural transfiguration of architectural discourse. One of the greatest influences on Willems's compositional practice is indeed architecture, both in the conception of spatial conjunctures and structure, and its oscillation between surface and volume, line and plane. In a recent discussion, the composer pointed out the powerful influence of Japanese architecture, particularly its sophisticated treatment of building and texturing surface facades, on the score of *The Loss of Small Detail*.[9]

At other times, Willems's creation of acoustic environments, particularly those spatialized over multiple loudspeaker channels, almost matches Forsythe's investigation of the three-dimensional trajectories drawn by the dancers in and through space. Even if sound source spatialization is in and of itself nothing new in theatre sound design contexts (although it has been less exploited for dance), what is distinctive is the way in which the spatial trajectories of moving sound and the localization of specific sound sources in space compositionally emulates Forsythe's organization of the movement of bodies on stage, creating an equally complex movement of acoustic bodies in the aural realm. Inspired by the spatial harmony (*Raumharmonie*) or *choreutic* theories of Rudolf von Laban, who saw the body as a dynamic generator of spatial trace forms – intricate geometries of cubic, isocahedric and polygonal networks of patterns akin to living architectures, Forsythe's exploration of these living architectures produced by moving bodies is met with the techniques of an equally live acoustic architecture.[10]

This movement of sound that helps form the acoustic environment is best illustrated in Willems's striking score for the second part of Forsythe's *As a Garden in This Setting*, entitled *And Through Them Filters, Futile*. As dancers cross the stage attached to massive bungee cords that continually pull them back to where they began in a Sisyphean ritual, Willems's multi-channel score orchestrated from *gagaku* samples simultaneously slaps and jumps across the multiple loudspeaker arrays in the ceiling and around the theatre like so many boomerangs whose sounds disintegrate in mid-flight as they pass our ears. At other times, frenzied dancers move on a destabilized centre of gravity, appearing as if their limbs were being wrenched from their body by multiple forces while Willems's time-stretched sounds of the Japanese *sho* (mouth organ) and percussive strikes destabilize the listeners' sense of the stereo field by shifting the sound behind, above, and in front of them. Starting at one location in the room, these sounds only return to their origin in a severely altered timbral or rhythmic manner. Like the disintegration of bodies and relationships that Forsythe choreographs within a theatrical environment filled with actions that lead nowhere, and terrifying ovular objects moving, sounding, and responding on their own volition without regard to human presences, the acoustic environment enveloping the spectator and listener is no less disconcerting.

Willems's transformation of space through the positioning and moving of sonic structures recalls the great coupling of space, architecture, and sound pioneered in Philips Pavilion for the 1958 Brussels World's Fair by Varèse, Xenakis and Le Corbusier. Varèse envisioned that his *Poème Électronique*, a multi-channel tape composition of electronically produced environmental sounds and noise structures projected from an array of approximately 325 loudspeakers, would follow the geometry of curves set out in Xenakis and Le Corbusier's mathematically derived architecture. Forming a set of 'sound routes' that would 'zip the sound spatially on, up and over the walls', Varèse and Xenakis's visual plans of such routes almost suggest the bodily-produced dimensional planes of Laban's choreutics (Treib 1996).

As a Garden in This Setting is unique in its exploitation of spatialization for affect but Willems's sonic environments for other Forsythe works have also explored how the architectural positioning and placement of sound sources can directly couple with on-stage body architectures by creating a three-dimensional space. Although most of his works shy away from the electro-acoustic music trademark of panning point source sounds around in space among a battery of loudspeakers, Willems has always been preoccupied with the division of the acoustic environment into different zones, accomplished by the precise positioning of specific frequency ranges in his compositions within a technical sound reproduction infrastructure composed of arrays of multi-channel loudspeakers.[11] 'The music cannot be two dimensional. A musical space must be created that has a foreground, background and sides. The Ballett Frankfurt always understood that music and sound are critical and thus, invested in and developed a sonic infrastructure that was on the same level to the choreography' (Bayerischer Staatsoper 2004: 15).

A more extreme example of spatialization occurs in Forsythe and Willems's first collaboration, *LDC*. The composer's score, consisting entirely of a drone constituted by the harmonic series of a single B flat, is spatially diffused through Forsythe and Michael Simon's scenographic environment. Instead of working with moving sound sources from stationary speakers, however, the sound is blasted from a wall of speakers placed on the massive turntable of the Frankfurt Opera House stage that gradually revolves around to face the spectators during the course of the ballet. Using both the resonances of the colossal stage as well as the actual physical movement of the sound-producing source through space, the harmonics and amplitude of Willems's tape-based composition are attenuated and amplified depending on where the speaker array is physically positioned not only in space but also in time.

The sheer grandiose scale of the Frankfurt Opera house has further been used by Forsythe's sonic collaborators: in particular, with Ryan's work with the trombone processing in *Eidos : Telos*. The understanding of spatial scale coupled with musical scale almost renders the intensity of the trombone sonorities into a higher dimension, in which, through the particular electronic processes, the scale of sound becomes a function of the scale of physical space. The complex, not well understood relationships between the perception of time and its influence on the perception of space is one of the more fascinating aspects of Willems's collaboration with Forsythe. Even though music and choreography are rarely designed to illustrate each other, Forsythe's pursuit of 'an unregulated space of time' for the dancing body is also exploited by Willems, in particular through his extensive use of repetitive structures. Though strongly influenced by the so-called minimalist movement, the use of repetitive structures in Willems's scores is different from the ostinato-fuelled work of composers of the 1960s like Philip Glass, Steve Reich, and Terry Riley and even Willems's teacher Andriessen. Such composers normally employed an extremely reduced series of notes (like Riley or Reich), as in the *tala* structures of Indian classical music or the interlocking rhythmic cycles called *kotekan* in Javanese gamelan, which saturates the listening space with a dense, continual pulse.[12]

Instead, in scores like *The Loss of Small of Detail*, where the beginning chordal structures and melodic appoggiaturas resurface as leitmotifs throughout the piece and are directly mirrored at its conclusion, or in *As a Garden in This Setting*, where a wandering melodic line changes at a painstaking pace by developing over an extended 40-minute period, Willems uses repetition in a decidedly more structurally narrative manner by slowly expanding melodic motifs or syncopated rhythmic structures over the macrostructure of a work. Creating both a sense of stasis and yet, simultaneously, forward movement, this elasticizing of time also heightens our perception of the space around the dancers, making it appear and sound at times to slow down and at other times to accelerate. Just as Forsythe often opens and closes the visual field of the stage through creeping or abrupt shifts in lighting, so too does Willems's sound produce multiple spaces of time around the body; acoustic bodies that move at different rates than the human body itself.

Conclusion

The role music and sound perform in Forsythe's choreographic work transcends the traditional use of sound in dance through their dramaturgical status, the ways in which they are technically generated and manipulated for specific spectator affect, and finally, the forging of new relationships with space and time. The perceptual transformation of the body's spatiality as defined by the rigid rules and power relations inherent in ballet that Forsythe sought to overturn conjoin with an equally rigorous challenge to utilizing music for dance strictly as emotional illustrator and narrative device.

Through the enrolment of actors, techniques, systems, and materialities both machine and human, the careful precision of composition-design, production, and diffusion of sound by Willems and others reinforces Forsythe's own quest to depict the dancing body itself as a beautiful technology – one capable of mechanically perfected precision and simultaneously, an atavistic flux of energies.[13] The attention to technologically enhanced systems, instruments and whole acoustic scenographies that yield their underlying but hidden structures in the breathtaking theatrical displays of aural, visual, and not least, physical virtuosity that constitute the work of Forsythe, Willems and other musical collaborators assures us that the place of audition in Forsythe's *oeuvre* is central.

Notes

1 http://intranet.woodvillehs.sa.edu.au/pages/resources/thearts/DanceNotes/ williamforsythe/forsythecollaborationwithThomWillems.doc. No date indicated.
2 Conversation with the author, June 2007.
3 Even a glance at reviews of Forsythe's works reveals the continual bias towards Willems's music, as if it was an unnecessary addition to the dance. In reviewing *Eidos : Telos* in Brooklyn in 1999, former *New York Times* dance critic Anna Kisselgoff described Willems's music as 'electronic chords that often provide a basic beat'. Other critics have been far less generous even, depicting Willems's music as 'assaultive', 'cacophonous', 'loud', 'noisy', or 'consisting of electronic blurps and beeps'. Perhaps the most aggressive critique comes from a British

critic who claimed in one review that 'Forsythe has a partner in crime in his composer Thom Willems, who likes to lift a measure of music from some iconic ballet score (from Tchaikovsky in *Impressing the Czar,* from Stravinsky in *Eidos : Telos*) and then torture it on the rack of his synthesizer, making it groan and scream'.

4 See Roads 1996 for a further discussion of the perception of harmonic relationships through spectral analysis.

5 See Salter 2010: 206–7 for more details.

6 A multi-tap delay line is a digital delay process where an output signal is stored in memory for a specific period of time. A multi-tap incorporates several discrete delay lines, each with its own delay time, level (amplitude) and panning.

7 Like all of the work in the development of *Eidos : Telos*, the second act went through multiple iterations. Originally the dancer was to wear an acceleration sensor built by Ryan that would control the signal processing techniques applied to the violin as well as the lights in the Frankfurt Opera House auditorium. This proposal proved technically too risky, particularly when it was discovered that Ryan's STEIM built sensor input/output device The Sensor Lab would have trouble communicating to the house lighting console. See Salter 1997.

8 See the archived site of the Forum Neues Musiktheater that developed the Max/MSP software used in *You made me a monster*. http://www.fnm.de/index2.php. Also see cycling74.com for an overview of the Max/MSP programming environment.

9 Conversation with the author, Amsterdam, March 2006.

10 Forsythe's interest in the spatial technologies of Laban is most explicit in the digital dance tool *Improvisation Technologies*, a CD-rom released by the Center for Art and Media (ZKM) in 1994.

11 Willems's interest in positioning different frequency zones by means of multiple loudspeakers similarly recalls Varèse and Xenakis's attempts in the Philips pavilion. See Treib 1996: 203–205.

12 Repetitive musical structures have long been studied for their ability to provoke trance-like effects in the listener. See Mertens 1998 for an analysis of minimalist techniques, McPhee 2000 for a description of the affects of gamelan, and Rouget 1985 for studies of music, trance, and possession.

13 The concept of actor here references the work of anthropologist Bruno Latour. See Latour 1996.

References

Artaud, Antonin (1976) *Selected Writings*, Susan Sontag (ed) Berkeley, CA: University of California Press.

Barthes, Roland (1967) *Writing Degree Zero*, A. Lavers and C. Smith (trans), pp. 40–2, New York: Hill and Wang.

Bayerischer Staatsoper (2002) *Takt: The Magazine of the Bayerischer Staatsoper* (December).

Cox, Christoph and Warner, Daniel (eds) (2004) *Audio Culture: Readings in Modern Music*, New York; Continuum.

Deleuze, Gilles (2003) *Francis Bacon: The Logic of Sensation*, Daniel Smith (trans) Minneapolis, MN: University of Minnesota Press.

Forsythe, William (2003), Interview by John Tusa for BBC Radio, broadcast 2 February 2003. Available at http://www.bbc.co.uk/radio3/johntusainterview/forsythe_transcript.shtml. (Accessed 10 May 2010).

Jacobs, Laura (1999), 'Meaningless Enchainments' in *New Criterion*, February 1999, Volume 17.

von Laban, Rudolf (1966) *Choreutics*, Lisa Ullmann (ed) London: MacDonald and Evans.

Latour, Bruno (1966) *Pandora's Hope*, Cambridge, MA: Harvard University Press.

McPhee, Colin (1979) *A House in Bali,* Oxford: Oxford University Press.

Mertens, Wim (1983) *American Minimalist Music,* London: Kahn & Averill.

Mumma, Gordon (1967) 'Creative Aspects of Live Electronic Music Technology', *Audio Engineering Society, Papers of 33rd National Convention*, AES, New York.

Papadakis, Andreas and Libeskind, Daniel (1995) *Moving the City Boundaries: The Groningen Experiments*, London: Academy Editions.

Roads, Curtis (1996) *The Computer Music Tutorial*, Cambridge, MA: MIT Press.

Rouget, Gilbert (1985), *Music and Trance: A Theory of the Relations between Music and Possession*, Chicago: University Chicago Press.

Ryan, Joel (1992) 'Effort and Expression: Some Notes on Instrument Design at STEIM', in Strange, A. (ed) *Proceedings of the 1992 International Computer Music Conference*, pp. 414–16, San Francisco, CA: Computer Music Association. Available at http://www.steim.org/steim/texts.php?id=3. Accessed October 22, 2009.

Salter, Christopher L. (1997), Unstable Events: Theater at the Verge of Complexity. Unpublished dissertation, Stanford University p. 96.

Salter, Christopher L. (2010) *Entangled: Technology and the Transformation of Performance,* Cambridge, MA: MIT Press.

Salter, Christopher L., Baalman, Marije and Grigsby, Daniel (2007) 'Schwelle: Sensor augmented, adaptive sound design for live theater performance' in *Proceedings for the 7th Annual Conference in New Interfaces for Musical Expression (NIME)*, New York: ACM (Association for Computing Machinery).

Trieb, Marc (1996) *The Space Calculated in Seconds: The Philips Pavilion, Le Corbusier and Varèse*, Princeton, NJ: Princeton University Press.

Willems, Thom (2004) sound recording of *The Loss of Small Detail*, Musidisc.

Willems, Thom (2006) sound recording of *Enemy in the Figure*, Accord.

Wishart, Trevor (1996) *On Sonic Art*, London: Routledge.

Xenakis, Iannis (1992) *Formalized Music: Thought and Mathematics in Music*, Hillsdale, NY: Pendragon Press.

6 Dancing music

The intermodality of The Forsythe Company

Freya Vass-Rhee

An auditory turn

In November 1984 William Forsythe presented a three-part evening of existing work entitled *Audio-Visual Stress* at Frankfurt's Schauspielhaus. The evening consisted of *France/Dance*, an intriguing homage to Balanchine featuring a sound collage of Bach, animal sounds, and text spoken by a dwarf moving between cutouts of historic monumental buildings; *Say Bye Bye*, which paired the ensemble's tough aggression with Stan Kenton's jaunty 'The Peanut Vendor' and the percussive music of Chinese New Year; and the shadowy film *Berg Ab*.

Forsythe's works have continuously challenged audiences with their sonic as well as their visual qualities. Covering a broad range of vocal elements ranging from the complex generational grammars of *Artifact* to the whispered, shouted, and synthesized texts of *The Loss of Small Detail*, and from the sweet lyricism of *Trio*'s repeating Beethoven phrases to complex weaves of texts and movement in works like *Kammer/Kammer* and *Woolf Phrase*, Forsythe's vocal deployments have shared many of the performative qualities that distinguish his choreographic *oeuvre*: engagement with the thresholds of visual and aural perception, saturation of performance spaces with competing sensory information, and thwarting of expectations through unexpected shifts or interruptions. The contrapuntal visual but also aural structures of Forsythe's choreography, which render it deeply musical and simultaneously highly challenging, demonstrate intense choreographic research on the connections between seeing and hearing.

Since the turn of the millennium, Forsythe has produced a range of new works in which the sounds of bodies in motion have become an increasingly salient feature. The ensemble's investigation of the sonic potentials of dance movement, which began in the final years of the Ballett Frankfurt, has produced a number of innovative choreographic strategies that link vocalization to the action of dancing in ways that highlight the common cognitive ground shared by visual and auditory perception. This connectedness of the senses is revealed in the language of synesthetic metaphor, which refers to sounds as being bright or dark, and colours as loud or quiet (for example, see Marks

1982). The interchangeable use of the terms theatre (literally, viewing place) and auditorium (hearing place), as well as of spectator and audience, further instantiates the linguistic reflection of perception's merged nature.

When the Forsythe Company's works and working methods are viewed through recent research on intermodal perception, or perception across different senses, and on social cognition, or how thinking in and about group situations takes place, one can understand the choreographic structures of its repertory as profoundly intermodal. Dancers produce movement but also sound within choreographed and improvisatory frameworks, and within complex, dynamic systems of structured relations that emerge within and across the modes of vision and audition.

I will focus here on *Three Atmospheric Studies* (the music for Part 2 is composed by David Morrow, that for Part 3 by Thom Willems) which was developed during The Forsythe Company's first year, as well as on several of the ensemble's recently produced works. The choreographic structures of *Three Atmospheric Studies*'s three parts illustrate several key methods and parameters the ensemble has developed that performatively engage with the interaction of vision and audition. These include 'breath scores', the production and optimization of intermodal counterpoint structure, translations of danced movement into vocal sound and vice versa, strategies of composition and aural *mise en scène* employed by the ensemble's musicians and sound designers, and collaborative composition of sound – and by extension, of movement, as I will argue – among musicians, dancers, and sound technicians. Together, these examples illustrate how the ensemble's research into the possibilities of making dancing music continues to advance.

Breath scores: performative tools for synchrony

Forsythe's musical accompaniment has undergone a substantial qualitative and quantitative shift since the early 1990s. Thom Willems notes that his compositions for Forsythe, for whom he has produced music since 1985, have become 'more objects and less progressions'. He refers to them as 'The music of disappearance, more or less … it's become immaterial, and I enjoy that' (interview with Thom Willems, Dublin, 20 April 2008). Forsythe's shift away from dominant music has left the sounds generated onstage more audible to audiences, as well as to the dancers themselves. Willems says that in turn 'You gain the energy of the theatre, the energy of the dancers, and the focus on the dancers; the more they are creating, the more the focus is on them'.

Niels Lanz and Dietrich Krüger, the ensemble's current sound and video design team, have worked with Forsythe since 1992 and 1995 respectively, and in 2007 received a Bessie Award for their collaborative work on *Three Atmospheric Studies*. Krüger delineates distinct periods of sonic engagement leading up to The Forsythe Company's current work. He recalls that while relatively few pieces from his early period with the ensemble involved the dancers dancing to classical compositions or easily parsable newer scores, many pieces relied on 'clock time', the use of digital time displays as an aid to navigate musical scores without easily distinguishable structural features. Krüger notes that in the mid-1990s Forsythe began creating more works with only minimal sound accompaniment. The score of *Duo,* for example, interpolates a faint, shimmering accompaniment by Willems, while the score of *N.N.N.N.* consists only of a few quiet fill-ins. However, these works also crucially involve precise and distinctive breath scores that the dancers use to synchronize, connect, and counterpoint their actions. These scores consist not only of the breath sounds of the performers but may also include slides, footfall, slaps, falls, stamps, and other vocal and contact sounds. The dancers thus navigate space and time not only by means of visual cues but also by referring to aural cues generated onstage.

Breath scores are direct products and reflections of the action onstage. As such, they share the choreography's emergent timing and dynamic structures. In Part One of the currently performed version of *Three Atmospheric Studies,*[1] which Forsythe describes as 'a very complex acoustic composition', the breath score supports a physical dramaturgy of tension and unpredictability. *Three Atmospheric Studies* Part One consists of set group choreographic structures interspersed with scheduled improvisational solos and passages with others. The dancers, however, are afforded leeway to determine the precise timing of their cues, as well as the length, timbre, and specific content of danced passages. This autonomous aspect, an essential component of much of Forsythe's choreography, promotes a deft and sustained spontaneity of response among the dancers. As they run, fall, and make physical contact, cycling and reversing through rapid-action fragments of the event described later in the work, it is critical that they attend to the timings of the symphony-like breath scores' sounds and silences for cues for action and to create the work's moving synchronies and precise, photographic stops.

Many earlier Forsythe works performatively address aural perception through obscuring techniques such as high or low sound volume thresholds, or dense, overloaded sound scores.[2] By contrast, subtle amplification is used to highlight the relatively quiet breath scores of *Three Atmospheric Studies* Part One and other works. Lanz and Morrow recall first amplifying breath scores during the Ballett Frankfurt's 2003 tour to São Paolo, Brazil, where the premiere audience, unaccustomed to extremely quiet dance pieces, made so much noise that the musical fill-ins of *N.N.N.N.* and *The Room As it Was* were rendered inaudible. Amplification of ambient stage sound, deployed in São Paolo as a strategy to generate audience focus, was retained in subsequent performances of these works and was also added to the work *Duo.* In *Three Atmospheric Studies* Part One the volume levels of two shotgun microphones positioned in the front wings and contact microphones mounted in the sprung floor are slowly increased by Lanz a few minutes after the work begins, and then are continuously balanced against the intensity of the danced performance.[3] Krüger explains that the aim of *Three Atmospheric*

Studies Part One's amplification is the re-creation in larger venues of the intimacy of the premiere of *Clouds After Cranach*, at which an audience of only 75 followed the action from the edge of the Bockenheimer Depot stage. However, the scaling up of *Three Atmospheric Studies* Part One's breath score in addition to bringing the voice closer to the audience, simultaneously offers a fuller, more visceral experience of the scene's extreme tension. In addition, accentuating the sounds of the dancing additionally foregrounds the physical effort involved in dancing – a factor fully obscured both visually and sonically in classical ballet.

Three Atmospheric Studies Part One's carefully balanced intermodality is perceptually performative along multiple complementary lines. In addition to enabling temporal navigation and synchrony among the dancers, the sounds of the breath score productively augment the sensory complexity and intensity of an environment already highly saturated with visual information. Performer and audience attention are intensified by a dual distribution of the performance's percepts: physically, across the performance space, and intermodally, across the modes of vision and audition. The density of information and the relentless momentum of onstage events confront viewers with the limits of their perceptual abilities, fostering awareness of their active search for meaningful structure and their attempts to take in as much information as possible; in short, of the attentional economics of their own performance of perception.

Three Atmospheric Studies Part One's intermodal cueing system supports the piece's dramaturgy of trauma by tapping into innate attentional proclivities related to causality and intention. Current research on intermodal perception shows that though human beings bear a cognitive imperative to attempt to infer the structural coherence of complex intersensory events, our attention is also innately drawn to amodal perceptual events, in which perceptual information is redundant across more than one sense modality. The sonic qualities of knuckles knocking on a door, for example, bear direct and synchronous relations to the location, timing, and visually perceivable effort of the action of the knocking.[4] In effect, *Three Atmospheric Studies,* Part One's breath score perceptually snares spectators between the contrasting attentional draws of amodal perception, which ratifies the connectedness of information across the senses, and the perception of crossmodal events that potentially offer parsable relational structure. A visible sonic or gestural cue at one side of the stage may motivate or interrupt one or more centres of visual or sonic action elsewhere, prompting spectator-auditors to make rapid attentional choices within an environment that, as in many other Forsythe works, complicates attempts at holistic perception through surfeits of competing information.

In addition to producing a radical and performative distribution of both performer and audience attention, *Three Atmospheric Studies* Part One's mix of visual and sonic cueing also permits performer-gaze to be directed elsewhere than at cue-givers. Directed gaze, gestures such as pointing, and certain vocal and manually produced sounds, constitute instances of attention-gathering interactions that are used to draw and direct the attention of others. These deictic corporeal and vocal gestures, to which humans are attuned from the earliest age, essentially allow us to read others' minds by discerning their attentional focus and intentions.[5] Crucially, *Three Atmospheric Studies* Part One's inclusion of both sonic and visual cues permits performers' gazes to be deployed as deceptive indicators of attention and intention. The inclusion of other attention-gathering gestures like pointing, slaps, and stamps, increases the potential for onstage action to mislead. As the sources and relations of sounds and actions are sought within the melee onstage, *Three Atmospheric Studies* Part One's unpredictable and dense interplays of intention, deception, cause, and effect thus underscore the tense atmosphere of suspicion and fear which characterizes the full work, offering an embodied metaphor of traumatic experience.

Striking a balance: intermodal counterpoint

Throughout his choreographic career, Forsythe has created works that deploy the division of audience attention as a performative strategy. His works typically offer manifold, simultaneous focal centres: for example, *Limb's Theorem*'s shifting stage dissected by light and architectural elements, the polycentricity of *In the Middle, Somewhat Elevated*, *The Second Detail*, and many other works; or, the multiple concurrent group passages of the 'Bongo Bongo Nageela' section of *Impressing The Czar*. Since early in the Ballett Frankfurt's second decade, Forsythe has remained keenly interested in counterpoint, which he defines as 'a form of dialogue [which describes] the intermittent alignment of things'.[6] Although this organizational concept is almost exclusively associated with music, his works show that counterpoint is not necessarily modally explicit. As the ensemble's dancers produce sound and movement within frameworks of choreographed and improvisatory tasks, complex dynamic webs of counterpoint structure emerge between visual and sonic events, within individual bodies, and across the members of an extended ensemble which, as I will discuss in more detail below, also includes musicians, sound designers, and sometimes video artists.

The balancing of sound is a key factor in optimizing counterpoint and the division of attention in The Forsythe Company's performances. Subtle amplification also figures in Part Two of *Three Atmospheric Studies*, where complex competitions for attention are staged across the modes of sight and sound for both performers and audience. As *Three Atmospheric Studies* Part Two begins, Jone San Martin, the mother figure who opens Part One by announcing that her son was arrested, sits far downstage on a chair next to two speakers that periodically emit the faint sound of a woman weeping. She attempts to dictate an account of the arrest to Amancio Gonzalez, who sits at a table and is engaged in transcribing her description into Arabic. A third performer, David Kern, kneels between the two other seated performers, describing a marketplace scene in miniature with gestures and a barely audible voice. Gonzalez eventually suggests that San Martin move closer to him so as to hear him better and she does so, indicating that the weeping sounds are interfering with her ability to concentrate on the task at hand. Kern's voice is then amplified and he begins overcutting the translation dialogue with authoritative vocal and gestural descriptions of figures found in the pictorial compositions that lie on another table. The added voice renders both informational streams difficult to follow, forcing upon the audience an attentional choice that is also played out on-stage by San Martin, who becomes increasingly frustrated in her attempt to focus on the translation of her account.

Krüger notes that the shifting, delicate sonic balance between the three dancers' voices and composer David Morrow's live musical accompaniment is fragile and difficult to achieve, and not all performance venues possess acoustics capable of producing ideal results. However, this balance is critical to creating the dissonant attentional effects that serve as a metaphor for the mother's state of turmoil. In the sound booth, Krüger, Lanz, and Morrow monitor and adjust volume and sound qualities as they follow the spoken text and action of the dancers, blending into and highlighting sections of

Figure 6.1 David Morrow, Dietrich Krüger, William Forsythe, and Niels Lanz in the sound booth during a performance of *Three Atmospheric Studies* in Dublin, Ireland, 2008 (Permission of Freya Vass-Rhee)

the physical and verbal discourse in response to the intensity of the dancers' physical performance and the specific acoustics of the venue. Forsythe, likewise monitoring the performance from the booth, requests fine adjustments of microphone levels and accompaniment qualities, and conducts distortion effects and musical cutoffs. When San Martin describes a further section of her account in monologue, freezing, stuttering, and fragmenting her words and movements as if caught on a malfunctioning videotape, she leads an intricate three-part visual and four-part sonic counterpoint. Her gestures conduct David Morrow's abrupt instrumental punctuations and ominous *sforzandi*, while the quartet's two remaining members – Gonzalez, quietly transcribing words at his table, and Kern, interjecting staccato words and poses far upstage in dappled light – counterpoint their words and gestures in response. Additionally, each of the three performers on-stage composes intermodal counterpoint structure not only externally, across the ensemble of performers, but also internally, between their own voice and movement. Kern describes his experience of this section as a kind of juggling act in which he shuttles attention between his own speech and action and those of the other performers, watching and listening for gestures and words which indicate the temporal distance to upcoming hook-ups, or choreographed points of gestural or textual synchrony.

The precise choreography of sound and movement in *Three Atmospheric Studies* Part Two reveals how Forsythe divides the attention of both performers and audience across the modes of vision and audition by combining and counterpointing polycentric visual action with manifold sound elements. Multiplicities of physical and textual discourse produce an environment in which audience members, attempting to parse coherence out of the synchronous streams of textual and movement information, are confronted with the limitations of their own perceptual systems. The embodied experience of audio-visual stress onstage in *Three Atmospheric Studies* Part Two thus delivers its audience a visceral experience of the distraught mother's psychological duress through a performative underscoring of the inherent limitations of perception.

Translating movement, moving audiences

Forsythe's exploration of the performative potentials of dance's sounds has coincided with his increased production of danced installations. A number of these intermodally extend Forsythe's improvisational modality of translating visual scores into movement, which he first employed in *Limb's Theorem*. In that work's final section, a dancer converts the complex two-dimensional geometry of a drawn instruction into a three-dimensional solo. In the newer paradigm, first developed during the making of *Decreation*, movement is translated into fully vocalized sound, producing an aural rendering of the dancing. This choreographic mode, which physically acknowledges the contiguity of the body's muscularity and inner and outer surfaces, dissolves the body's external–internal boundary, extending the conceptual domain of dancing to its interior spaces and presenting dancing in both visual and sonic form.

In subsequent The Forsythe Company works, the ensemble elaborated the vocalization of movement by conceiving of the vocal apparatus as exquisitely sensitive and responsive to movement generated virtually anywhere in the body and refracted across its spaces. In *You made me a monster*, this operation was coupled to the translation of visual scores. Performers reel through the audience-filled space translating the large, twisted sculptures of paper skeleton pieces and pencil tracings of the skeleton sculptures' shadows into vocal and corporeal gestures. (Its improvisational tasks are sometimes performed as an installation entitled *Monster Partitur*.) The simultaneous reading and translation of multiple locations of the score elements into movement and sound radically divides performer attention, causing a disruption of physical coherency that engenders unpredictable sounds, movements, and trajectories. The commingling of audience and performers within the dark, close space of the installation physically ensnares the audience in the work's thematic of the xenophobic fear of corporeal invasion.

The intermodal score of *Heterotopia*, created the following year, is distributed across series of looking, listening, and responding performers linked in intricate networks of contrapuntal cause and effect across the space of the installation. The work, which Forsythe has referred to both as concert and oratorio, is performed in a divided space in which sounds from the first table-filled room are conveyed into the almost empty adjoining second room via strategically placed microphones and a large bell speaker. Muted sound also passes between the rooms through the floor-to-ceiling screen that separates them. Vocalizations engender movements and vice versa as the dancers conduct each other or, responding to direction, translate others' actions and sounds into a visuo-sonic composition of artificial human and animal languages. Manifold streams of movement and sound constitute and compete with improvisational tasks as prompts for response, motivating audience members, who are free to move about the installation's spaces, to choose among perspectives and select among multiple targets of attention.

Heterotopia divides spectator attention between aural and visual aspects of the performance, between the performance's multiple spaces, and between spectatorship and the activities necessary to navigate through the populated audience space. The work's intermodality and spatiality comment wryly on the hierarchization of vision in dance. Similarly, Forsythe's film installation *Antipodes I/II* subtly heightens attention and generates audience action through the spatial distribution of the installation's aural and visual components, including those provided by the audience itself. Two screens at opposite ends of a darkened room show Forsythe filmed with trick camera setups similar to those used to make Fred Astaire appear to dance on a ceiling in the 1951 film *Royal Wedding*. (Forsythe quips: 'It's cheap, but it's fun'.) The audio speaker placed by the inverted image of Forsythe dangling from a table at the top of the screen delivers the ambient sounds of his breathing, sliding, and the clicks of his wedding band against the table. The other image – Forsythe zanily floating and flipping between two standing tables – is accompanied only by Ryoji Ikeda's thin, high musical atmosphere and draws occasional murmurs and punctuations of quiet laughter from audience members. Attention is drawn back and forth not only by the installation's multiple and diversely composed visual and aural percepts but also by the audience's own response as it turns, looks, and comments. *Antipodes I/II*'s audience thus enacts an ensemble performance of perception, its members' actions prompting those of others in a subliminal counterpoint which emerges in the cinema-like darkness.

By tapping and extrapolating the vocal potential of movement, Forsythe has extended his translational processes across the boundary of the senses. This merging of percepts creates the potential for structuring intermodal counterpoint in which danced and vocal gestures are improvisationally united into audio-visual performance that is both symphonic and perceptually challenging. The interrelated visual and aural information in these installations, together with audience staging that elicits visible, audible, and sometimes tangible reactions among spectators, thus also divides audience attention intermodally while harnessing it as a performative element (Vass-Rhee 2010).

Translating music: compositional re-vision

The composition and execution of *Three Atmospheric Studies* Part Two's musical score illustrates parallels between Forsythe's sound team's processes of translating and performing musical material and those undertaken by Forsythe and the dancers with choreographic material. The stage action of Part Two in its current version is augmented and undercut by a musical score which ranges from delicate, random-sounding tones to insistent, weighted accents. Morrow recalls playing sections from Monteverdi's 'Il Combattimento di Tancredi e Clorinda' during preliminary studio rehearsals for the 2005 version of *Three Atmospheric Studies*. (Forsythe also choreographed *Tancred und Clorinda* to this work in 1981.) For Part Two of *Clouds After Cranach* (*Three Atmospheric Studies*'s current Part Two), Morrow reduced the passages to specific harmonic progressions and played them on a MIDI-generated harp, while Krüger and Lanz processed part of a recording of the Monteverdi music into high-pitched crystals or needles that are played around the perimeter of the audience space at Part Two's beginning and end.[7] The sound, according to Krüger, is meant to arouse the audience's aural attention while simultaneously delineating the environment of the theatre: 'We draw a space; we make a box with the needles'.

Two other sonic layers of *Three Atmospheric Studies* Part Two derive from an 'Arabian tone scale' that Morrow generated by selecting among existing harp harmonic samples in his audio library. He assigned numbers to the pitches of the scale, which complements the harmonic progressions he derived from the Monteverdi score, and applied two calculations based on the Golden Section to them. The first of the two number sequences, the Golden Ratio or decimal value of Pi, ranges to infinity and dictates the selection of the pitches Morrow plays on his keyboard during the beginning of Part Two. The second binary calculation, the Golden String or Fibonacci 'Rabbit' Sequence, generates a non-repeating pattern of zeroes and ones that guides the rhythm of the trombone accents, rumbling chordal frictions, and dense vectors he plays later during San Martin's distraught 'aria'. Morrow employs these formal structures while playing in responsive relation to the dancers' movements and dialogue. The group section described above, he says, is 'more of a linear counterpoint conducted by [San Martin], while her solo section is more of a timbral one and more of an emotional counterweight to her state of conflict ... I introduce dense sound vectors which pull against Jone's torsions, because Bill said it's like she's going down the drain' (discussion with David Morrow, Salzburg, 5 July 2008).

Like the dancers, the musicians improvise within distinct compositional parameters, counterpointing the action of the dancing with sound. The constraints they employ produce demands for intermodal attention and calculated physical thinking that often reflect those elicited by Forsythe's choreographic operations. The pitches of Morrow's tone scale for *Three Atmospheric Studies* Part Two, for example, are distributed across his keyboard in a nonlinear order, with the result that what he hears does not correspond to the keyboard's normal tonal progression. Morrow further notes that for *Three Atmospheric Studies* Part Two, the keyboard pitches are actually inverted, with the highest tones played by the little finger of his left hand. 'I have to reverse my hemispheres when I perform the piece' (discussion with David Morrow, Salzburg, 5 July 2008), he remarks. However, as he emphasizes, such practices do not exclusively determine musical execution. Thom Willems, who also employs mathematically and structurally constrained compositional strategies in works like *Limb's Theorem*, *The Loss of Small Detail*, and *Eidos : Telos*, concurs: 'The construction is a thing to build on, to start working with, but the final decision is a musical intuition' (discussion with David Morrow, Salzburg, 5 July 2008).

Other works in The Forsythe Company's musical repertory involve similar processes of translation of material used during rehearsals or early performances. During rehearsals for *Yes We Can't*, Forsythe returned to the *Srimpi* (Provisions for Death), a gamelan composition from the Javanese court of Surakarta that he had previously used in the Ballett Frankfurt's productions *Pivot House* and *Endless House*. During the first few weeks of the rehearsal period, Morrow analyzed the musical structure of the 60-minute work and, with the team's assistance, produced a scrolling plasma screen display of coloured bands and visual accents for Forsythe and the dancers to use as an aid in navigating the repetitive, hypnotic score. Shortly before the work's premiere, Forsythe decided not to use the *Srimpi* recording; however,

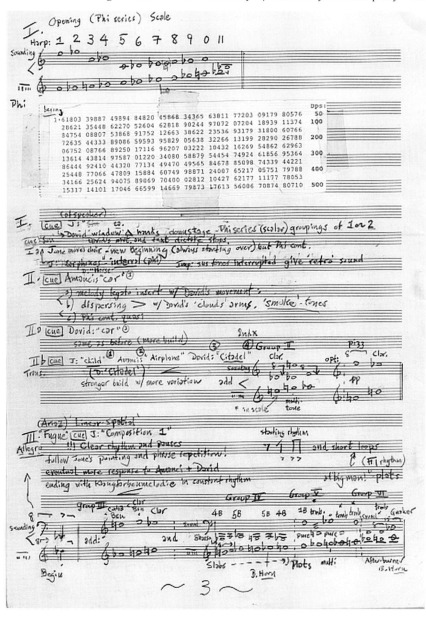

Figure 6.2 Excerpt from David Morrow's score for Part Two of *Three Atmospheric Studies* (Permission of Freya Vass-Rhee)

he explicitly requested the ensemble to retain the physical dynamic that the music had evoked during rehearsals.[8] Forsythe began reworking dance material produced while rehearsing with the *Srimpi*, splitting duets and trios and continuing to elaborate dramaturgical themes of unsustainability and prolongation of tactile sensation. Concurrently, Krüger and Lanz set to work deriving material from the original gamelan recording. They produced two loops that are used in performance: an ominous, repetitive bass motif and a thundering sub-bass loop whose fluctuating volume level Forsythe conducts by hand during performances. Just as *Three Atmospheric Studies'* crystals are not recognizable as the original Monteverdi, neither of the gamelan loops resembles or evokes the original *Srimpi* recording. Additionally, Krüger and Lanz recorded a high-pitched rock-and-roll style vocal riff produced by dancer Roberta Mosca during rehearsal and converted it into two loops, one of which closely resembles the sound of an electric guitar. These materials, together with other samples from the musicians' sound libraries, disjointed piano motifs played by Morrow from the wings, and spoken and sung content from the dancers, constitute the full sonic score of *Yes We Can't*[9] (in April 2010, Forsythe produced a fully new version of *Yes We Can't* set to a live improvised piano score by David Morrow).

The applications of compositional constraint by Forsythe's sound team, like those employed by Forsythe himself, are exercises in economy of means that nevertheless result in extravagantly complex and dramaturgically poignant structures. Both playful and cerebral, these practices reflect a delight in compositional challenge and in the engendering of autopoietic systems.

Sonic improvisation technologies: intermodal collaboration

In several The Forsythe Company works the sonic output of the dancers is co-generated by vocalizing performers and one or more sound technicians working with audio technologies. Forsythe has explored collaborative performance between musicians in the booth and performers onstage since works like the 1987 version of *The Loss of Small Detail*, in which a data glove[10] was used to generate sound, likewise in *Eidos : Telos*, the first work in which Forsythe employed Max/MSP, an algorithmic programming environment which enables the design or physical modelling of responsive virtual instruments, such as what Forsythe describes as a '10-foot velvet gong'. The distribution of performative agency between dancers and musicians via interactive sound technologies opens consideration of mediated real-time choreography as a social process of co-creation that extends beyond the space of the stage to include other performers whose input can be heard as well as seen.

In *You made me a monster*, for example, the dancers' vocalizations, breath, and gestural sounds are picked up by head-mounted microphones they wear as they translate the visual score of twisted skeleton pieces and their shadows into sound and movement. The sounds are altered, augmented, and fed back in real time into the performance space by composer-programmer Hubert Machnik using a Max/MSP interface. One of the voice programs used in *You made me a monster* produces a delayed gated overtone scale in response to varied sound qualities, with uptake and processing contingent on the point within the program's temporal cycle at which they are uttered, while another program responds almost immediately to the sonority and volume of vowels, altering them and feeding them back in a shifting variety of echoing pitches and qualities. Thundering, wailing, and chiming through the space of the piece, the voices of the Max/MSP feedback offer distorted, unpredictable, but clearly related aural accompaniment to the movement and sound being produced and provide an additional, emergent improvisational resource for the performers.

The dancers treat the Max/MSP programs as instruments that they play with their whole bodies as they read the visual scores of twisted paper bones and lines, dividing their attention across the multiple spaces, surfaces, and streams of sound. The specific characteristics of the three Max/MSP programs used in *You made me a monster* enable the programs to be learned and their responses to be predicted to a certain degree by the dancers. However, the cyclic nature of information uptake, Machnik's real-time optimization of the programs during performance, and the visual and sonic input provided by the other moving, vocalizing performers together generate a level of unpredictability which requires the dancers to remain intensely

Figure 6.3 David Kern, Roberta Mosca, and Christopher Roman in *You made me a monster* (Permission of Julieta Cervantes, copyright 2007)

aware and responsive to the aural environment. Machnik, along with Krüger and Lanz, responds to the information in the room, watching and listening to the improvising dancers and their mobile audience and tempering the performance as it emerges. Thus, the improvisational feedback loop is open at both ends for all performers involved.

In Part Three of *Three Atmospheric Studies*, the Max/MSP interface is used to viscerally emphasize Forsythe's assertion that 'People are dangerous'. Ander Zabala's vocalizations are translated into a roaring, shrieking, sonic image which, along with the sounds of dancers hurling themselves against the miked wooden wall and slamming the clanging door (played manually from the booth by Willems), is counterpointed by ballistic dance action and David Kern's non-stop, animated description of relationships between cloud formations. Zabala plays other dancers with his voice and movement, sometimes roaring a demand at the sound booth for more sonic power. The stage darkens and the terror intensifies, augmented by staticky interpolations from Willems. In this scene, Willems says, 'I just try to put energy in … It's not so much about music, it's really a moment about energy. If I see that it's getting too low or it's building up, I just jump in and give articulations and details with sounds, to give it a push' (interview with Thom Willems, Dublin, 20 April 2008). Later, Kern delivers a breathless report of a bombing as the dancers, following the sonic paths of Zabala's vocalized missiles and flying debris, repeatedly dive for cover. Lanz, in the sound booth, throws the experience of terror at the audience and dancers by rapidly trajecting

Figure 6.4 Ander Zabala and Yoko Ando in Part Three of *Three Atmospheric Studies* (Photograph by Stephanie Berger)

the huge sounds between speakers. 'It's like making a building fall into the auditorium' (dsiscussion with Niels Lanz, Salzburg, 5 July 2008), he says. Finally, as Gonzalez lowers a mute, numbed San Martin to the floor, Willems underscores Dana Caspersen's drawling baritone platitudes with faint, ironic bombs and faded fragments of Bach.

Forsythe's crossmodal linkage of sound production and improvised movement, combined with the iterative processes of intermodal translation, render the dancing a product of choices made both onstage and in the sound booth. The outcome of both the danced and sonic performance of the mediated dancers in *Three Atmospheric Studies* Part Three, *You made me a monster*, and other similar works is thus determined jointly by the dancers and several unseen individuals. This accords with Edwin Hutchins's theory of distributed cognition, which he developed in his seminal analysis of large-scale modern navigational practices. Hutchins argues convincingly that cognitive activity is not limited by 'the boundary of the person'; instead, both thought and action are distributed across individuals, artifacts, and technologies, and thus extend throughout the environment in which these agents are situated. This shared cognition is constrained by the distinct knowledge and technologies of each of the group's individuals, the structure of the group's interactions, and the group's culture as a whole (Hutchins 1995). By virtue of the ensemble's intermodal improvisatory collaboration, mediated onstage performances are thus the result of the interactive decision-making, inference, memory, and reasoning processes of not only the dancers working with their specific action potentials and constraints, but also of the musicians and sound technicians working with and within theirs, along with those of Forsythe, who monitors the overall timbre of the performance and its audience, modulating the output of this extended ensemble. The refiguring of performance as distributed between the spaces of the stage and the sound booth and throughout a larger ensemble of performers complicates the ideas of performance space and choreographic agency in ways that question both the visuality of dance performance and hierarchies of choreographer, dancer, musician, and technology in dance performance.

In summary, Forsythe's turn to the auditory has offered the ensemble a new range of compositional and staging strategies, enhancing the visceral impact of the danced performance through the intermodal division of performer and audience attention. In making dancing re-sound, Forsythe has also shifted the parameters of collaboration among the members of the extended performing ensemble, redistributing choreographic agency in a manner that refigures the roles of dancer, choreographer, and musician. Forsythe has again interrogated traditional perceptions of what dancing is and suggested new ways that it can be conceived and produced.

The danced research of Forsythe and his ensemble thus continues to question ideas about dancing and its perception by exploring and extending classical-conceptual form beyond its historical scope, refiguring performance environments, and honing the sensing perception of dancers and audiences alike. Forsythe's manifold extension of the body's physical and perceptual capabilities has involved not only the discovery of new ways that the body can move, but new ways that bodies and performance environments can be organized. In moving dancing into the realm of the sonic, The Forsythe Company's en-visioning of dance's sound, which highlights the multisensory nature of perception and deploys the merging of the senses as a performative device, continues Forsythe's interrogation of dance and the extension of the dancing body.

Acknowledgements

I am deeply grateful to Dietrich Krüger, Niels Lanz, David Morrow, Thom Willems, William Forsythe, and the dancers of The Forsythe Company for their support.

Notes

1   The 2005 version of *Three Atmospheric Studies* consisted of two parts, the second of which became Part Three of the current version. *Clouds After Cranach*, which premiered in November of the same year, consisted of the work's current Parts One and Two performed on two stages facing each other, with the audience relocating between the two sections. *Three Atmospheric Studies* was first performed as a three-part evening in Berlin in early 2006.

2   It is interesting to note, for example, that the dancers in *One Flat Thing, reproduced*, like those in *Three Atmospheric Studies* Part One, both contribute and selectively respond to a dense score of visual and sonic accents that are cues for global or localized action. However, the choreographed sounds of *One Flat Thing, reproduced* are substantially, though not completely, masked by Thom Willems's dominant, throbbing musical score. Though the moving dancers in *One Flat Thing, reproduced* intently focus on both movement and the sounds of footfall and table slaps, slides, slams, and verbal cues that sometimes must be shouted to be heard, the work's total in-performance soundscore foregrounds the visual cueing over the aural, with the result that audiences see more of the work's intermodal choreographic structure than they hear. The soundscape components of *One Flat Thing, reproduced* can be compared by toggling the audio settings of the work's video score at the Synchronous Objects for *One Flat Thing, reproduced* project at www.synchronousobjects.osu.edu/content.html#/fullVideoScore

3   For *Three Atmospheric Studies* Part One, pad floor microphones are typically only deemed necessary in larger venues and are thus not always used.

4   In Elizabeth Spelke's pioneering studies of infant intermodal perception, infants were presented with video images of two toy animals bouncing at different rates, accompanied by a recorded sound which corresponded to the impacts of one of the animals but not the other. The infants tested preferentially looked at the toy whose impacts were in synchrony with the sound rather than the out-of-sync stimulus. See Bahrick and Hollich (2008) and Spelke, ES (1976, 1979).

5   See Zukow-Goldring (1997) and Baron-Cohen (1995).

6   Quoted in audio commentary of Synchronous Objects for *One Flat Thing, reproduced*.

7 DSP (Digital Signal Processing) programing and voice treatments for *Three Atmospheric Studies* and *You made me a monster* were executed by Andreas Breitscheid, Olivier Pasquet, and Maunel Poletti in collaboration with the Forum Neues Musiktheater of the Staatsoper Stuttgart.

8 Forsythe has frequently used and subsequently jettisoned music during production phases. Glen Tuggle, Forsythe's ballet master from 1990 to 2004, recalls Forsythe playing and later abandoning a recording of Jessye Norman singing 'Dido's Lament' from Purcell's *Dido and Aeneas* during rehearsals for *The Vile Parody of Address,* the original version of which premiered in 1988. Forsythe has also explained that he created the choreography for his film *Solo* (1995), which features music by Thom Willems, while listening to hip hop music and Stravinsky's *Capriccio for Piano and Orchestra*, to which George Balanchine choreographed *Rubies.*

9 In April 2010, Forsythe produced a fully new version of *Yes We Can't* set to a live improvised piano score by David Morrow.

10 'The Hands' data glove was designed by Michael Waisvisz of the Studio for Electro-Instrumental Music (STEIM), The Netherlands.

References

Bahrick, L.E. and Hollich, G. (2008) 'Intermodal perception' in M. Haith and J. Benson (eds.), *Encyclopedia of Infant and Early Childhood Development*, vol. 2, Amsterdam & London: Elsevier Ltd./Academic Press.

Baron-Cohen, S. (1995) *Mindblindness: An Essay on Autism and Theory of Mind*, Cambridge, MA: MIT Press/Bradford Books.

Hutchins, E. (1995) *Cognition in the Wild*, Cambridge, MA: MIT Press.

Marks, L. (1982) 'Bright Sneezes and Dark Coughs, Loud Sunlight and Soft Moonlight', *Journal of Experimental Psychology: Human Perception and Performance*, 8(2): 177–93.

Spelke, E.S. (1976) 'Infants' intermodal perception of events', *Cognitive Psychology*, 8: 533–60.

Spelke, E.S. (1979) 'Perceiving bimodally specified events in infancy', *Developmental Psychology*, 15: 626–36.

Vass-Rhee, Freya (2010) 'Auditory Turn: William Forsythe's Vocal Choreography', *Dance Chronicle*, 33(3): pp. 388–413.

Zukow-Goldring, P. (1997) 'A Social Ecological Realist Approach to the Emergence of the Lexicon: Educating Attention to Amodal Invariants in Gesture and Speech', in Cathy Dent-Read and Patricia Zukow-Goldring (eds) *Evolving Explanations of Development: Ecological Approaches to Organism-Environment Systems*, Washington, DC: American Psychological Association.

7 Choreographic objects

William Forsythe

An object is not so possessed by its own name that one could not find another or better therefore.

Rene Magritte

Choreography is a curious and deceptive term. The word itself, like the processes it describes, is elusive, agile, and maddeningly unmanageable. To reduce choreography to a single definition is not to understand the most crucial of its mechanisms: to resist and reform previous conceptions of its definition.

There is no choreography, at least not as to be understood as a particular instance representing a universal or standard for the term. Each epoch, each instance of choreography, is ideally at odds with its previous defining incarnations as it strives to testify to the plasticity and wealth of our ability to re-conceive and detach ourselves from positions of certainty.

Choreography is the term that presides over a class of ideas: an idea is perhaps in this case a thought or suggestion as to a possible course of action. To prohibit or constrain the substitution or mobilization of terms within this domain is counterintuitive. The introduction and examination of the effect of terminological substitutions that reveal previously invisible facets of the practice is key to the development of procedural strategies.

Choreography elicits action upon action: an environment of grammatical rule governed by exception, the contradiction of absolute proof visibly in agreement with the demonstration of its own failure. Choreography's manifold incarnations are a perfect ecology of idea-logics; they do not insist on a single path to form-of-thought and persist in the hope of being without enduring.

Choreography and dancing are two distinct and very different practices.

In the case that choreography and dance coincide, choreography often serves as a channel for the desire to dance. One could easily assume that the substance of choreographic thought resided exclusively in the body. But is it possible for choreography to generate autonomous expressions of its principles, a choreographic object, without the body?

The force of this question arises from the real experience of the position of physical practices, specifically dance, in Western culture. Denigrated by centuries of ideological assault, the body in motion, the obvious miracle of existence, is still subtly relegated to the domain of raw sense: precognitive, illiterate. Fortunately, choreographic thinking being what it is, proves useful in mobilizing language to dismantle the constraints of this degraded station by imagining other physical models of thought that circumvent this misconception. What else, besides the body, could physical thinking look like?

The blind French resistance fighter Jacques Lusseyran, writing about the inner sense of vision which enabled him to see and manipulate forms and thoughts, famously described it as being like a boundless mental canvas or screen which existed 'nowhere and everywhere at the same time'. The blind mathematician Bernard Morin described his envisioning of the process of everting a sphere in a similar manner. And so it is with the choreographic object: it is a model of potential transition from one state to another in any space imaginable. An example of a similar transition already exists in another time-based art practice: the musical score. A score represents the potential of perceptual phenomena to instigate action, the result of which can be perceived by a sense of a different order: a transition via the body from the visual to the aural. A choreographic object, or score, is by nature open to a full palette of phenomenological instigations because it acknowledges the body as wholly designed to persistently read every signal from its environment.

I make this comment in relationship to Lusseyran and Morin to introduce the manifold possibility of our practice. Lusseyran's inner vision enabled him to see topographies and project strategic movements of groups of people. Morin saw an event in the space of his mind that he then translated with haptic skill into sculptures and subsequently into the universal yet somewhat hermetic language of mathematics. Their quite substantial bodies, put into action by the force of their ideas, left very discernable traces of those ideas in the real world; from nowhere to somewhere, not everywhere, and no longer exclusively within their bodies.

But what if we, for a moment, look at the situation of the choreographic act. Historically choreography has been indivisible from the human body in action. The choreographic idea traditionally materializes in a chain of bodily action with the moments of its performance being the first, last, and only instances of a particular interpretation. The idea's enactment is not sustained and cannot be repeated in the totality of its dimensions by any other means. As poignant as the ephemerality of the act might be, its transient nature does not allow for sustained examination or even the possibility of objective, distinct readings from the position that language offers the sciences and other branches of arts that leave up synchronic artifacts for detailed inspection. This lack of persistence through time, like the body itself, is natural and suspect at the same time. The irretrievability of the choreographic enactment, though possibly engendering a nostalgic thrill, perhaps also reminds the viewer of the morbid foundations of that same sentiment.

Are we perhaps at the point in the evolution of choreography where a distinction between the establishment of its ideas and its traditional forms of enactment must be made? Not out of any dissatisfaction with the tradition, but rather in an effort to alter the temporal condition of the ideas incumbent in the acts, to make the organizing principles visibly persist. Could it be conceivable that the ideas now seen as bound to a sentient expression are indeed able to exist in another durable, intelligible state?

A choreographic object is not a substitute for the body, but rather an alternative site for the understanding of potential instigation and organization of action to reside. Ideally, choreographic ideas in this form would draw an attentive, diverse readership that would eventually understand and, hopefully, champion the innumerable manifestations, old and new, of choreographic thinking.

8   Decreation

Fragmentation and continuity

Dana Caspersen

My body has given me powerful lessons regarding the nature of both fragmentation and unity. It has taught me that how we think about a thing determines whether or not we are able to see its wholeness, and that apparent disjuncture is often just the presence of an intricate set of detours.

I have been working as a dancer and choreographer for the last 30 years, 20 of those years in close collaboration with Bill Forsythe, first in the Ballett Frankfurt and, since 2004, in The Forsythe Company. Some of the questions that I have been steadily preoccupied with during this time have been: How are the details and fragments of complex motion and pattern shaped by the whole? How is the whole shaped by the details and fragments? How does detailed articulation emerge in the body? Of what is the wholeness of the dancing body composed?

My spine has some unusual twists and shifts in it that can have the effect of dis-integrating my body, causing it to act as separate parts. Through practice, I discovered that I needed to learn the skill of thinking my body into a whole, even in situations where my body was not actually whole. I realized that even when we are not aware of it, we are always already engaged in some thought version of our bodies. I saw that the experience of fragmentation was a form of the experience of unity; the apparent breakdown of continuity was actually a glimpse into the interior workings of integration. My body showed me that a dive into detailed fragmentation can allow for an understanding of a richly counterpointed whole.

My years of work with Bill have provided the opportunity to notice that this experience of dilation between fragmentation and unity is taking place constantly, and in many domains. Two central areas of investigation that we have been engaged in, which have been illuminating for me in this regard, have been the use of gaze and the emergence of detailed counterpoint within the body. In the piece *Decreation*, these two areas of research merged in a new way, raising questions for me of what it is that constitutes a body. What are the different bodies involved in the creation of a new work and what holds them together?

Bodies

A company of performers and creators can be seen as a kind of body, and the work that a company creates can be viewed in the same way; as a body that is composed of our thoughts and the differing ways that our individual bodies are thinking. As a company, we are engaged in a daily, functional practice of rehearsal and performance, and simultaneously engaged in a delicate and powerful ensemble sensing. We sense—notice—when it is time to move into a new area of research, revisit an old one, when to redirect a work that is losing energy or when to let it fail and collapse. This sensing is not always a conscious action but arises out of our communal practice.

The form of collaboration that we engage in to create new work differs from piece to piece, but generally Bill functions as an instigator and an editor. He offers areas of interest or groups of ideas as catalysts, hoping that something that he hadn't thought of will then emerge. An exchange then begins where these ideas are taken up by the dancers, interpreted in new ways and countered with other ideas, which are then further transformed by Bill's interpretation or juxtaposition of the dancer's thoughts.

An unmade piece is a question in the collective mind of the group. Together, during the rehearsal process, we develop, gather, and assimilate an immense amount of information, such as movement, text, images, rules, etc. We experiment with forms of relationship and states of being, we articulate fine details, investigate larger structures, and finally develop a vibrant and divergent group of events that expands until it reaches the point where it needs to coalesce, to collapse, to explode; to transform.

At that point, instead of thinking the parts—the individual scenes or movements—the group begins to think the whole. The piece begins to precipitate in the minds and bodies of the company. Then, and often over the course of many years, we practice discernment. We practice committing completely to what is being developed at the moment while remaining prepared to jettison whatever doesn't work out. Pieces can start from any point, and every point within each piece contains the essence of the whole. Pieces can arise after years of deep research and months of work, or sometimes they just sneak up on us, fully formed.

Dancing is a curious blend of dogged, repetitive practice and mediumistic transmission. Differentiating between subtly different states requires tremendous physical skill, which in turn requires years and years of daily practice. Dancers practice remaining consistently curious, being willing to move into the complex, mutable energetic structure of a piece that is being born. They practice understanding that freedom is not the absence of external pressure, but an internal ability to remain fluid and engaged under demanding circumstances. It isn't possible to know what a piece is in advance, or if the fragments that are encountered along the way are connected to each other, or to the piece itself. So dancers become accustomed to riding multiple, sometimes apparently conflicting, energetic waves to find out where they might go.

Internal Structures

Like a weather system, where clouds are the visible result of the interaction of force and matter, each new piece has its own internal system that determines how it functions, and what can successfully occur within it. A cloud always reflects its environment; you can't force a thunderhead to appear when the conditions for a clear sky are present. Similarly, a new piece has its own inherent forces that interact with the thoughts, energies, and bodies of the performers and choreographer(s) to shape the nature of its flow and the events that appear within it.

Sometimes, what appeared at first to be the heart of the piece has to be thrown out later because it no longer works within the total body of the whole. This process of things dropping away takes many forms. Sometimes it will be just sections of choreography that get thrown out, sometimes an entire piece will need to vanish in order for the piece to be reborn in another way. For example, when we made *The Room As it Was*, Bill had choreographed two 20-minute works that he tossed out on the morning of the premiere. We then went back to a series of scenes, which we had previously abandoned, that were based on rules of relationship, and we created a new piece, extrapolating out from those rules that instigated timings, form, interaction, and dynamic.

For a piece to function, each performer must be willing to experience, to embody, its inherent energies. The process of creation can feel like failure, struggle, or like exultation. The performers and the choreographer need to be willing to wait, to fail, to not know, to be outrageous, disciplined, clairvoyant. They must be willing to change, to abandon what they understood to be right.

Gaze and thought

The body of a piece is a confluence of energies, and the body of the individual dancer is similarly a complex system of energetic counterpoint. Experienced internally as a matrix of counter-currents, these systems of dynamic, direction, and opposition are made visible to the viewer in a number of ways, including the use of gaze.

The second version of *The Loss of Small Detail* marked a change in the direction that Bill and the Ballett Frankfurt were taking with regard to understanding the body and its relationship to gaze as a state of thought. We began to investigate the nature of trance states and to work on a kind of movement that sought to achieve speed and complexity without force. We began to develop what we called dis-focus, a kind of seeing that is not a diminishing of vision, but rather a widening of vision, backwards.

In some pieces, such as *Limb's Theorem*, *Artifact*, *In the Middle, Somewhat Elevated* or the first act of *Loss,* called *The Second Detail*, gaze is used as a kind of compass. This kind of gaze forms the basis of classical ballet's *épaulement*: a set of complex relationships between the eyes, head, shoulders, hips, arms, hands and feet in the balletic form. The body, in *épaulement*, is a series of curvilinear forms—or directed lines or volumes—in angled relationships. The strong, outwardly directed, linear gaze of *épaulement* emerges as the result of the body's inner directional refractions. The angle of the gaze reflects the angles upon which the body orients itself. By focusing strongly in one direction, this gaze, or directed seeing, illuminates all the other directions that exist in relationship to it. It exteriorizes the geometries that dancers intuit through their experience of having a body. It extends this geometry past the body into the room, and it expands and delineates the space and the relationships between the dancers, the stage, and the audience.

In the second act of *The Loss of Small Detail,* however, we began to consider a different kind of gaze, one that was not outwardly directed, but rather that moved at inverted angles to the coordinations in the body. We disassociated our eyes from their balletic relationship to the body and thought of turning our gaze backwards, as if we were seeing the space far behind us. In this state of dis-focus, the principles of relationship, the complex, internal refractions that are the learned reflex of *épaulement*, are inverted or twisted, so that the relationships, or the quality of relation remains, but the form that they take is altered; it is an inverse body that flows backward from the gaze.

Using proprioception—the body's ability to sense where it is in space— and the learned reflexes of *épaulement*, we began to create a situation that enhanced our sense of the kinetic potential of space. Dancers develop a very keen proprioceptive ability, which enables them both to sense and to imagine their bodies with a high degree of exactitude. Taking in information within the kinesphere—the space that the body's movement occupies—involves sensing the body where it cannot be seen. For example, you cannot see your shoulder blade, but you can sense where it is in space, and in relationship to the rest of your body. This ability of the body to create an internal image of itself also allows for the possibility that the body can create an image or sense of itself where it does not exist, or for it to imagine itself orienting along lines, planes, or volumes in ways that are not actually possible. For example, I can imagine that I can fly, or that I have four arms, or that the curve of my arm is a line or volume of direction that I continue to sense even as it moves out into space, far beyond my body. I can imagine how it would feel to move in these situations. The proprioceptive field seems to expand to include a space that my body does not actually occupy. This ability to imagine multiple versions of the self, a proliferating, projective equation that moves out from where the body is to where the body might be, creates a situation where space seems to be inhabited by a complex, fluid matrix of potential motion and form, of which the body is part.

In *The Loss of Small Detail,* the character that I embody is experiencing two kinds of vision at once; I see the stage, with its visible people, objects, and empty space, and at the same time I see the space around me as alive with potential, invisible forms, and lines of movement. I am continually ambushed by, caught up in, this welter of doubled vision. I have the sense of seeing these two visual worlds simultaneously, and of speaking of one in the other. My real and imagined bodies are in a constant state of exchange through the medium of my eyes; they incorporate the ideas of motion present in one visual world, and express them in the other. This quality of being in multiple states at the same time is one that is often present in Bill's work, and has been developing throughout the years. The challenge for the dancer is how to react to multiple inputs with precision and fluidity. How to perceive what something is, to look at its internal components—the details of its parts and then to investigate what makes it whole and what else it might also become. This multi-streamed state is something that we have worked on, and are still working on, in many pieces, but that is particularly strong in *Decreation*.

Decreation

Decreation was a tricky process; it was full of deep-dwelling things that were reluctant to surface. It seemed to be composed of impossible things; contradictory and divided things. We began the process by considering the state of jealousy that arises from fragmentation, and the fragmentation that arises from jealousy. We thought about the nature of the contiguous and the singular, the nature of restraint and communication. We started working on a language of indirectness and fragmentation. For example, Bill created the task of walking while setting in motion a sort of diachronic physical ricochet in the body, which was accomplished by sending the eyes in one direction, jaw in the other, rib cage in one direction, hips in the other, etc. Most motion in *Decreation* takes place in this state, which is a further development of dis-focus, and so a further development of *épaulement*. It is the interconnectedness of the multiple patterns moving through the bodies that creates the oblique, twisted gaze of *Decreation*, and it is the gaze of *Decreation* that creates the complex of patterns moving through the room that is the body of the piece. As we progressed through the rehearsal process, we tried to both fragment and connect ourselves, as individuals and as a group. We bound ourselves together with ropes and tried to move. We each created what we called a '10 point' sequence, where we tried to connect and observe 10 points on our body while attempting to adhere to impossibly restrictive rules of behavior. We engaged in various experiments to see if two bodies could be in complete and constant contact with one another. We tried to make a book of the body. We covered our bodies in charcoal and, remaining in these states of restricted behavior, approached a paper-covered wall in the studio, making a huge mural of markings, drawings, imprints of the body.

We translated the fragmentation, and the attempts at unification, from the body to the voice. We made up ridiculous operas, sang for days in a seamless flow of evolving scenes, finally creating physical arias, movements that produced sounds that were the result of the body voicing its attempts to see itself within these restricted states. These arias began with the idea of trying to create a catalogue of all conceivable body movements in 60 seconds, as a way to bridge the past and future, to become a ball of memory, to become everything at once. We made scenes where one text moves through many people, where the body speaks what the voice cannot, where one person speaks what another cannot. We tried all these things, and many others. We failed constantly in entirely new ways, and slowly it became clear to me that this dynamic knotted-ness that we were after was exactly the kind of inner ricochet that is always going on in my own body.

Most of the tasks employed in this piece involved extreme isometric tensions and, because of my back, it was literally impossible for me to do most of the things that Bill was suggesting without ending up in a cramped heap on the floor. So, in this *Decreation* process I encountered these things that I could not do. I needed to re-think what it was that the piece required from me. I began to consider how the piece itself necessarily contained within it these junctures of struggle/obstruction. I considered how my own body, with its many areas of twisting, can only function effectively in a state of integration with its whole self, which, in my case, means integration through thought, as my actual structural wholeness is disturbed, or detoured. As with my own body, the nature of the piece that we were making was counterpointed torque. The body of the piece spoke though its own detours; it could only be present where a state of constant, oblique tension was the norm. This was, in fact, its wholeness. In order for the piece to speak, each instance of communication needed to take place in a state of mediation, or translation.

One movement method that came out of this we refer to as shearing. It is a state that the body enters into where no approach, neither physically nor vocally, is ever made directly. For example, as we approach a microphone, or a person, our thoughts move in that direction, but our gaze and our bodies ricochet backward, off the thought, in a series of oblique refractions. In *Decreation*, the body becomes a proliferation of angular currents flowing backwards out from the point of desire; the body enters into a state of complex, fragmented reaction.

Eventually, I realized that in order to enter into the torqued states that the piece required, which would normally be disastrous for my body, I had to understand what my body was thinking. I had to understand that it was already engaged in thinking about the whole room: about the form and direction of the body of the piece and the nature of the information that I was receiving from the bodies and the voices of the other performers. I needed to notice that I was part of a flow that was bigger than my own body, and that I only ran into problems when I tried to construct the flow rather than allowing myself to enter into it. I realized, for example, that the task of creating this physical ricochet of eyes, jaw, rib cage, hips, and so on, actually became possible if I allowed it, in my thought, to be not an activity, not something that I constructed, but rather a state that traveled through my body and connected me to the room.

Complex chains of events in the body, like *épaulement*, or like the physicalities we use in *Decreation*, can be experienced as either disjuncture—collections of discrete parts—or as a fluid, lively whole. Inside *Decreation*, everything is fragmented: the bodies, the text, the voices, and the characters. The body of the company is possessed by several voices that migrate between the dancers' individual bodies. For example, in the first scene I am engaged in a dialogue in which I speak both of the roles. I let the idea of the two separate voices move through me in a kind of sheared way, so that my body is kept in a state of tense counter-twist, facilitated by the device of pulling my clothes to affect distortion in my face, my gaze moving at oblique angles to my body.

The gaze in *Decreation* is both the outcome and the origin of the dynamic, refractive angles of direction within the body. It is a method of achieving a balance, an integration, which allows for motion. In the first scene, the relationship of my gaze to my body sets off a ricocheting pattern of motion that passes through me and sets the text in motion throughout the group. The disjuncture/fragmentation in the self, in the group, and in the piece is never solved, but is held. The bodies of the dancers and of the piece are made whole only by the shearing torque of the patterns of tension that connect us internally: in our individual bodies, as a group, and as elements of the larger structure of the work.

One night after a performance of *Decreation*, I was talking with a woman who had been in the audience. She was in a wheelchair and had a spastic condition that torqued both her body and her voice. She asked me why we moved the way we did in the piece, which reminded her of the way she moved. I explained some of what we were doing, which made sense to her, and then the woman, her husband, and I talked about detour and communication. How when integration is seamless and apparently without effort, then the mechanics of integration are sometimes not visible. But when faced with a situation like hers, or mine, or like *Decreation*, where there are substantial detours necessary to make communication possible, then the nature of integration and wholeness becomes simultaneously more evident and more mysterious. The energetic body of a whole can be present both in a state of coordinated ease and in one characterized by fragmentation. Experiencing fragmentation is another way of experiencing connection. The way that we think about a thing determines whether or not we are able to understand it as a whole.

How does the body think? What does it see? In *Decreation*, the body of the piece is in motion through time and the bodies of the performers are in motion in relationship to it. Our bodies think themselves into motion, the performers, all together, think the fragments of the piece into a whole. The piece, then, in turn, unites the individual performers into the time-body that it is. *Decreation* lets me notice, in a new way, that the presence of obstacle is not the same thing as the absence of unity. A body can be broken and still be whole. How we look at fragmentation affects the unity of the body. If we allow ourselves to be a unity composed of detailed fragments, then we can see more clearly both the fragmentation and the unity of what we are: the body thinking itself into the flow of the world, and the world itself flowing into the thinking of the body.

9   Inside the knot that two bodies make

Steven Spier

The film *From a Classical Position* is a fully collaborative work between a notable dancer and performer and a notable choreographer, being danced, directed, and edited by Dana Caspersen and William Forsythe of the late Ballett Frankfurt. By looking closely at the film, its origins, and its process of creation, we gain an understanding of Caspersen and Forsythe's way of collaborating and their interest in working with other media and formats. Uncompromising if not difficult for a general dance audience, it is also somewhat didactic and offers us insights into some of the Ballett Frankfurt's methods of generating movement, choreographic structures, and the importance of classical technique to a distinctive movement vocabulary: '[The film] was also a little message to the British, who I'm sure were curious about us. It was a little missile to them, saying yes we are the Ballett Frankfurt, yes we perform before so many seats in the Opera House. We are the same people and this is what we do … There is the obvious classical training and this is how we are dealing with it' (Forsythe 1999).[1]

The Ballett Frankfurt scrupulously avoided a formal hierarchy among its dancers, often listing them in a programme alphabetically, but Caspersen was unmistakably a prominent performer and contributor. Since joining the company in 1988 after leaving the North Carolina Dance Theatre, she had been a dancer, actress, author, director, choreographer, and film editor both with the company and on her own.[2] She won many awards as a dancer. She was nominated in 2001 for the Laurence Olivier Award for Outstanding Dance Achievement; won a Bessie, the New York Dance and Performance Award for Outstanding Creative Achievement, in 1999; and was named 'Best Dancer' by critics in *Ballett International's* annual poll for 2000–1, 1996–7, and 1994–5.

Forsythe was artistic director of the Ballett Frankfurt from 1984–2004 and has long been recognised as one of the world's leading choreographers. (He is also acknowledged to be an exceptional lighting designer.) He dances when he is teaching in rehearsal, but rarely performs publicly.[3] He has a long history of working with people in other fields, including literature, music, architecture, and film, and has frequently worked with a dramaturg. Similarly, he has involved company members in choreography, costume design, making videos, and writing texts and music. While working collaboratively with dancers is not a new idea, it is unusual in a ballet context; and through his extensive collaboration at the Ballett Frankfurt, Forsythe has sought to break down the traditional hierarchy between choreographer and dancer. Programme notes from as early as *Pizza Girl (Ninety One-Minute Ballets)* have credited the choreography to the dancers and himself. He has often referred to the Ballett Frankfurt as a choreographic ensemble.[4]

The idea of Caspersen and Forsythe dancing with each other and of making a film came from the creation of *Tight Roaring Circle* (now referred to as *White Bouncy Castle*), an installation in London by Caspersen, Forsythe, and Joel Ryan commissioned by Artangel. Over the four years from first conversation to inception, the installation changed numerous times, but the ideas of making a film and of Caspersen and Forsythe dancing together were recurring (Caspersen and Forsythe 1997).[5] This was a period of extremely active collaboration between them. As full collaborators they made *White Bouncy Castle, The The*, and *Firstext* (with Antony Rizzi). Caspersen also contributed significant parts to pieces by Forsythe. She directed and choreographed him in part one of *Endless House*; choreographed parts of *Small Void, Alien/a(c)tion*, and *Quintett*; and wrote texts for *Endless House, Sleepers Guts, Eidos : Telos, Of Any If And, The The*, and *Alien/a(c)tion*. She danced or performed in all those pieces except for the first part of *Endless House*.

The making of *White Bouncy Castle* took a form of collaboration that is as complete as in the film, and Caspersen's description of creating *White Bouncy Castle* equally applies to *From a Classical Position*:

> There is the kind of collaboration where people work on different aspects of one project to create the whole, there is the kind where someone organises the seminal parameters of an event and enables others [to] move into this field to find their own version of it, and then there is the kind of collaboration which is the coming together of two or more minds with the intent to carry out the difficult and lovely work of letting something take root and form in the expanded and complex space of minds thinking together about one task.
>
> (Caspersen 13 July 1997: fax to the author)

The installation also displays some of the preoccupations of the collaborators that are taken up again in *From a Classical Position*, even if it is, as the world's largest bouncy castle,[6] rather more populist. The most important impetus was to recapture authentic impulse, the joy of moving, the sheer delight with one's body that everyone has as a child. These may sound like obvious starting points for a choreographer and dancer, but they are often subsumed:

> Choreography should serve as a channel for the desire to dance. Often, when I [Forsythe] make ballets for other companies, I sense a loss of the

joy of dancing. … I'm not talking about being on stage, I'm talking about *dancing* … not at how they perform 'the choreography'.

(Sulcas 1995)

The use of a bouncy castle makes all this simply fun if not silly as one is literally destabilised and thus forced to move in a way that makes one aware of one's body in space and its relationship to gravity. Through heightening one's sense of proprioception, the awareness of what one's own body is doing, it hints at the sophisticated spatial awareness that trained ballet dancers have. The installation also uncovers the existence of rules or systems that define spatial relationships with other people or choreographic structures, though in this case an instinctive order that prevented people from colliding. It is these themes of collaborative making, the joy of movement, and uncovering means for organising bodies and movement in space that are also central to *From a Classical Position*.

Another important reference for *From a Classical Position* is *The The*, a piece that looks at how the body moves under different parameters. '*The The* is a richly articulate knot, wound by two women. Thinking intently through the curves and tensions of their bodies, the women engage in a conversation of limbs, spoken in a precise, tangled dialect of beauty' (Caspersen, 26 May 2003: email to the author). In each of four stagings between 1996 and 2000 *The The* opens with two people (a man and a woman, but two women in the latest staging in Brussels) downstage sitting next to each other, still for the first minute or so. They dance while seated in a complex counterpoint with each other. (*The The* soon became the first piece in an evening's performance entitled *Six Counterpoints*.) As the piece continues it is punctuated by meditative periods and a dancer's display of a hip, rib, or sole of a foot. Occasionally the dancers stand up to move to a different part of the stage and continue there. Sporadically Caspersen calmly calls out words that sound like cues, 'one', 'together', 'two', 'stop' to the faint background of traffic noise. In it some of the same physical coordinations and theatrical means as those in *From a Classical Position* are explored. There is an interest in isolating certain upper torso coordinations – shoulder–hip and rib cage–shoulder. The limbs sometimes seem cadaverous, other times brittle; generally they react to the actions of the torso and not the other way around as in *épaulement*.[7] The scale of the movement (that it occurs while the dancers are sitting), the absence of music, and the bare stage all demand that the viewer concentrate his or her gaze.

From a Classical Position has Caspersen and Forsythe dancing on a bare sound stage for 25 minutes. Though shot in colour, it looks black and white. The editing is crisp; the music by Forsythe's long-time collaborator Thom Willems comes and goes, as does the sound of the dancers themselves. The lighting is generally even. There are solos, pairings, extreme close-ups that resemble landscapes or hyper-real sculpture, and sound that not always corresponds to what one sees. A close look at the first 55 seconds shows the film's complexity. Forsythe encircles and twirls around a stationery Caspersen for about 10 seconds before the title comes on the screen, then a thumping sound as Caspersen and Forsythe repeatedly tumble to the floor; the sound, however, is subtly out of sync with the movement apparently generating it. Then they are sitting next to each other, looking for a point on each other with which to continue: Caspersen with her hand on Forsythe's forehead, his hand on her knee, he then taking her finger and leading her hand away from his forehead. This fades to them dancing upright to piano music; the sound of them dancing comes in; jump cut to them sitting on the floor dancing; a rhythmic banging noise that is asynchronous but clearly represents Forsythe's elbow hitting the floor as he collapses; jump cut; Caspersen solo with piano music; sound of her dancing and then slapping noises; Caspersen falling to the ground; the frames of her falling to the ground repeated; Forsythe entering the frame to reposition her. Soon afterward we have the first of 18 extreme closes ups, this one of his hand wrapped around one of her limbs as the camera slowly pans up his forearm, accompanied by the sound of a rhythmic thump, then piano music, an ear, Caspersen's hands gripping Forsythe's arm, the creases of Caspersen's arms against her upper body. At the very end Caspersen and Forsythe are entwined.

The primary nature of their relationship in the film is spatial, about the shape of another body from the interior, defining the space between them, making visible 'the interior of the knot' (Caspersen 1999) that two bodies make. Forsythe's description of the process of using drawings by Tiepolo in the making of *Hypothetical Stream* shows this interest in the space of two bodies entangled:

> There are all these human knots that Tiepolo had floating about as sketches ... And so *Hypothetical Stream* is simply people trying to solve these problems, unravel these knots.
>
> (BBC Radio 3 1999)

In the same interview he says he understands ballet as a 'geometric inscriptive art form'.[8] His instructional CD-Rom, *Improvisation technologies [interactive multimedia]: a tool for the analytical dance eye,* is the culmination of such explorations with its origins in teaching dancers new to the company how to understand his way of understanding the body in space.

The obviously strong physical understanding between Caspersen and Forsythe, however, helps make their exploration of the space between two bodies not only formal but personal as well. This ambiguity can be seen especially in the instances where one body is rearranged by the other person. Forsythe, for instance, sits down panting, and Caspersen takes his chin in her hand. This becomes the point with which to begin the next movement. Similarly, Forsythe lies down and Caspersen takes his wrist to swing him around so that he is prone and lays her arm across his back so her hand is on his shoulder. He then twists around and up with Caspersen's hand on the back of his neck and then jumps back; the music comes in, and he is alone dancing. Forsythe may say that, 'Here is a man and a woman who obviously have a very connected relationship but … without any kind of innuendo. There's no other thing going on except a man and woman dancing together, [which] can compose a relationship. And that's what it is.' (Forsythe 1999), but certain scenes are emotive as well as geometric. Caspersen understands that her training as a dancer allows her to see the world geometrically and admits a viewer might also see other kinds of relationships:

> What is interesting about dancing is that we come to live in a physical world which understands the geometry of space … You can realign a partner, for example, in some way to help them; or, not to help them. [Dancers] can put those kinds of internal psychological activities into space. I might see Bill [Forsythe] as himself, but I also see him as a collection of curves and lines. I might realign him on a purely geometrical level, from my point of view. But humans understand intuitively that it has another level.
>
> (Caspersen 1999)

The methods used to generate movement for the film were some of the many methods used at the Ballett Frankfurt. For example, a dancer generates a movement alphabet: small, short, gestural movements that are intuitively associated with a letter (Caspersen 2000). These become the basis of a phrase, and the physical configurations or operations that make up that phrase become what the dancer's body remembers. They become the building blocks for further choreography, duos, or group dances, or they become altered to inform the choices dancers make in a structured improvisational setting. Caspersen and Forsythe worked with their phrases off and on for about five weeks. They created duets not in order to learn steps but as a process of becoming entrained to allow them to improvise successfully together (Caspersen 1999):

> What we were doing was improvising all sorts of combinations we had made. So we had a big database in our brains of what basically are relational positions or relational movement directions. We could sense after a while: if I did this he could sense that I was basing it on some part of some phrase and he would react in some appropriate way … That's one of the benefits of having endlessly rehearsed those combinations: your body then has them. There's a kind of body awareness which functions very quickly, almost faster than your brain … You intuitively understand how one connection connects with another connection, and how those timings might hook up with something else … It's an intellectual activity, but it's not something that you stand around and consider.
>
> (Caspersen 1999)

Caspersen describes this process as 'a simultaneous building of counterpoint'. Forsythe comments that,

> Even at my age, more than the physical part, it was the intellectual part that required keeping that amount of information flowing at that speed and not getting habitual. It's really an unbelievable intellectual task. Dancers, it's perhaps a good thing that they're distracted from it, because if they started to acknowledge it it's really a giant task. I think perhaps in our case it's a big task because our dances are hyper-complex.
>
> (Caspersen and Forsythe 1997)

While some of the same methods for generating movement in live performances were used, performing for a film required a different kind of presence than for the stage, which they had not expected:

> We got in there on that first day and did it all. It was exactly like every horrible film we had ever seen. [They had watched all the dance films they could find.] We did all those bad things. It was amazing. Film is different for sure. It has to do with focus, I find. The kind of performance focus, dance focus you use on stage doesn't work with films … What we found worked best was to keep our gaze in a smaller sphere than we were used to.
>
> (Caspersen 1999)

They were so surprised by the difference of dancing for film that after they watched the first day's rushes they threw out all the material. They then,

> took two days off, contacted the Royal Ballet who gave us their studios, rehearsed there for two days, [and] structured all the material as improvs as opposed to choreographed sequences. Although there are some [vestigial] choreographed sequences in there too.
>
> (Forsythe 1999)

As Caspersen puts it,

> We threw out the actual choreography, the steps we had worked out … I think seven different duets. A lot of work, a lot of time was spent going, 'Okay, your right arm … no!' And then … we had to redo everything … and had four days to shoot, which is not very much time for a half-hour film. We went in there … and just did take after take … and improvised.
>
> (Caspersen 1999)

Caspersen and Forsythe danced without a final sequence in mind, and so the editing process involved finding a structure in order to reduce four days' footage to the precise length required for a film made for television. Forsythe likens the editing process to the choreographing of *Hypothetical Stream*, 'where you have material with no agenda except making sense out of the material' (Forsythe 1999). They had early on decided that the film should concentrate on the movement and so avoided special effects, which led to the use of a simple camera strategy of lots of steadycam work and straightforward editing techniques like cutting on the motion. (Forsythe, though, had been interested in using desynchronised sound for some time, and they agreed to use that technique.)

> We didn't have any problems deciding on what materials would go in, just how it would go together, the sequence, because we had nothing set up at all. We just picked out the material that looked good. Then we picked out sound. A lot of it was based on different kinds of sound and also desynchronised sound.
>
> (Caspersen 1999)

Though the film was not scripted or storyboarded and did not have a traditional cinematic structure to allow it to be cut together (Kaplan 2002), there is a logic to the way Caspersen and Forsythe move with each other. What had remained from the first day's shooting was their sense of entrainment (Caspersen 1999) and a coherence based on their classical training: 'When we were making the film we discovered that when we didn't use classical systems it became harder to read. They're very useful as an orienting tool, for the eye' (Caspersen 1999). Forsythe adds, 'They're very good for counterpoint. The work we were trying to do at that point was very contrapuntal' (Caspersen and Forsythe 1997).

An issue in the editing process was finding a way to collaborate, for Caspersen and Forsythe work very differently:

> We've got a very strong physical understanding of each other, how we move and how we dance. So the dancing by itself was just delightful to do ... The editing was very difficult and maybe that does have more to do with how we each think about choreography. We agreed on a lot of things but we disagreed about the process because we work very differently. I like to set up a lot of larger structures and then move into the work and see what happens. Bill likes not to know what's coming; he likes to let things go. I like sometimes to take more time and stick with something if it's not working, to work on it. He'll just, well, if it's not working he'll throw it right out.
>
> (Caspersen 1999)

As Forsythe says,

I think the problems are probably methodological. I'm quick. Da dee, da duh. I'm very impulsive. Dana's very methodical. I'm entirely instinctive and Dana is far more, she makes things minutely, step-by-step. I tend to instinctively throw things out there and then deal with them afterwards.

(Forsythe 1999)

Caspersen agrees, saying,

Bill gets frustrated sometimes because he can't choreograph as quickly or as intricately as he can dance because it comes from his body, it's an intelligence in his body. That's what he said the other day. So for him, choreographing is dancing, it comes right out of him like you turn on the tap ... But for me choreography is completely different ... I think of the whole thing as bigger than me. I don't feel it all in my body. I feel it more in the room, the choreography as a whole, as a piece.

(Caspersen 1999)

They interviewed a number of film editors and chose to work with Jo Ann Kaplan. Not only did she have a greater knowledge of editing techniques than they did, but she is also a filmmaker. Her role was not only technical but also to help find a logic for the film; this often meant getting between Caspersen and Forsythe with her own ideas.

As a truly collaborative work the film cannot be pulled apart into its constituent contributions, though one can find characteristics in it of both Caspersen's and Forsythe's own work and influences. Caspersen had worked with film techniques and paradigms previously, but unlike Forsythe had not actually made a film before. It can be convincingly argued that Forsythe has been drawn to film and its techniques more consistently than other cultural stimuli (Sulcas 2002).[9] Indeed, his interest in collaboration with dancers can be likened to the role of a film editor. Caspersen and Forsythe have continued to collaborate with each other and to work with some of the elements of film and of editing. *Endless House* physically forces the viewer to choose between the numerous things happening around him or her, to edit together a coherent performance that has different emphases depending on what one sees and hears as moveable screens and lighting, like on a sound stage, physically alter what is in view. Forsythe's own *Kammer/Kammer* is even more obviously filmic, with movable walls forming rooms and dance occurring live but mostly out of sight and projected onto screens hung over the stage. In his *Decreation* the theatre at the Bockenheimer Depot resembles a sound stage in its vastness and is set with keyboard, microphones, video cameras, and a screen on which are shown various performers, often in almost unrecognisable close up.

Arguably one of the greatest influences of film on Forsythe has been that of editing, for instance in structuring the choreography of *The Loss of Small Detail*:

I envy the idea in film that you can edit several different versions of the same action, then choose the one you like, so in part two I simply put more than one version of certain sequences onstage.

(Suclas 2002)

While Forsythe's work is well known for having multiple centres of interest, of often being so busy that the audience does not know what to concentrate on, film allows one to have almost complete control of what the audience sees, even if, as in this case, it remains fragmented:

Basically it's a dance you never see ... completely. You're always given a piece of it. You can't see the whole thing, you build motion and a dance out of the art of editing as opposed to stringing steps together or motions together.

(Forsythe 1999)

But the extremely focused nature of *From a Classical Position* is not only inherent to film but characteristic of Caspersen's choreography, and the use of the sounds of dancing – breathing, squeaking of moving feet, hands slapping the floor – give the film a presence that is almost contrary to the usual distance of dance on film. Forsythe's description of *Kammer/Kammer* could apply to parts of *From a Classical Position* and gets at its finely perched ambiguity between narrative and abstraction, intimacy and pure form:

Initially I knew that I wanted to use film, but as I was working on the piece it became clear to me that it was going to be a live filming, a sort of hybrid. I wanted to bring film into the theatrical medium, like a fabulous magnifying glass. The piece is partly about intimacy, and film allows you to go up close, to get that thing that people miss in the theatre.

(Sulcas 2002)

Notes

1 *Firstext* for the Royal Ballet was the first piece by Forsythe (with Caspersen and Rizzi) to be danced in Great Britain. The company did not dance there until November 1998, at Sadler's Wells.

2 Her own choreography consists of *Solo for One Man* (2003), Ballett Frankfurt; *The Use Of* (2001), Ballett Frankfurt; *Work for Three* (1999), commissioned by Klapstuck Festival; Endless House, Part One (1999), Ballett Frankfurt, directed and choreographed by her; *Prelude 17* (1998), CaDance Festival, Den Haag, commissioned by Korzo Theater; *Work #2* (1998), Ballett Frankfurt; *Work #1* (1998), Holland Dance Festival, commissioned by and for Sylvie Guillem. She has collaboratively choreographed, in addition to *From a Classical Position*, *The The*, Ballett Frankfurt, with William Forsythe; *Firstext*, The Royal Ballet, with William Forsythe and Antony Rizzi. Within Forsythe's works she has choreographed parts of *Small Void*, *Alien/a(c)tion*, and *Quintett*. She has written text for the following Forsythe works: *Endless House, Sleepers Guts,*

Eidos : Telos, Of Any If And, The The, and *Alien/a(c)tion*. For *Endless House* Part Two she was co-dramaturg. With William Forsythe and Joel Ryan she created the installation *Tight Roaring Circle* (now *White Bouncy Castle*).

3 Antipodes I/II (2007), Wanda Golonkas's *An Antigone* (2002); Part One of *Endless House, From a Classical Position*, and *Solo* for Sylvie Guillem's film *Evidentia*. He joined the Robert Joffrey Ballet School in 1969 and danced with the Joffrey Ballet until 1973, when he joined the Stuttgart Ballet under the artistic directorship of John Cranko. The company had a policy of developing new choreographers and Forsythe created his first professional work there in 1976: *Urlicht*. He subsequently made more pieces for Stuttgart Ballet and for other companies and by 1980 had stopped performing.

4 For instance, from 'A Conversation between Dana Caspersen, William Forsythe and the architect Daniel Libeskind' at the Royal Geographical Society, London, 7 March 1997. Peter Cook substituted for an ill Libeskind.

5 Among earlier ideas was a giant camera obscura, giant turntables, the installation of a huge red circular staircase, dancing on that staircase, and them dancing on a strip of sand, leaving their traces and filming it with sequential video cameras.

6 The work was installed in Frankfurt in December 1999 at the Bockenheimer Depot and was in Vienna in September 2003 and in Frankfurt again in December 2003. The company now refers to it as *White Bouncy Castle*. For a thorough description of the piece and the issues of collaboration and ordering movement see Spier (2000).

7 'The slight twist in the torso, from the waist upwards, which tilts one or other shoulder slightly forwards, thus giving an extra three-dimensional quality to a pose'. From Debra Craine and Judith Mackrell (2000), *Oxford Dictionary of Dance*, Oxford: Oxford University Press.

8 For an extensive description of Forsythe's relationship to geometry and drawing see Spier, 'Dancing and Drawing, Choreography and Architecture', *Journal of Architecture*, vol. 10 no. 4. 2005, 349–363.

9 *Sulcas* (2002) traces his interest in film, its effects, and techniques through Gänge, *Berg Ab*, whose original title was *Three Orchestral Pieces – a Motion Picture, Die Befragung des Robert Scotts, Slingerland, The Loss of Small Detail, As a Garden in This Setting, Alien/a(c)tion, Pivot House, Eidos : Telos, Endless House*, and *Kammer/Kammer*. The author attended the interview that formed the basis of her piece.

References

BBC Radio 3 (1999), 'William Forsythe: Seeing your finger as a line', interview by Christopher Cook with Deborah Bull, William Forsythe, Daniel Libeskind, Ann Nugent, and Roslyn Sulcas, broadcast 14 March. (The Ballett Frankfurt had performed at Sadler's Wells Theatre, London, November 1998.)

Caspersen, Dana (1999), interview with the author, Brussels, 2 July.

Caspersen, Dana (2000), 'It Starts From Any Point: Bill and the Frankfurt Ballet', *Choreography and Dance* (special issue on William Forsythe), vol. 5 part 3: 25–39.

Caspersen, Dana and Forsythe, William (1997), interview with the author, London, 25 March.

Driver, Senta (ed.) (2000), *Choreography and Dance* (special issue on William Forsythe), vol. 5, part 3.

Forsythe, William (1999), interview with the author, Frankfurt am Main, 21 October.

Forsythe, William, *et al.* (1999 [2003]), *Improvisation technologies [interactive multimedia]: a tool for the analytical dance eye/a CD-ROM*, Karlsruhe: ZKM Karlsruhe, distribution Hatje Cantz Verlag.

Kaplan, Jo Ann (2002), telephone interview with the author, 17 May.

Spier, Steven (2000), 'A Difficult and Lovely Work', *Choreography and Dance* (special issue on William Forsythe), vol. 5 part 3: 103–14.

Sulcas, Roslyn (1995), 'Kinetic Isometries: William Forsythe on his continuous rethinking of the ways in which movement can be engendered and composed', *Dance International*, Summer: 8, p. 8.

Sulcas, Roslyn (2002), 'Forsythe and Film: Habits of Seeing', in Judy Mitoma, Elizabeth Zimmer and Dale Ann Stieber (eds), *Envisioning Dance on Film and Video*, New York and London: Routledge.

10 Aberrations of gravity

Heidi Gilpin

For Tracy-Kai Maier-Forsythe, dancer, 1961–1994

> It was night itself. Images which constituted its darkness inundated him. He saw nothing and, far from being distressed, he made this absence of vision the culmination of his sight ... . Not only did this eye which saw nothing apprehend something, it apprehended the cause of its vision. It saw as object that which prevented it from seeing.
>
> Maurice Blanchot, *Thomas the Obscure*, pp. 14–15

I felt violent shaking, I heard everything crashing around me, but I saw nothing. To see the earthquake was to see those moments of instability that are the focus of this text: moments that are invisible until after they have passed. You see the wreckage of the forces that shifted during the Los Angeles quakes, but that moment of shifting is inaccessible, even in memory. I saw nothing. I have only a memory of the sounds and sensations of physical shifts in the walls, in the ground. This inability to see that moment of movement is the paradox of performance. Movement is a traumatic event.

The survival of traumatic events involves complicated nonlinear transformations—moving from the experience of a life-threatening event to consciousness, where actual experience, perceived experience, and memory collide and invent other realities. Cathy Caruth, who has written extensively about the relations between repetition, trauma, recollection, memory, and history, discusses the functions of post-traumatic stress (a condition familiar to many, and much commented upon in the media in the aftershocked phase of the 1994 L.A. quake) in a way that illuminates the function of the denial, or elimination from our understanding, of experience:

> While the traumatized are called upon to see and to relive the insistent reality of the past, they recover a past that enters consciousness only through the very denial of active recollection. The ability to recover the past is thus closely and paradoxically tied up, in trauma, with the inability to have access to it. And this suggests that what returns in the flashback is not simply an overwhelming experience that has been obstructed by a later repression or amnesia, but *an event that is itself*

constituted, in part, by its lack of integration into consciousness. Indeed, the literal registration of an event—the capacity to continually, in the flashback, reproduce it in exact detail—appears to be connected, in traumatic experience, precisely with the way it *escapes* full consciousness as it occurs.

> (Caruth 1991a: 418–19, first emphasis mine)

In relation to movement performance, which I will discuss here, the performance of absence is what enables us to recognize the performance of presence. To escape full consciousness is both to acknowledge a presence (of mind, of perception) and to enact the denial of presence. Performance, in this sense, is an act of escape from full consciousness—from full vision, full perception—for both performer and spectator. Performance, then, and our relation to it, positions itself as a traumatic event.

Traumatic recall remains insistent and unchanged to the precise extent that it has never, from the beginning, been fully integrated into understanding. According to Caruth, 'in its repeated imposition as both image and amnesia, the trauma thus seems to evoke the difficult truth of a history that is constituted by the very incomprehensibility of its occurrence' (Caruth 1991a: 419). The connections here to an absence and failure of comprehension, and to repetition, offer powerful evidence that such terms of alienation— amputation, disappearance, disfiguration—propose relevant and suggestive ideas through which to examine various expressions of trauma and history in the work of contemporary performance genres. These terms not only seem to arise organically from the complex issues of late twentieth-century experience, they are immediately recognizable in the recent work of a genre-breaking form I call movement performance.

There is a lightness inherent in performance that is similar to the absence found in trauma: that always sought after but never realized or articulatable void that engenders *Entstellung*. Lightness can be considered both a displacement and a movement. Freud suggests that the word *Entstellung*, or distortion, signifies not only disfigurement, but also *dislocation*:

> We might well lend the word 'Entstellung' (distortion) the double meaning to which it has a claim but of which today it makes no use. It should mean not only 'to change the appearance of something' but also 'to put something in another place, to displace'.
>
> (Freud 1960a, p. 43)

Lightness is a condition where something happens—an accident, a traumatic event, a failure, a disappearance—outside of the capabilities of some form of notation. These issues can be played out via the work of performance choreographer/director William Forsythe. In Forsythe's work, lightness is a quality that emerges out of failure, disappearance, and disequilibrium. But first it is necessary to map out some of the complexities of failure and disappearance that conceptually guide the trajectories of other terms discussed here.

Failure

Failure contains within it notions of absence, of lack, as well as very distinct elements of movement and performance. Notice in the following definitions the kinds of terms that are used to describe failure and failing, terms which point to performance, physicality, and movement: to fail comes from the Latin *fallere*, which means to deceive, to disappoint. To fail is to lose strength, to fade or die away, to stop functioning, to fall short, to be or become absent or inadequate, or to be unsuccessful. A failing is 'a usually slight or insignificant defect in character, conduct or ability'. Failure addresses an absence or lack: 'an omission of occurrence or performance; a state of inability to perform a normal function; a fracturing or giving way under stress; a lack of success; a falling short, or deficiency; deterioration, decay'; and finally, 'one that has failed' (*Webster's Dictionary*, 9th ed).

Sigmund Freud articulates issues of absence or lack in relation to failure in *The Psychopathology of Everyday Life* (1901), where he discusses failures and errors of action, thought, and speech, which in English are called parapraxes. Parapraxes are not arrests but events, oscillations, in that they are failures of movement of some kind. The German term Freud first used to describe such misperformances, absences of memory, or slips of the tongue, is *Fehlleistung*, which is described in the editor's introduction to the *Standard Edition* as 'faulty function'. The definition of the masculine German noun *Fehl* is 'fault, blemish, failure' (*Cassell's*). The feminine German noun *Leistung* bears the following definition: 'performance, execution; achievement, accomplishment, work; production, output, result, effect'. 'Failed performances', such as these, articulate the fundamental interaction of failure and performance in the movement they generate. Displacement, as a movement, is a potential source for configuring the interpretation and composition of performance, but here its importance is in relation to failure. Freud uses the term *Vergreifen*, translated as 'bungled actions', to describe 'all the cases in which a wrong result—i.e. a deviation from what was intended—seems to be the essential element'. Such deviations, or wrong results, are thus linked to the failed performances and the movements they describe or cause. In terms of the genre of movement performance at issue here, deviations or errors are significant markers for how to enact as well as interpret movement.

Failed performances ultimately describe movement: movement of a physical and psychic nature, and multiple movements of the body, of memory, and of the unconscious. If these ambiguous movements actively fail to be fixed by any singular meaning, then failure, it seems, can be regarded as a positive, enabling force of movement. Failure functions within the work of contemporary European movement performance directors as a significant strategy both for the composition and interpretation of movement. The work of Forsythe at issue here presents the failure to maintain the balletic vertical. Although contemporary choreographers employ failure in many different ways, what is interesting is how exactly failure functions to produce new movement, new scenic and spatial compositions, and new interpretations. Their examples point to ways that movement can be performed in a three-dimensional space while engaging imaginary spaces through which a body is constantly in a state of multidimensional falling. Failure contains within it notions of movement, of performance, and of the enabling ambiguity that produces movement.

The idea of absence and negation, of what we don't know offering up possibilities that might enable different perspectives, other visions, other movements, is the subject of Barbara Johnson's essay 'Nothing Fails Like Success'. Johnson writes:

> If I perceive my ignorance as a gap in knowledge instead of an imperative that changes the very nature of what I think I know, then I do not truly experience my ignorance. The surprise of otherness is that moment when a new form of ignorance is suddenly activated as an imperative.
>
> (Johnson 1987: 16)

The movement involved in the process Johnson describes is significant. Where there is movement, there is the potential for constant and infinite movement. Stasis is impossible. 'Activation' is the operative term, shifting the concept of failure from that of a gap of static space to that of an imperative that causes dynamism. Rather than a space of absent experience, nonfulfillment, and living death, movement is an art of becoming (Deleuze and Guattari 1987). But the process of becoming is a constantly shifting, goalless experience. The traditional notion of movement, of dance, is that there is a moving toward something, and that that something is fixed. And yet, according to Johnson, this movement, this system of gestures, this dance keeps discovering that there is no something, that the something is not fixed, but keeps changing. The development of these dynamic movements of failed performance involves a certain disappearance of the source of movement and oscillation. Dance finds stillness the way language or music finds silence. Its dynamism is located in its stability; its static nature engendered by instability.

Disappearance

What does it mean to disappear? This too is a term of performance and movement. The *Oxford English Dictionary* offers:

> 1a. To cease to appear or be visible; to vanish from sight. b. Of a line or thing extended in space, which ends by gradually ceasing to be distinguishable, or 'dies away' by blending with something else; *to be*

traceable no farther. 2. To cease to be present, to depart; to pass from existence, pass away, be lost (emphasis mine).

Disappearance is 'the action of disappearing; passing away from sight or observation; vanishing'. The first example the *OED* offers for disappearance dates from 1712: 'Not likely to be remembered a Moment after their Disappearance'. The act of disappearing, then, involves both movement and the cessation of movement: to pass from sight and to cease to be present. It also registers a lack of representationality: the disappeared can no longer be represented because they can be traceable no farther, they can no longer be notated, they have vanished from sight, which also suggests that they have vanished from existence, from presence. According to dictionary definitions, dying is indistinguishable from disappearing. Death, like disappearance, is a passing from presence to absence, a movement from figuration to disfiguration—physically and in memory. The possibility that presence, once it is no longer traceable, is also no longer part of our memory of it, is deeply disturbing. How is it possible to forget what was once present? How can such a forgetting be tolerated responsibly? How do we enact this memory, even if it is through a performance of absence? How can absence be performed?

That the disappearing person, object, or idea is not likely to be remembered immediately after its disappearance, is a topic Caruth addresses via latency and the act of forgetting, again in relation to traumatic events. Caruth writes:

> It is not so much the period of forgetting that occurs after the accident, but rather the fact that the victim of the crash was never fully conscious during the accident itself: the person gets away, Freud says, 'apparently unharmed'. The experience of trauma, the fact of latency, would thus seem to consist, not in the forgetting of a reality that can hence never be fully known; but in an inherent latency within the experience itself. The historical power of the trauma is not just that the experience is repeated after its forgetting, but that *it is only in and through its inherent forgetting that it is first experienced at all* … . If return is displaced by trauma, then, this is significant in so far as *its leaving—the space of unconsciousness— is paradoxically what precisely preserves the event* in its literality. For history to be a history of trauma means that it is referential precisely to the extent that it is not fully perceived as it occurs; or to put it somewhat differently, that *a history can be grasped only in the very inaccessibility of its occurrence.*
>
> (Caruth 1991b: 17, emphasis mine)

Thus disappearance paradoxically manifests precisely what we presume it makes absent. It enables not only appearance, but perception, apprehension, experience, and memory. If, as Caruth suggests, forgetting an event allows us to experience it for the first time; if the departure of movement preserves movement; and if history can only be grasped in its ungraspability, then the fundamental fact of performance is that it is enabled by its vanishing, that it exists through its disappearance. The points of instability and disequilibrium that engender such vanishing acts are precisely those that cannot be recorded, as the work of Forsythe demonstrates.

William Forsythe: the dynamics of stasis and absence

> Something strives for a form, for a wholeness, and excitement is really only created at the cracks, where suddenly everything goes wrong.
>
> Wim Wenders, *siteWORKS*

Forsythe, American-born choreographer and artistic director of the Ballett Frankfurt in Frankfurt, Germany, thrives on the thrill of accidents. His choreographic work has consistently attempted to expose states of concentration where accidents happen to produce exquisite and unexpected possibilities. With displays of vertiginous danced virtuosity and stunning visual and sonic performance, Forsythe has created a new genre of balletic performance, a genre some critics have described as the ballet of the twenty-first century. Although the Ballett Frankfurt dancers are trained in ballet (and other) techniques, and although the women frequently dance on pointe, it would be difficult to describe many of Forsythe's choreographies as ballet or simply dance. In this form of movement performance, texts appear frequently, either spoken by dancers or presented on supertitles or scrims on stage; movement vocabulary ranges from classical ballet to breakdance; and modes of presentation range from austere pure dance sequences without sets to musicals and gospel mixed with Kabuki. At the least, Forsythe frequently manages to surprise and disturb his audiences with a powerful mix of dance, technology, contemporary and ancient cultural artifacts, theoretical explorations and an eye for the exquisite in space—whether it is through a late-twentieth-century fairy tale whose narrative is nonexistent and therefore constantly sought, through a musical that humorously deconstructs the familiar Broadway genre, through strident references to xenophobia present in the audience, or through an environment of darkness and shadow that challenges how we think about the moving body in space, and what we expect from danced performance.

Forsythe's strategies of composition and performance differ significantly from those of other contemporary movement performance director/choreographers. He is extremely committed to working within already existing paradigms of dance, even if he attempts to transgress, augment, and explode them in the process. Forsythe celebrates dance to such an extent that, at least in some of his productions, the body disappears. Although an ambivalence about the dancing body still exists for Forsythe, he plays it out in other ways: he displays the dancing body's dizzying beauty while at the same time forcing its loss of identity.

In recent productions, Forsythe seems to be pushing dance through invisibility to see what possibilities this strategy might offer. Literally, shadows, limited and carefully positioned lighting, and near-darkness often inhabit the stage of the Ballett Frankfurt. Such performance environments highlight the nonvisibility of the dancers, forcing the audience to strain to see or imagine the body that is producing the movement whose traces are all that can be discerned. Movement itself does not disappear, but the body that performs it does. Conceptually, through new forms of vertiginous dynamism, Forsythe eliminates visibility via the performance of movement.

As an architecture of disappearance, Forsythe's performative events display movements where the presence of the body is no longer assured. Forsythe dismembers the deceptive unity of movement operative in classical ballet, explodes it into a space we take for granted, and culls its residual motions to offer new forms. He presents the speed of intense concentration on a complex network of movement operations. Unlike other directors of performance genres, Forsythe focuses on the specific residual effects of failure in movement explorations. Forsythe inscribes failure in, on, and with the body as an attempt at technical and intellectual precision, as a vertiginous thrill of exactitude. In such a process, failure can be lifesaving. In this way the Ballett Frankfurt dancers display movement that is derived from but is no longer traditional ballet. With Forsythe, both the body and classical balletic vocabulary are being challenged in order to discover, or uncover, other directions and forms of movement.

Laban's model of spatial possibilities

In uncovering possibilities of movement composition, Forsythe's working methods draw significantly from the work of Rudolf von Laban, one of the movement pioneers of the early twentieth century, who devised a system to understand and record the possibilities of human movement. In a work entitled *Choreutics*, Laban develops his ideas about *Raumlehre*—literally, space instruction—and elaborates the notational system we refer to today as Labanotation, or Kinétographie.[1] This system of notation is designed to be able to record, with equal precision, the movements of a dancer, a woman giving birth, or an assembly line worker, using a series of carefully defined geometric symbols. Although Laban was a proponent of his own form of free dance, which departed from the tradition and constraints of classical ballet, the theoretical premises of his systems draw significantly on the essentially axial model of ballet. Laban argues that 'dance and architecture are the two basic arts of man from which the others derive'(5), and his notion of *Raumlehre* rests on a metaphor that likens human movement to architecture: 'Movement is, so to speak, living architecture—living in the sense of *changing emplacements* as well as changing cohesion. The architecture is created by human movements and is made up of pathways tracing shapes in space [which] we may call "trace-forms"' (5, emphasis mine). Accordingly, recording movement requires drawing a groundplan like that of an architect, with at least two elevations in order to convey 'to the mind a plastic image of the three-dimensional whole' (5).

The cornerstone of Laban's system is the idea of the *kinesphere*— the spherical space around the body delineated by easily extended limbs 'without stepping away from that place which is the point of support when standing on one foot' (10). Moving beyond the kinesphere, where the rest of space lies, involves transporting the kinesphere to a new place. According to Laban, the kinesphere remains in a fixed relationship to the body, and as a constant always travels with it. In order to represent the kinesphere, Laban likens it to a cube that surrounds the body to the front and back, right and left, top and bottom. This cube assumes the *stability of a single central point* in the body from which all movement emanates and through which all axes pass. The kinespheric model unfolds into a virtually infinite number of possible planes delineated by the axes that transverse the body at that centre point. For Laban, 'a multilateral description of movement which views it from many angles is the only one which comes close to the complexity of the fluid reality of space'(8). Laban's model suits the movement vocabulary of classical ballet particularly well, since both employ one central point in the body as their structuring element.

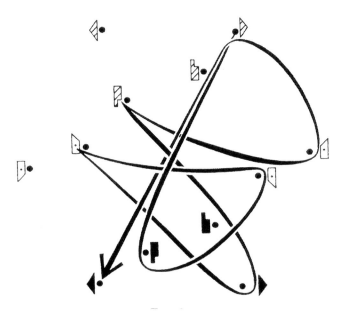

Figure 10.1 Diagram of Labanotation from Rudolph von Laban

Exploding the kinesphere

But if, as Forsythe asks, a movement does not emanate from the body's centre, or if there were more than one centre, or if the source of a movement were an entire line or plane, and not simply a point, then one would have to assume a whole array of collapsible and expandable kinespheres, and reassign their centres infinitely throughout the body. In Forsythe's dismantling of Laban's model, any point or line in the body or in space can become the kinespheric centre of a particular movement, and the kinesphere is permeated with an infinite number of points of origin that can appear simultaneously in multiple points in the body. An infinity of emerging rotating axial divisions may have as their centres the heel of the right foot, the left ear, the right elbow, the back of the neck, or an entire limb, for example.

Laban's kinesphere is one stable, nonvertiginous entity that remains in a fixed relation to the body it surrounds. Its relation to space, however, is not fixed, for the kinesphere responds in relation to the movement of the body's centre, so that for Laban, as the body moves, the kinesphere moves with it. Yet these movements are generated by a profound unalterable sense of balance. Laban imagines dream movements only as far as the boundaries of equilibrium: 'dream-architectures can neglect the laws of balance. So can dream-movements, yet a fundamental sense of balance will always remain with us even in the most fantastic aberrations from reality' (5). For Forsythe, the body is not the equilibrated unified form that Laban imagined it to be: as the centre point of a *designated* kinesphere moves, that kinesphere moves with it.

The kinesphere's relation to the ground, in Laban's model, is a vertical one that corresponds to a standing body: the cube rests on its bottom plane, and the upper and lower, side, and diagonal planes are clearly delineated. Gravity responds to the verticality and central point of Laban's model, while in Forsythe's movement research process, one could imagine a number of different relations with gravity, primarily because verticality as a rule has disappeared. This loss of verticality has dynamic effects.

Although Laban never articulated his model's potential as a destabilizing source of movement, Forsythe explores precisely that—the extrakinespheric moments when the boundaries of equilibrium are transgressed, when falling is imminent because something has failed. That something is balance. Fundamentally, ballet as movement spectacle invites a narrative of physical grace, poise, and style: the *telos* of classical ballet implies and assumes—at the very least—physical balance. This assumption and its consequent attitude toward beauty are interrogated by Forsythe. He elevates the failure to maintain balance as the most important project in his movement research. He constantly challenges the dancers to confront moments of failure and vertigo, moments where balance is lost. Laurie Anderson exposes this concentrated state:

> You're walking ... and you don't always realize it but you're always falling. With each step ... you fall. You fall forward a short way and

then catch yourself. Over and over … you are falling … and then catch yourself. You keep falling and catching yourself falling. And this is how you are walking and falling at the same time.

(Anderson 1987: 68)

It is curious that we generally repress this vertiginous yet intense state of concentration, that we choose to overlook it, to tame it by calling it 'walking' or 'moving', rather than to explore the very disorienting spatial and psychic possibilities that such a state offers up. The movement composition research of the Ballett Frankfurt attempts to expose and examine precisely these disturbing moments of lost attention. In such choreography, the double-edged tension of disequilibrium is a state that emerges from the infinite operations that dismantle historically established bodily configurations. This state reveals what is always in the process of disappearing; the dancing thereby highlights the continuous vanishing moments of movement, and offers a redefinition of dance as we have come to know it. Dance, as Forsythe's work suggests, is a process of embodied disappearance. Distinct from choreographers whose interactions with dance offer definitions of it as an ordered system or set of expectations, Forsythe performs a redefinition (some might say a disfigurement) of dance that alludes to contemporary notions of becoming and embodiment whose references are always already absent. This work embodies a process that can only be witnessed in the act of its disappearance.

How to maintain vertigo: spatial inscriptions

In Forsythe's strategies of movement composition, invisible moments of discontinuity and absence are the connectors of movement. Missing parts are precisely those that create continuity. The source, the event that engenders other events, is located in a gap, in a void. There is a confrontation, manoeuvred in distinct ways, with absence.

In order to maintain a vertiginous state, Forsythe works with various operations, exploring the rules and limits of games of expression (mimicry), games of competition *(agon)*, games of chance *(alea)*, and games of vertigo *(ilynx)*, among others, often in relation to Roger Caillois' classification of games in his 1958 *Les jeux et les hommes*. After suspending and dispersing Laban's model, Forsythe literally permeates the resulting structure with a network of terminology. Terms of quantity, order, change, form, dimension, and motion, among many others, are the basis of Forsythe's operations on movement. In conversations since 1989, Forsythe describes one such operation, 'universal writing', as:

a continual reassignment of effort and shape; a loss of strict categorization in which desired randomness, with residual aesthetic logic, allows any form—like the linear components of a letter of the alphabet, for example—to be written prepositionally, in, on, with any part of the body.

He characterizes universal writing as having 'a refractory quality; the object is to scatter the material, in proliferation and perfect disorder'. Comparable operations have included: 'arc and axis', 'cross and pass', 'tubing', and 'video scratch'. Many are descriptive, mimetic acts, which both reassign movement and generate its unavoidable and unforeseeable residues. Forsythe argues: 'I don't want to know what's going to happen. I want to be ambushed by the results'. He does this by creating ever-multiplying systems of movements, which in turn regenerate themselves through variation.

The explosion of form

Rather than retrieving and reproducing classical balletic forms that are fixed entries in the roster of movement, Forsythe bursts open these forms so that previously hidden moments in balletic movements are made plainly visible. In doing so, not only are movement and form given a new life and a new set of possibilities, but so is ballet in general. Failure and falling, for example, are retrieved and revalorized as intrinsically necessary and equally valid structural components of classical dance. What Forsythe moves towards is an opening of the apparently immutable, because historically sanctioned, assumptions of his discipline. Linearity, and verticality in particular, is lost when Laban's kinespheric model is exploded, when the symmetrical grid is actually found to be constructed of decentred and multiplicitous spaces. Forsythe demonstrates that the unity of the dancing body is fallacious and deceptive.

In order to sustain the vibrations of disequilibrium and disappearance in his work, Forsythe is forever throwing the question of impermanence into play. His productions contain traces of the ephemeral within the very processes he chooses to explore. Instability permeates these processes. When Forsythe asks the dancers to 'sustain the reinscription of forms', he is trying to maintain a state of vibration, a moment of trembling devoid of stability, devoid of permanence. Quaking moments; endless aftershocks. He also uses improvisation to display impermanence; as he declared in 1989: 'the whole point of improvisation is to stage disappearance'. Finally, Forsythe constantly plays with details, changes sections and even entire structures, as was the case with *The Vile Parody of Address* (1988), of which at least six radically different versions have already been performed. At the Paris Opera premiere of *In the Middle, Somewhat Elevated* (1987), he reset the order of the sequences and informed the dancers just before the beginning of the performance. During his 1989 America Tour, he 'let the linear formations disintegrate' only hours before the performance of *Behind the China Dogs* (1988). In one of the (December 1992) Ballett Frankfurt's most recent evening-length productions, *Alien/a(c)tion*, Forsythe continues

Figure 10.2 Tracy-Kai Maier-Forsythe in *Limb's Theorem* (Permission of Dominik Mentzos)

to alter texts, songs, and movement material in the third section so that apart from the costumes, it is virtually unrecognizable, or at least radically different, from the premiere version. He purposely keeps everyone—the dancers, the audience, and himself—on an edge, always geared to expect the unexpected.

In such a process, reproducibility is anathema in all of its manifestations. Forsythe is not interested in the survival of his work as an object; that would fetishize the work as a finished, categorizable, reproducible object. He is similarly adamant about the fact that his choreographies, unlike classical ballets, cannot be recorded using Labanotation. A Labanotation expert confirmed in 1990 that the operations performed on movement could be recorded generally, but that sequences of movements themselves were impossible to notate.

The 'explosion' model Forsythe uses encourages his audiences to confront assumptions about linearity, space, and ultimately, the linearity of history. Forsythe focuses on moments of rupture and discontinuity and participates in the sort of history that Michel Foucault writes about:

> Discontinuity was the stigma of temporal dislocation that it was the historian's task to remove from history. It has now become one of the basic elements of historical analysis.
>
> (Foucault 1972: 8)

Forsythe's work certainly betrays a measure of indebtedness to balletic traditions. Yet he is also immersed in a current effort to interrupt the mechanics of classical balletic syntax. Ultimately, the question of representation is at stake with the obscured layers of processes that engender movement. Forsythe challenges both the spectator and performer to apprehend and perform the invisible strata that we take for granted in even our most prosaic gestures. He liberates formal coordinates so that they no longer resist vertigo. The performer becomes an agent; at once an inscriber and a transcriber, the dancer performs operations that dismantle an assumed, logical structure. The forgotten elements of deceptively unified and coherent sequences are reassembled spatially. Performances fail where they forget their own histories of discontinuity and disappearance. In this way choreography—the memorized, fixed, fetishized object—disappears.

In rehearsal and in performance, Forsythe and the dancers study forms of division and moments of invisibility that are actually the joints of movements: they question the notion of a unity of movement, attempt to scatter it, and offer the refracted, incomplete motions as sources for new forms. They employ movement operations on already existing phrases of movement to generate unavoidable and unpredictable residual movement. This fallout enables observers to witness gaps, moments of discontinuity and absence which so often go unnoticed. Our attention is drawn precisely to moments we might otherwise have overlooked, namely, moments of falling; of the failure to maintain balance. Simultaneously we observe the emergence of unanticipated residual movement. Through the strategies of manifesting disequilibrium, slowness, invisibility, almost imperceptible speed, and attention, Forsythe exposes previously invisible dimensions of movement and stasis.

As in the case of the operation of universal writing, often textual material is created as a source of movement research: for *Limb's Theorem* (1990), a production I worked on as dramaturg, we were working with a number of ideas for both conceptual and physical enactment, including but by no means limited to circles and spirals, the shape of the letter *U*, Archimedes' principle of displacement, and Aldo Rossi's idea of the fragment as an object of hope. I combined mathematical, architectural, and physical terms with terms of action and motion, change, form, order, dimension, quantity, relation, difference, and time to construct an extensive series of directives called U-lines. These short phrases were then given to the dancers to be applied as operations onto various movement material in a virtually infinite number of ways. Some of these U-lines were, for example: U invert difference; U arc indivisibly; U project solids; U solidify angles; U extend impulse; U divide pressure, U precede seizure; U suggest vortex; U displace contraction; U locate depth; U moderate verticality; U deviate laterality; U arrange remainder; U uncover weight; U organize appearance; U relocate symmetry; U retrograde spirals; U outline aberrations; U radiate concavity; U classify repetition; U fragment volumes, U rearrange revolutions, etc.

Forsythe works with various operations like U-lines to explore the rules and limits of the games of expression, competition, chance, and vertigo discussed above. As these operations and games fail to meet the requirements of their own rules, they offer up maps of decomposition as results that can continually be reassigned in, on, or with any part of the body. The result of such processes is the generation of forms produced by the research apparatus itself, not some series of fixed, seizable, and repeatable movements. It is a serious and concentrated process of exploring unknown physical, intellectual, psychic and spatial realms. As Forsythe has said, 'if you are consumed by the act, nothing else exists: it's insanely beautiful'. Although he made this statement a year before the U-lines were used as a choreographic strategy, the pun on the subject of U/you still maintains what Forsythe's work displays in manifold ways: that with the disappearance of the body, the self disappears.

In such a process, the notion of perfection or success has little if any meaning; the only criteria are one's concentration as a dancer and one's imagination as an observer, and both are potentially limitless. The notion of the procedural, of repeating attempts in an effort to capture a moment of exploration rather than specific results of an exploration, is essential to Forsythe's work, and it maintains the concept of failure as the central principle of organization.

If, as Johnson claims, nothing fails like success, then perhaps Forsythe's movement performance work presents the productive aspects of failure, opening up the realm of possibilities to the point where we may no longer want to know what succeeds, but rather, how else failure could function. Ultimately, such acts and enactments of reading, as those of the Ballett Frankfurt, represent a process whose failures offer up previously unanticipated possibilities, and point to the enabling and productive nature of movement systems that derive their stability from constantly shifting instabilities, from accidents. This is a strategy of exploring the possibilities of how else failure, disappearance, and vertigo can function if we let go of the visible, stable, unified body.

Insofar as performance presupposes the absent body—and the impossibility of notating or recording that body—in the very moment of its presence, Forsythe foregrounds this absence as a site of trauma, and of lightness, throughout his movement performance oeuvre. His repeated displays of disappearance itself—whether via the instability of movement, the failures to create symmetrical emplacements, or the making invisible of bodies—align themselves with much critical writing about trauma. If movement can embody the dynamism of vertiginous spatial models and engender other movement via residue, as well as celebrate the reemergence of altogether absent bodies, then earthquakes might be survivable, even without sight. The experience of survival is traumatic, it seems, only if vertigo is not a constant. The task is not to attempt to see the invisible, or to notate the ephemeral, but to applaud these manifestations of impossibility as the sources for further composition and breathing. So that the absence of vision becomes the culmination of sight.

Note

1 Subsequent references to this edition appear in parentheses in the text. 'Choreutics' and 'choreography' are derived from the Greek term *choreosophia*, meaning literally, the knowledge or wisdom of circles. Choreutics may be defined as the practical study of the various forms of more or less harmonized movement.

References

Anderson, Laurie (1987) 'Words in Reverse', in Brian Wallis (ed.) *Blasted Allegories*, Cambridge, MA: MIT Press.

Blanchot, Maurice (1988) *Thomas the Obscure*, trans. Robert Lamberton. Original French edn 1950, Barrytown, NY: Station Hill Press.

Caillois, Roger (1961), *Man, Play, and Games*, translated from the French *Les jeux et les hommes* (Paris: Gallimard, 1958) by Meyer Barash. New York: Free Press of Glencoe.

Caruth, Cathy (1991a) 'Introduction', *Psychoanalysis, Culture, and Trauma (part 2). American Imago*, 48(4 Winter): 418–19.

Caruth, Cathy (1991b) 'Unclaimed Experience: Trauma and the Possibility of History', *Yale French Studies 79, Literature and the Ethical Question*, pp. 181–192.

Deleuze, Gilles and Guattari, Félix (1987), *A Thousand Plateaus: Capitalism and Schizophrenia*, trans. and foreword by Brian Massumi, Minneapolis MN: University of Minnesota Press.

Foucault, Michel (1972), *The Archaeology of Knowledge and The Discourse on Language*, trans. A.M. Sheridan Smith, New York: Pantheon.

Freud, Sigmund (1960a) *Moses and Monotheism*, in *The Standard Edition of the Complete Psychological Works of Sigmund Freud*, translated from the German under the General Editorship of James Strachey, in collaboration with Anna Freud, assisted by Alix Strachey and Alan Tyson, vol. 23. London: The Hogarth Press.

Freud, Sigmund (1960b) *The Psychopathology of Everyday Life* (1901), in *The Standard Edition of the Complete Psychological Works of Sigmund Freud*, translated from the German under the General Editorship of James Strachey, in collaboration with Anna Freud, assisted by Alix Strachey and Alan Tyson, vol 6. London: The Hogarth Press. Strachey cites Freud's first use of the term *Fehlleistung* in a letter to Wilhelm Fliess of August 26, 1898. (p. xii)

Funk & Wagnalls Co (1958) *Cassell's German/English Dictionary*, revised and re-edited by Harold T. Betteridge. New York: Funk & Wagnalls Co., 1958. All definitions from the German are from this edition unless otherwise noted.

Gilpin, Heidi (1989–1994) Conversations with William Forsythe. Unpublished.

Johnson, Barbara (1987), 'Nothing Fails Like Success', in Johnson, *A World of Difference*, Baltimore, MD/London: The Johns Hopkins University Press, 1987.

von Laban, Rudolf (1966 [1939]), *Choreutics*, Lisa Ullmann (ed.), London: Macdonald and Evans.

Merriam-Webster (1986) *Webster's Dictionary*, 9th edition, Springfield, MA: Merriam-Webster. All subsequent definitions are from this edition unless otherwise noted.

Oxford University Press (1971) *Oxford English Dictionary*, Oxford: Oxford University Press. Emphasis mine. Subsequent definitions from this edition refer to the OED.

Wenders, Wim (n.d.) as cited in *siteWORKS, UCLA Architecture Journal,* vol. 3, p. 1.

11 The space of memory

William Forsythe's ballets

Gerald Siegmund

It's just a little bit of history repeating ...

In his essay 'De l'œvre au texte' from 1971, Roland Barthes outlines the idea of a certain pleasure, *plaisir*, that is inherent to the notion of text. This pleasure is different from the delight one might take 'à lire et relire Proust, Flaubert, Balzac, et même, pourquoi pas', as Barthes puts it, 'Alexandre Dumas; mais ce plaisir ... reste partiellement ... un plaisr de consommation', he continues. '[C]ar, si je puis lire ces auteurs, je sais aussi que je ne puis les ré-écrire (qu'on ne peut aujourd'hui écrire 'comme ça'); et ce savoir assez triste suffit à me séparer de la production de ces œuvres, dans le moment même où leur éloignement fonde ma modernité (être moderne, n'est-ce pas connaître vraiment ce qu'on ne peut pas recommencer?)', Barthes concludes (Barthes 1994 : 1216). The aim of this quotation, as I choose to read it, is twofold. First, it links modernity in literature and the arts with an ideal of text production as opposed to text consumption – or the 'scriptible' and the 'lisible', as Barthes calls it in *S/Z* (Barthes 1994: 558). Text is defined as an activity that constantly rewrites and reworks itself, thus claiming its modernity in a state of pleasurable production both on the side of the artist and the reader. In fact, the very relationship between work, author, and reader becomes re-defined. They all become entangled in the same activity of text production. It is, however – and this is my second point – a modernity that cannot abolish the past in a simple act of negation, but one which is forced to posit a certain relationship to the past and former modes of writing. Its texts therefore draw on history, despite the fact that there is a certain futility and even loss inherent in its artefacts. It is a futility, moreover, which constitutes and marks my very modernity as a melancholy one.

What holds true for literature certainly holds true for classical ballet with its outdated fairy stories and ideals of courtly love. In interviews, William Forsythe, director of Ballett Frankfurt since 1984, has repeatedly stated that ballet is a futile activity and that, as an art form, it may have come to an end (Fischer 1999). The choreographer, who was trained as a classical dancer at the Joffrey Ballet School in New York City, mourns ballet as an art form for which contemporary society has no use any longer outside the realm of, as Roland Barthes would put it, unproductive readerly consumption. Ballet today has no choice but to painfully exhibit the loss of a hierarchically structured model of society, exactly the order that was constitutive for its birth. It cannot help but mourn the loss of linear perspective, the device that created its very subjects by distributing them along lines of visibility in the eighteenth century, as Michel Foucault has shown in *Surveiller et punir* (Foucault 1975). By spacing them according to value and rank from *élève* to *étoile*, it created a space in which they could be easily seen, overseen, detected, and judged. Thus ballet's use of space corresponds to the disciplinary model of power enforced in schools and prisons. Finally, after the social and scientific upheavals of the twentieth century, it cannot even rely on the model of the upright body anymore, a body secure in its axis and verticality as one that denotes reason. When Forsythe somewhat apodictically states: 'I speak the language. I don't recite the language' of ballet, he makes it perfectly clear that he is not content with a simple re-reading of the classics by spelling its vocabulary correctly. Forsythe knows that he cannot 'write like that' anymore. He still believes that 'ballet is a very good idea', because it is 'a body of knowledge' that inevitably connects him with the past. Although ballet is history, it is remembered by being re-membered, taken apart and assembled anew, by speaking the language.

While abolishing ballet, Forsythe opens up a space of memory for ballet that keeps it very much alive in the very act of disappearance. By reorganising space, sound, light, the body, and its movements, Forsythe's ballets become texts that refuse to yield an object, an artefact, in favour of a melancholy art effect. They make use of an original loss of small detail that does not give the subject of ballet what it wants, but rather destabilises it in the very act of remembrance of something that cannot be remembered. I would like to explore these ideas a little further here. I will refer to two of Forsythe's full-length ballets as examples, which are aptly titled *Artifact* and *The Loss of Small Detail*. It would like to draw your attention to three different modes of memory in these texts: an acoustic, a spatial, and a bodily memory.

Sound space: the echo chamber of *Artifact*

Artifact,[1] which had its premiere in Frankfurt in 1984, begins with a bald greyish figure – the programme identifies it as 'Other Person' – walking across the stage in next to complete darkness. Only a single spot brightens the floor on the left hand side of the empty stage. A 'Person with Historical Costume' with long cape-like sleeves billowing imperiously enters and takes centre stage. She claps, and on cue the music starts, Eva Crossman-Hecht's 'Bach Variations', which are followed by Bach's Chaconne in D minor in Act II. 'Step inside', the woman invites us. Behind her, in the twilight of the stage, the shadow of another figure appears, the 'Person with Megaphone'. 'I forget the dust. I forget the rocks', his tinny disembodied voice can be heard to say. 'I remember a story and it went like this. She stepped outside and she always saw it. She stepped inside and she has always seen it'. The head and torso of the Other Person appear in a trap door on the stage floor. The man with the megaphone bends down and addresses the figure, saying: 'I forget the story about you. Remember, remember, remember'. 'Good evening. Remember me?', the woman in historical costume chips in, in a glitzy showbiz manner. But her words are not her own. She is admonished by the man with the megaphone to use the correct words, and she obeys grudgingly, until they end up quarrelling loudly and unrestrainedly in Act III.

A little later, the Other Person appears from her trap door to engage in powerful *ports de bras*; moving her arms together in front of her body and above her head, she claps each time. An almost invisible line of dancers answers her calls with a double clap on the off-beat from the depths of the dark stage. Towards the end of Act I and at the beginning of Act II, she stands in front of the *corps de ballet* like a teacher whose students pick up her basic arm and leg movements – *avant, arrière, croisé* – in a repetitive exercise.

Sound, movement, and even the sparse use of light in *Artifact* function in a similar way. And yet, they work independently of each other. The respective sign systems are structured individually, and yet, they follow the same paradigm like the words of a poem forming a dense web of meaning. On all three levels, the ballet follows the structure of the double or the spectre. The artefact that we think we see is therefore indeed only an art effect, the illusion of a thing long since past when we think we are actually seeing it. The Other Person is mirrored in the Person With Historical Costume. They both make extensive use of *ports de bras*, while their respective positions on stage are diametrically and symmetrically opposed: one is up, the other down, one is lavishly dressed, the other almost stripped bare. She appears unmarked, the overexposed white acting as a negative foil to ballet's marked history that she teaches to the *corps de ballet*.

The list of binary oppositions continues. While the historical woman rearranges words by emptying them of their meaning within a given grammatical structure, the woman in grey rearranges the ballet vocabulary. Act II consists of two *pas de deux* framed by various corps formations. Every now and again the curtain drops with aplomb over the scene thus disrupting the viewing continuum. Every time it rises the formations have changed position: from lining the three walls of the stage to forming the apex of a triangle to a single line at the back, to two lines on either side of the stage. By refusing to choreograph smooth transitions, which would only gloss over (historical) gaps and rifts, Forsythe emphasises the structural possibilities of the line by isolating every single position in time and space. Both languages become devoid of meaning as their signifying elements are isolated and played out against one another without any context. Words swap places as in a grammar exercise. Remembering equals forgetting equals thinking, seeing, and hearing, simply because they appear in the same structural position. In this sense, they can be considered echoes of one another, paradigmatic resemblances where the one present remembers the absent ones. The result is a mind-boggling but fascinating opening-up of a potential of thought and perception. Out of a strictly limited number of basic words and a number of strictly limited movements infinite possibilities arise. By stripping ballet and language bare to its skeletal structure, Forsythe reassembles its bones and echoes.

William Forsythe describes his approach to movement in *Artifact* as follows:

> What I began to do was imagine a kind of serial movement and, maintaining certain arm positions from ballet, move through this model, orienting the body towards the imaginary external points. It's like ballet, which also orients steps towards external points (*croisé*, *efface*, ...) but equal importance is given to all points, non-linear movements can be incorporated and different body parts can move towards the points at varied rates in time.
>
> (Sulcas 1995: 59)

By emptying the centre and focusing on those points of the kinesphere that are furthest from a centre, the stabilising centre is only ever evoked, but never actively reached. While trying for these exterior points, the dancers, with extremely arched backs, their bodies pulled out from behind or engaged in little jumps that direct feet and calves away from the centre, destabilise and rearrange the axial model of the body of ballet.

The spectral structure is not only a structure of fragmented and repeated movements. It is also, and this was my emphasis here, an acoustic one. In fact, sound and movement function in parallel universes that mirror each other. By means of the technical device of parallelism, they open up individual mental spaces that intertwine. Words or, rather, the quality of their sound material, their signifiers, take over the role of music as accompaniment for the dance. The ballet's four distinct characters – Other Person, Person with Historical Costume, Person with Megaphone, and the *corps de ballet* as an entity – strongly relate to one another by echoing sounds. *Corps* and Other Person are linked by echoing claps. The clapping is equally a call for attention and a cue for synchronicity, for being together, which runs as an imperative through ballet's historical formation.[2] The historical figure is linked to the megaphone man by echoing his sentences. His voice is separated from his natural body and given a second body in the shape of a technical instrument. It isolates the dis- and re-embodied voice by giving it a metallic ring, which emphasises both its mechanical qualities and its imaginary ones. It becomes a source of fascination and fantasies precisely because it is turned into an object, a self-contained thing-in-itself available to be desired.

The voice as object approaches us from a distance. Like the telephone voice, it bridges a distance between two separate realms of time. By doing so, it creates a third space as an intermediate space where the borders of past and present become blurred. After all, how can we be sure that the voice we are hearing is actually still alive? Perhaps it is only a signal that was delayed in the process of transmission. *Artifact* is an echo chamber of ballet's past. Its echoes are effects, repetitions of fragments without a body, of voices without a self or an origin. Its origin is split, distracted, deviant in that it bounces back from some oblique other to lose itself in repetition after repetition. It thus marks its own disappearance in the very act of being present by being repeated.[3]

The presence of ballet is therefore only an effect of its absence. Its present is shot through by history, which in turn is only constituted by reverberating sound effects. It is absent because, as Forsythe states, 'when you speak about the vocabulary of classical dance, you are talking about ideas' (Sulcas 1995a: 9).[4] It is only an idea or *langue*, one that only comes alive in an act of *parole*, of dancing.[5] The individual dancer does not do an *arabesque*. He or she goes through an arabesque as through a hologram, thus evoking the figure only retrospectively. Forsythe can therefore claim that *arabesque* does not exist. It is the sum of all possible *arabesques*, whose numbers are endless. By emphasising the *performative* aspect of ballet language, he is able to conceive dance and movement differently. It is no longer an essence to be incorporated more or less perfectly (one particular ballerina being better than another one), but a spectral shape whose ontological state is absence. The language of ballet ceases to be the *logos* of a pre-scription, of a text anterior to the performance that has only to be realised on stage. Rather, it becomes an in-scription in the body of the individual dancer as he or she moves through it thus divesting him- or herself of ballet history. If ballet vocabulary is no longer thought to be an essence, it may suddenly mutate and be related to other shapes in any conceivable way.

Visible space: *The Loss of Small Detail* as palimpsest

If the echo chamber serves as a model for *Artifact*, then the palimpsest functions as a frame of reference for *The Loss of Small Detail*.[6] Originally meant to describe either an ancient parchment, whose inscriptions were scraped off in order to save writing material, or a geological formation in which traces of an even older formation are still visible, the term palimpsest is used here to describe a kind of memory that is paradoxically preoccupied with defacing memory in the very act of remembering. To remember is to invent, to produce new meaning on top of the hieroglyphs of the past.

The making of the piece itself reflects such a layering. A first version was premiered in 1987 in Frankfurt, but was quickly forgotten until, in 1991, Forsythe presented a completely new version, which in turn underwent another radical reworking in 1992. The ballet is set in a white cube that resembles a museum. Its walls can be scrolled up and down like roles of parchment, while functioning as the basis for all kinds of projections. A few minutes into the ballet snow begins to fall softly on the stage, covers it in a metaphorical layer of forgetfulness while hushing up its sounds. Lines from Yukio Mishima appear on the backdrop only to be rolled up again: 'Each passing year, never failing to exact its toll, keeps altering what was sublime into the stuff of comedy. Is something eaten away? If the exterior is eaten away, is it true, then, that the sublime pertains by nature only to an exterior that conceals a core of nonsense? Or does the sublime indeed pertain to the whole, but a ludicrous dust settles upon it?' (Ballett Frankfurt 1991).

Two films are projected in the lower right-hand corner backstage. Amongst fierce strobe light and thunderous noises, an electronically distorted voice can be heard. After the thunderstorm has died down, a naked figure stands perched upon a chair. His body is painted white and he sports black dots, as if he were indeed covered in snow or as if the 'ludicrous dust' mentioned in the Mishima quote as a cover of the sublime essence of things had indeed settled upon him. The snow/dust has turned his appearance, that in another time and context would have been that of a sublime warrior or a shaman, into something ridiculous and comic. But the body paint also turns him into the negative of the regular black film images at the back. In the programme, Forsythe describes an imaginary scene, some elements of which form part of the actual scene on stage: 'very very slowly the film fades to black. It is snowing. apparently, it has been snowing for quite some time. The light that now increases reveals several figures that are watching a film of primitive people portrayed by contemporary performers. The figures are snow covered as are the primitive Performers in the film, the film watched in printal negative. The snow is black. The primitive performers, white. They are watching a scene in a contemporary film, printed in negative. It is also snowing in this film, white. The real snow falling On STAGE is back-lit by the film, and appears to be black' (Ballett Frankfurt 1991).

This complex shifting of frames finds its equivalent on stage in the performer portraying a primitive in printal negative as if he had indeed stepped right out of a film. On top of the visible space an intermediate area is established where we can no longer distinguish between inside and outside, between what is film and what is theatre, who is watching and who is being watched. It is a disconcerting intermediary space where spectres of the past, such as the primitive, are allowed to come forth, albeit only in their comic guise. In history, as Marx said, everything is bound to happen twice. Once as a tragedy and the second time as a farcical repetition. Once he is allowed to come forth, the performer portraying a primitive cannot help but turn the other performers on stage into ghosts as well. It is the disconcerting aspect of history that it disrupts the present to suspend its reality. Faced with his radiating presence, the others too become shapes in the negative version of a film, which they incidentally are seen watching while they sit on the stage floor listening to the ghosts' disembodied utterances. Their identity as performers or characters becomes overridden by layer after layer with historical sedimentation.

This device also becomes evident in another crucial scene of the ballet. A female dancer is sitting behind a table centre front, while another dancer is lying on the floor to her right. She engages the dancer in a question and answer ritual. From her notes and translations she reads out questions like 'What is the door?', or 'What are the two sides of the river?', trying to wrench some meaning out of old prehistoric tales that Forsythe has taken from a collection of stories by Jerome Rothenberg. The second woman interprets her questions in explicitly sexual terms with the doorstep becoming a crocodile, its handle a penis, the two sides of the river a man and a women. But the sign on the table reads 'Version III A', implying an infinite number of other possibilities that could be brought to light if the session were continued, other questions or indeed somebody else asked. Everything can indeed mean everything because of an original loss or the loss of an origin, the loss of small detail to which the title refers, that guarantees a stable origin and thus a safe ground on which to base one's interpretation.

The Loss of Small Detail stages the loss of an *Ursprung*, which leads to a production of meaning even out of possible misunderstandings. To forget is viewed here as a productive activity. It is considered necessary for making new developments possible. Forsythe explains:

> But our attempt to read that page is initially frustrated because we have not yet agreed upon a common basis from which to comprehend these glyphs as a system of language. Let us assume that this text could nonetheless be deciphered in some way – perhaps by repositioning ourselves? Then again, we could consider repositioning the text. Perhaps the spatial redeployment of these glyphs would enable us to approximate their meaning.
>
> (Ballett Frankfurt 1991)

Such a spatial redeployment of the text of ballet is acted out by the dancers' movements. At the beginning, a female dancer slowly draws herself up from the floor, her arms extended, her body curling inwards. She seems to float upwards, her body almost boneless and liquid. A male dancer dressed in black approaches to bring her a stool. She sits down, facing the woman behind the table who will question her later. Suddenly she walks to the table and folds her body around it, legs stretched out underneath, arms resting on top. The man in black carries her away, holding her stiff body horizontally in his arms like a plank. The phrase is repeated several times and indeed marks the ballet's first instance of forgetting: the forgetting of something that has been done before, even unsuccessfully so, and yet is repeated over and over again without having left a trace in the dancer's memory. It is a movement that is bound to disappear every time it is re-enacted. The specific quality of movement of the ballet is an incredible softness and transparency. The dancers seem to have given up all strength. They slide to the floor repeatedly, only to rise again in bizarre curling movements. This is brought about by a technique Forsythe calls 'disfocus' (Siegmund 1999: 16). The focus of the dancers vision is not directed to some point in front of them, which serves as the body's axis. It is directed towards the back of their own head, which enhances the dancers' proprioperception. Their ability to perceive their surroundings diminishes in favour of a heightened awareness of their own limbs and internal muscular alignment. These 'internally refracted co-ordinations' prevent the dancers from dancing the way their 'body has been trained as a ballet dancer. It's not that you destroy the foundations', Forsythe explains, 'you just end up in an opposing state of support. The small detail that is lost is your physical orientation. Your body gives up one kind of strength, but another comes into play' (Sulcas 1995a).

The shift of the focus from the outside to the inside redeploys the body of ballet. It does not destroy it, however. The historical body continues to shine through as one layer underneath the body's current reorientation. The body of ballet perceives itself for the first time, it gains self-awareness and perhaps even a self-consciousness that undoes it at the same time that it comes into its own. The result of this turning in on oneself, of folding the body over, is an overriding of its historical text, which cannot be written anymore, an effacement which makes the body illegible. You cannot read these bodies anymore because they refuse to become signs in an economy of exchange. They refer to ballet's vocabulary as a trace in their bodily memories, but they do not stand in for it. The dancers have absorbed the historical language of ballet into their bodies only to make it implode by undoing its coded relations. The moving body here does not so much create kinaesthetic space but rather internalises space, thereby imploding both visible space and body in the process. Those bodies represent nothing else apart from the truism that on stage every body represents at least a body.

Mnemonic space

When Forsythe suggests a 'repositioning of ourselves' towards the illegible palimpsest, so that we may find a way to decipher it, Roland Barthes' notion of pleasure comes into play again. It should have become clear that this pleasure cannot be a pleasure of consumption, the pleasure I get when re-reading an old story. It is the pleasure of writing myself into this text, which consists of soundscapes and theatrical landscapes weaving past and present into a mnemonic space. It is precisely because the body becomes illegible that it enters into play, which is not only a play between signifiers but above all a play with the limits of the subject. The stage no longer functions as a mirror providing an imaginary image of the whole (social) body, as in classical ballet. The scene is not one of representation but that of its imaginary other. Looking at Forsythe's bodies on stage, the stage refuses to give to you what you want. A narcissistic identification with these bodies must necessarily fail. What they offer instead is a desire towards the Real of the body, towards the impossible cathexis for which Lacan's *petit objet a* stands in. Yet the small object of desire, whose detail is always already lost, never actually takes shape here. It remains a trace of something originally lost in the body, of something that was never there in the first place, i.e. movement. One can therefore call it a melancholic movement, melancholy according to Freud being that state of the subject in which it does not know the object mourned, in which the object refuses to divulge itself because it never was an object to begin with (Freud: 193–212). The melancholic subject loves a void: the spectral memory of a spectral memory. In that sense, movement with Forsythe remains a memory, insubstantial and ghost-like, as it disappears with every movement, thereby resisting reification as an object even as it is desired as an object. It is a phantom, a phantasm that plays with the phantasms of our own body.

Movement works towards its own vanishing point in the gap between inside and outside of what Laurence Louppe calls the *fonds corporel*: a pre-articulate phenomenological body that is the residue of meaning but never meaningful in itself (Louppe 1997: 72). If in dance movement is at the same time that which is produced and that which produces, if the dancing body is simultaneously an agent without a consciousness of itself and its own interpreter, who must keep movement at a distance by the very act of analysing, then movement is never given or transparent to itself. It is, as Jacques Derrida has pointed out in relation to the gesture of a painter, in its presence already 'un acte de mémoire' (Derrida 1990). Movement is generated in the liminal space between I and Not-I, a mnemonic space which hands over every movement to the past in its very state of emergence. Movement is always in a state of emergency, a matter of life and death which also implies the life and death of ballet I referred to at the beginning of my paper. It is this gap, however, that opens up a space that enables movement to think: it is the pre-articulate time-space of effort where choices are made. In the case of Forsythe, this liminal space, which is neither inside nor outside, which, as Donald Woods Winnicott has outlined, neither belongs to the subject nor to the object (Winnicott 1971: 11–12), comes into being when the dancing subject gives up control. The disfocus allows the body to enter another state of semi-consciousness where it literally 'stumbles into'[7] new movements at the same time as it leaves the old ones behind. Movement, like the ghost of the primitive in the intermediate space between past and present, film and theatre, thus becomes a mnemonic trace of a potentiality, of a future.

To conclude, I would like to quote Forsythe again, who sums up these thoughts admirably:

> The more you let go of your control, and give it over to a kind of transparency of the body, a feeling of disappearance, the more you will be able to grasp differentiated form, and differentiated dynamics. You can move very fast in this state, and it will not give the same impression – it won't give the impression of violence. You can also move with

tremendous acceleration provided you know where you leave the movement – not where you put the movement, but where you leave it. You try to divest your body of movement, as opposed to thinking you are producing movement. So it would not be like pushing forward into space and invading space – it would be like leaving your body in space. Dissolution, letting yourself evaporate. Movement is a factor of the fact that you are actually evaporating.

(Forsythe 1995)

Notes

1 I have repeatedly seen live performances of the ballet in Frankfurt's opera house. Additionally, to check my memory, a video recording of the performance of 26 February 1997 has been used.
2 William Forsythe has based an entire ballet, *Gänge*, on the 'togetherness' of line formations as the main structural element of classical ballet.
3 See also Gilpin 1996: 110.
4 See also Siegmund 2000.
5 For the linguistic aspect of *Artifact* see Gabriele Brandstetter 1997: 207.
6 I have repeatedly seen performances of the ballet in Frankfurt's opera house. As with *Artifact*, I have taken recourse to a video recording of 27 April 1996 for my analysis.
7 See also Brandstetter 2000: 102–34. Brandstetter's strong emphasis on the tumbling of the dancers in order to produce unforeseen movement seems to me, however, to be too limited an understanding of the dancers' movements.

References

Ballett Frankfurt (1991), Programme Notes, *The Loss of Small Detail*, Frankfurt: Intendanz Ballett Frankfurt.

Barthes, Roland (1994), 'De l'œuvre au texte', in *Œuvres completes,* vol.II, Eric Marty (ed.), Paris : Seuil.

Brandstetter, Gabriele (1997), 'Choreographie und Memoria. Konzepte des Gedächtnisses von Bewegung in der Renaissance und im 20. Jahrhundert', in Claudia Öhlschläger and Birgit Wiens (eds), *Körper-Gedächtnis-Schrift. Der Körper als Medium kultureller Erinnerung*, Berlin: Erich Schmidt Verlag.

Brandstetter, Gabriele (2000), 'Choreographie als Grab-Mal: Das Gedächtnis der Bewegung', in Gabriele Brandstetter and Hortensia Völckers (eds), *Re-Membering the Body*, Ostfildern: Cantz.

Derrida, Jacques (1990), *L'autoportrait: mémoires d'aveugle et autres ruines*, Paris: Gallimard.

Driver, Senta and the editors of Ballet Review (1990), 'A Conversation with William Forsythe', *Ballet Review*, 18(1, Spring): 96.

Forsythe, William (1995), Programme *Eidos : Telos*, Frankfurt: Intendanz Ballett Frankfurt.

Foucault, Michel (1975), Chapter III, 'Discipline', in *Surveiller et punir. Naissance de la prison*, Paris: Gallimard.

Freud, Sigmund (1982), 'Trauer und Melancholie', in *Psychologie des Unbewußten*. Studienausgabe vol. III, Frankfurt: Fischer.

Gilpin, Heidi (1996), 'Lifelessness in movement, or how do the dead move?', in Susan Leigh Foster (ed.), *Corporealities*, London: Routledge.

Louppe, Laurence (1997), *Poetique de la danse contemporaine*, Paris: Contredanse.

Siegmund, Gerald (1999), 'Interview with William Forsythe', *Dance Europe*, 23: 12–17.

Siegmund, Gerald (2000) 'Wir arbeiten, um uns arbeiten zu sehen: Ein Gespräch mit William Forsythe', *Frankfurter Allgemeine Zeitung*, Sunday, 23 January.

Sulcas, Roslyn (1995a), 'Kinetic Isometries', *Dance International*, Summer: 9.

Sulcas, Roslyn (1995b), 'William Forsythe: Channels for the Desire to Dance', *Dance Magazine*, 69: 52–9.

Winnicott, D. W. (1971), *Playing and Reality*, London/New York: Routledge.

12 Choreographic thinking and amateur bodies

Steven Spier

Putting together steps, illustrating a piece of music, making dance or even just movement: what is choreography actually? The question is seldom so bluntly posed and the answer not as obvious as it first seems. It is, however, a question central to understanding Forsythe's long career performing and choreographing. While he has always displayed an insatiable curiosity – such diverse fields as ballet, music, literature, mythology, philosophy, popular culture, geometry, higher mathematics and cognitive science, amongst others have all been influences – his central preoccupation is indeed the question of what choreography is and can be.

For Forsythe, 'choreography is about organising bodies in space, or you're organising bodies with other bodies, or a body with other bodies in an environment that is organised'.[1] The idea that the body itself must be organised in space would befuddle most people and the centrality he gives this idea challenges those in the dance world too. It also helps to explain his long and controversial interrogation of ballet. Forsythe was trained and practised as a classical ballet dancer, and finds the balletic to be a system that lends itself to multiple analyses. A ballet dancer is trained to imagine lines, arcs, planes, and vectors in order always to know precisely where the parts of his or her body are in three-dimensional space. Classical ballet connects the body's parts in established ways, which has allowed it to develop a high degree of formal and technical complexity. Forsythe's work with the Ballett Frankfurt can be seen as an investigation of ballet's most fundamental principles for organising the body. (It also helps to explain architects' affinity for his work, for his definition of choreography could as well be a definition of architecture.)

Forsythe's preoccupation with exploring the organisation of the body in space is paradigmatic in five of his pieces between 1997 and 2003 that confront the public with the choreographic, and often political, question of how the body moves and how bodies in space are organised. As Forsythe puts it: 'I was trying to figure out how I could create a choreographic environment, which [in these non-theatre pieces] means having the experience of interacting with an idea that changes the way you think about your body organising moving' (Siegmund 2001: 74). Forsythe views works such as

White Bouncy Castle, City of Abstracts, Scattered Crowd, and *Instructions* as choreographic objects, or scores (Forsythe 2011). Here, rather than working with trained dancers to create a choreographic system whose organisational principles are held in the bodies and minds of the performer, Forsythe works to create a choreographic event that can 'generate autonomous expressions of its principles, a choreographic object, without the body' (Forsythe 2011: 90). As Caspersen puts it:

> These are situations where, unlike in traditional performance, the choreographic principles are visible and persist over time. The public enters into the choreographic environment, and their bodies, trained or untrained, and the decisions that each person makes, become a perfect expression of the environment. However, the choreographic principles exist and are visible independent of those bodies and decisions.[2]

The very idea of organisational systems for the body in space and in movement would be a surprise to people who are not trained dancers or dance aficionados. The choreographic environments under discussion here are not laboratory-like experiments, however, and do also remind people of the sheer pleasure in moving, for, 'choreography should serve as a channel for the desire to dance' (Sulcas 1995).

White Bouncy Castle (originally *Tight Roaring Circle*)

Though already then an internationally renowned choreographer, Forsythe and the Ballett Frankfurt had not yet performed in Great Britain when Artangel, which commissions and produces site-specific, temporary works by contemporary artists, approached him in 1993 for what would eventually become *White Bouncy Castle*. In fact, his work had barely been performed in Great Britain. (The Ballett Frankfurt's first appearance in London would be as late as 1999.) He had, though, achieved some local notoriety for a piece commissioned by the Royal Ballet in London, *Firstext*, which was choreographed by him, Dana Caspersen and Antony Rizzi. Artangel's commissions were themselves well known and so the anticipation and expectations for *Tight Roaring Circle* were high when, on 26 March 1997, four years after the first approaches, the world's largest bouncy castle opened in London as a collaboration among Dana Caspersen, William Forsythe, and Joel Ryan. The critics were bemused; the audience physically thrilled.

The castle occupied the entire central space of The Roundhouse, a vast brick building built in 1846 to stable and service locomotives, which has subsequently achieved folklore status as a performance venue. It was the perfect foil physically: a soft, white, vinyl, bouncy castle with floppy castellations. There was a constant stream of music by Joel Ryan, variously rhythmic, atmospheric, and melodic, that referred to The Roundhouse and its imaginative space. At the base of the short ramp by which one entered the castle was a carpeted area with benches where people would sit to remove their shoes. One then waddled up the inflated ramp and entered the castle. People ran, hopped, or skipped across the huge space, some bounced in place, others loped, some deliberately crashed into the walls. Others gave less vent to the natural desire to be more acrobatic than in their everyday lives, and sat along the walls – resting, gazing, listening to the music. A few lay in the middle to admire the building's Victorian roof. (At the opening a few even refused to remove their shoes and enter it.) With *White Bouncy Castle* people were able to share the passion and recapture the instinctive joy and the fearlessness with one's body that children possess. This authentic impulse is so primal that one could not predict on any basis – generational, sartorial, class, race, or gender – how people would behave, though most behaved as children. The installation has since been restaged numerous times in various venues.

Creating a channel for the desire to dance is a previously cited preoccupation of Forsythe's as a professional choreographer and artistic director. *White Bouncy Castle,* however, introduces a lay audience, through the simplest or even silliest of means, to fundamental and conceptual issues about the body in space, and about engendering and composing movement. For example, from the moment one stepped on to that inflated ramp, the most taken-for-granted movements became exaggerated or distorted and thus noticeable to oneself. After exiting it the body felt very heavy indeed, for one is made physically and mentally aware of how the body moves.

Figure 12.1 From *White Bouncy Castle* (Permission of Frédéric Kiehn)

In *White Bouncy Castle* movement was individually based within a self-organising choreographic system. Even with the diminution of one's normal bearings and control, for example, enough order was maintained to allow everyone to interact within the destabilising mechanics of that environment and, critically, to avoid collisions. This ability of people to move together in complex patterns is based, in part, on proprioception and entrainment, phenonemena that have been of particular interest to Forsythe in his work with the Ballett Frankfurt. 'When dancers are dancing, they are encountering an inner vision that can be described as the experience of proprioception – the awareness of what one feels and sees one's body doing. And once you encounter this, you are opening yourself up to a whole lot of new information and new impulses that change one's dancing and approach to dance' (Sulcas 1995). If proprioception is about experiencing oneself, entrainment, the process that occurs when two or more people become engaged in each other's rhythms, when they synchronise, is about experiencing someone else. It is the phenomenon, for example, that makes talking to someone in person, where one has access to a menu of nods and gestures, different than on the telephone.

In a light-hearted way, then, *White Bouncy Castle* suggests to a lay audience, including both adults and children, knowledge that dancers have in their bodies and the means by which choreographers work. At the time of the piece Forsythe was particularly interested in processes that would produce movement that was in accordance with the principles of a work, but not determined by him in detail. In performance situations, Forsythe has frequently worked with improvisational systems where the dancers generate movement within variously prescribed parameters. Speaking of such work, Forsythe says that ultimately, 'We organise a potential for interaction, as choreographers, which is also what we're doing here'.[3]

City of Abstracts

Unlike trained dancers, lay people are generally unaware of how they move and how they look moving except perhaps when they catch themselves in a mirror, are injured or while playing sports. This is despite the proliferation of portable, even hand-held, video recording and playback devices having become increasingly portable. In order to have people see how they, as individuals, move, in *City of Abstracts* Forsythe simply records the audience moving unawares and plays it back to them with a slight time delay. But with this piece he is particularly interested in how people move in and occupy urban, public space, and so he captures us moving in the city and plays it back at an urban scale, on large outdoor screens or on to building facades.

In order to have the experience be more than a simple double-take, Forsythe distorts the images before he plays them back. Once one realises that one is up there, one can choose to participate actively or passively. In either case, the piece is in effect choreographed by those on screen. As with

Figure 12.2 From *City of Abstracts* (Permission of Julian Gabriel Richter)

White Bouncy Castle, reactions are individually determined. One can simply keep moving through the space, stop and stare, or try out movements and observe how one moves. By exaggerating the movement through distortion he lends the participants some of the proprioceptive abilities – or if one is not alone, entrainment – that professional dancers have. It is in fact a continuation of his work with improvisational techniques, by means of which he sets up a framework within which dancers improvise.

City of Abstracts has been installed in numerous cities and has taken a few different forms. In the original performance with Atelier Markgraph, an interdisciplinary design firm, it captured images of people in three different locations in Frankfurt, which were distorted and played back on screens at those locations, making a performance out of everyday situations. (It also included images of dancers in the studio that were blended with images of the public, thus rather didactically contrasting trained and untrained bodies. Subsequent performances have eliminated the dancers in the studio.) *City of Abstracts* is, like *White Bouncy Castle,* a way of setting bodies in motion in a choreographic environment. As Forsythe says, 'I feel the project of a democratic dance is perhaps almost impossible to achieve within a theatre. It seems that only by ambushing amateurs can you arrive at a truly democratic way of organising dance' (Siegmund 2001: 73).

Scattered Crowd (2002)

In its first incarnation at the huge Frankfurt Convention Centre *Scattered Crowd* was an invitation to people to explore the making of space as well as a lyrical critique of the inhuman scale and generic quality of some contemporary spaces. On entering Hall Seven, people were given two balloons strung together as a dumbbell. A white balloon was filled with helium and a clear one with air, so that the white one was at the top. You could leave your balloon wherever you chose in the space, and over the course of a day the space was collectively shaped by such individual choices. Because the height of the dumbbell was tailored to be each individual's height, the piece offered a lyrical suggestion, with human beings leaving transitory traces of themselves and giving definition and a human scale to an otherwise inhuman space.

The second and more frequently exhibited incarnation of *Scattered Crowd* again involves balloons, but this time the public does not design the space but must respond to it. A public interior space, for instance a museum, is filled with thousands of balloons by Forsythe's collaborators. To avoid knocking into them people bend, lean, and crawl in order to move through a probably familiar space in order to reach their destination. Other people run in to clusters of balloons, thus changing the configuration of the space. As in the previous two pieces, people move with purpose, with dignity, with abandon, with self-awareness, and with all states in between.

Figure 12.3 From *Scattered Crowd* (Permission of Julian Gabriel Richter)

Instructions

Commissioned to do a piece for *Nuit blanche*, the now-annual event when most public and cultural institutions in Paris stay open all night, and in collaboration with association edna/Boris Chamatz, and Siemens Arts Program, Forsythe devised 15 choreographic instructions that the public would encounter within the quotidian course of their day. They were distributed on electronic notice boards; on the screens at bus stops that announce when the next bus will arrive; in the magazine *Magazin Mouvement 2* as a pop-up; on the website mouvement.fr; and, on the radio. Following the instructions could thus take place in public or private, alone or with others.

As if to make even clearer that choreography is not primarily a visual but a physical experience instructional cards were also printed in Braille and distributed in public spaces, schools, libraries, and blind people's organisations. One such instruction is:

'I want to ask you to stop. Stop right where you are. Simply freeze, in place, for a moment, for just a moment and hold that position, for just a moment longer, thanks ...'

Figure 12.4 From *Instructions* (Permission of William Forsythe)

Bockenheimer Depot, with Nikolaus Hirsch

After ten years as the director of the Ballett Frankfurt, Forsythe had established it as one of the world's most important and innovative dance companies. He was also though, perhaps understandably, chafing at the demands of running a large, municipal ballet company, and the artistic constrictions of the opera house with its huge, traditional proscenium stage and seating capacity of 1200. Artistically he was moving away from exploring the spatial organisational system that is ballet and increasingly questioning the theatrical situation and relationships in which dance normally takes place (Siegmund 2004). *Endless House*, for example, captures the shift in his interests and the uses he would make of the TAT (Theater am Turm) at Bockenheimer Depot. The first half, directed by Caspersen, takes place in the Opera House and is both an ode and an elegy to the proscenium stage, revelling in the type of experience it can offer and literally exposing its infrastructure. For the second half the audience relocates to the Bockenheimer Depot, where it mills about at the edge of or within the performance, which has a multitude of concurrent performances of different scales. It is now often performed alone.

The TAT had been an important alternative, often politically engaged, theatre since 1953 with various incarnations and locations before it moved to the Bockenheimer Depot, a brick, former tram depot with three 75-metres-long bays, in the university quarter in 1995. (Frankfurt's significant budgetary problems, plus a historically difficult relationship with the TAT, led the city to close it in 2004.) Forsythe, its newest director in 1997, hired Louise Neri as artistic director for its final season. She put together a programme of theatre, dance, film, music, and lectures, many of which happened elsewhere in the city. This coincided with the city's deliberations, met with international outcry, to close the Ballett Frankfurt, ostensibly due to the aforementioned budgetary problems. During this fraught time Forsythe, with architect Nikolaus Hirsch, redesigned the interior of the Bockenheimer Depot. This four-month installation confronted the public with his ideas about choreographic thinking and made explicit previously subtle critiques of the privatisation of public space.

Forsythe describes taking what was strictly a performance space and turning it into a community space, a kind of park with a roof,[4] thus challenging central assumptions about the design and use of public or, better, non-private spaces. For one, the foyer could be entered for free, without having to buy a ticket for a performance, and was open much beyond the hours of a theatre interior; namely, from Wednesday through Sunday, from 14:00–24:00. Furthermore says Forsythe, 'I thought, how about a space where no one was trying to sell you anything or tell you how long you can stay or how to behave, where you don't have to spend any money.'[5] And so you could bring your own food, there were toys for children to play with, a library, a video library, and periodicals. There was even a restaurant, but

Figure 12.5 The Bockenheimer Depot interior, unoccupied (Permission of Nikolaus Hirsch and Michel Müller)

it was only take-away. 'We didn't have a permit for a restaurant so Heiner Blum came up with the idea of waiters with mobile phones and the menu was a collection of all the things available from all the neighbourhood take-away places. You just called up and it was there in 10 minutes. There was a regular big bar but I struck all logos; on all the glasses, for example. I had every logo removed.'[6] To be able to have several things happening at the same time Forsythe and Hirsch hung a grey felt curtain between the performance space and the foyer, and lay the same material on the floor to deaden the space acoustically. This also gave the huge industrial space of brick, iron columns, industrial windows, and timber roof a unity and a degree of warmth.

Forsythe likewise wanted to encourage the kind of physical behaviour not normally associated with a visit to the theatre or any public space. He and Hirsch designed lightweight, and therefore mobile, modular, three-dimensional frames on which to sit, lie down, and to use as tables. They were not actually furniture, though, since they had varying and non-standard heights and widths, thus gently challenging how the body's musculature and skeleton let the body occupy space: 'All of our benches and tables are ... wide enough to do other things than just sit on. They don't define just one specific position or function ... [People] are using more than just their backbones to support themselves. They are spreading their bodies out, their weight is differently distributed, different muscles are required' (Hirsch and Forsythe

2003). Likewise they were not designed for a specific use, size, or age of person. This is the opposite of ergonomics, which works with a standardised function and body. On these objects also lay big sheets of grey felt that could be moved, draped, twisted, folded, and curved in order to customise the way one wanted to be in the space. There were also big silver gym balls on which to drape oneself. As one might expect from a choreographer, 'the first decision concerned the floor … [that] people should get back to the floor [and] the space is very floor oriented' (Hirsch and Forsythe 2003). As Forsythe has said in a different context, 'Dancing is a conversation with gravity'.[7]

The individual freedom allowed by the foyer posed its own challenges for the designers. The architect says it was impossible to install the pieces the first time in a way that seemed right, which in retrospect is obvious since the piece is designed to allow and not determine action.[8] The programme of individuality and indeterminacy, 'of planning the unpredictable' (Hirsch and Forsythe 2003), challenges the way an architect designs and is a continuation of Forsythe's research in improvisational techniques. The foyer was a kind of laboratory for human movement and behaviour. Without the obligation to buy anything or the compunction to behave in ways that furniture compels us, the warmth and hush of the space helped induce an awareness of one's own body and how it occupies public space.

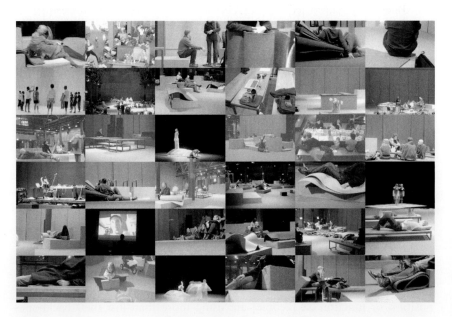

Figure 12.6 The Bockenheimer Depot interior, in use (Permission of Nikolaus Hirsch and Michel Müller)

Conclusion

The five pieces described in this chapter are paradigmatic of Forsythe's career-long interest in the question of what choreography is or can be. The means to investigate this question vary, be it a form of dance or of installation. Forsythe continues to look for choreographic incarnations that, 'do not insist on a single path to form-of thought and persist in the hope of being without enduring' (Forsythe 2011: 92). The work described in this chapter is sometimes playful, other times more lyrical, in the last example critical of the use of public space and resources, but ultimately they are all a way of setting bodies in motion. They are also a harbinger of the wide range of media and the crossing of art forms that has increasingly characterised Forsythe's work. Many of the pieces of The Forsythe Company, for example, can only be classified with the use of hyphens or double titles, such as the *Performance-, Raum- und Videoinstallationen* at the Festspielhaus Hellerau, or the performance installation *Nowhere and Everywhere at the Same Time*. In the end, they demonstrate in a condensed form Forsythe's fundamental questioning of what he does as a choreographer as well as the media – dancers, theatre, dance with which he works.

Notes

1 'A Conversation between Dana Caspersen, William Forsythe and the architect Daniel Libeskind' at the Royal Geographical Society, London, 7 March 1997. Peter Cook substituted for Libeskind who was ill; M. Figgis (Director), *Just Dancing Around*?: Bill Forsythe, Channel Four Version, Euphoria Films, 50'59", 1996. Broadcast 27 December 1996, Channel Four, 19.30.
2 Email to the author, 2 April 2010.
3 Interview with the author, London, 25 March 1997.
4 Interview with the author, 21 November 2007.
5 Interview with the author, 21 November 2007.
6 Interview with the author, 21 November 2007.
7 Caspersen, Forsythe, and Libeskind.
8 Interview with the author, Frankfurt, 23 April 2005.

References

BBC Radio 3 (1999), 'William Forsythe: Seeing your finger as a line', interview by Christopher Cook with Deborah Bull, William Forsythe, Daniel Libeskind, Ann Nugent, and Roslyn Sulcas, broadcast 14 March.

Forsythe, William (2007), interview with the author, Frankfurt, 27 November.

Forsythe, William, 'Choreographic Objects', in Chapter 7, this volume.

Hirsch, Nikolaus (2005), interview with the author, Frankfurt, 23 April, am Main.

Hirsch, Nikolaus and Forsythe, William (2003), 'Bockenheimer Depot/030306', in *Janus*, 14(03) pp. 64–8. (The interview is reprinted in Nikolaus Hirsch (2007), *On Boundaries*, New York: Lukas & Sternberg.)

Odenthal, Johannes (1992), 'Danced Space: Conflicts of Modern Dance Theatre' in *Daidalos*, 15 June, pp. 38–47.

Siegmund, Gerald (2001), 'Choreographic Thinking', in *Ballett Tanz International Yearbook*.

Siegmund, Gerald (2004), 'William Forsythe: Räume eröffnen, in denen das Denken sich ereignen kann', in Gerald Siegmund (ed.), *William Forsythe – Denken in Bewegung*, Berlin: Henschel Verlag.

Sulcas, Roslyn (1995), 'Kinetic Isometries: William Forsythe on his "continuous rethinking of the ways in which movement can be engendered and composed"', in *Dance International*, Summer, p. 8.

Alphabetical list of works

Choreographies

Alien/a(c)tion (1992)
Angoloscuro (2009)
Angoloscuro / Camerascura (2007)
Approximate Sonata (1996)
Aria de la Folía Española (1978)
Artifact (1984)
As a Garden in This Setting (1992, 1993)
Baby Sam (1986)
Bach Violin Concerto In A Minor (1977)
Behind the China Dogs (1988)
Berg Ab (1984)
Big White Baby Dog (1986)
Clouds after Cranach (2005)
Daphne (1977)
Decreation (2003)
Die Befragung des Robert Scott (1986, 2000)
Die Nacht aus Blei (1981)
Double / Single (2002)
Dream of Galilei / Traum des Galilei (1978)
Duo (1996)
Eidos : Telos (1995)
Endless House (1999)
Enemy in the Figure (1989)
Event 1, 2, 3 (1981)
Famous Mother's Club (1980)
Firstext (1995)
Fivefold (2007)
Flore Subsimplici (1977)
Four Point Counter (1995)
France / Dance (1983)
From the Most Distant Time (1978)
Gänge (1983)

Gänge, ein Stück über Ballett (1982)
Herman Schmerman (1992)
Herman Schmerman (pas de deux) (1992)
Heterotopia (2006)
How To Recognize Greek Art I and II (1985)
Hypothetical Stream II (1997)
I don't believe in outer space (2008)
Impressing The Czar (1988)
In The Middle, Somewhat Elevated (1987)
Invisible Film (1995)
Isabelle's Dance (1986)
Joyleen Gets Up, Gets Down, Goes Out (1980)
Kammer / Kammer (2000)
LDC (1985)
Limb's Theorem (1990)
Love Songs (1979)
Marion / Marion (1991)
Mental Model (1983)
New Sleep (1987)
N.N.N.N. (2002)
Nowhere and Everywhere at the Same Time (2007)
Of Any If And (1995)
One Flat Thing, reproduced (2000)
Opus 31(1998)
Orpheus (1979)
Pas./parts (1999)
Pivot House (1994)
Pizza Girl (Ninety One-Minute Ballets) (1986)
Quartette (1998)
Quartetto (1998)
Quintett (1993)
Ricercar (2003)
Rong (2006)
Same Old Story (1987)
Say Bye Bye (1980)
Self Meant To Govern (1994)
7 to 10 Passages (2000)
Skinny (1986)
Sleepers Guts (1996)
Slingerland (Part I) (1989)
Slingerland (Parts I–III) (1990)
Slingerland (Parts I–IV) (1990)
Small Void (1998)
Snap. Woven Effort (1991)
Square Deal (1983)

Steptext (1985)
Tancred und Clorinda (1981)
Theatrical Arsenal II (2009)
The Defenders (2007)
The Loss of Small Detail (1987, 1991)
The Returns (2009)
The Room As it Was (2002)
The Second Detail (1991)
The The (1995)
The Vertiginous Thrill of Exactitude (1996)
The Vile Parody of Address (1988)
Three Atmospheric Studies (2006)
33/3 (2002)
Time Cycle (1979)
'Tis A Pity She's A Whore (1980)
Trio (1996)
Two Part Invention (2009)
Urlicht (1976)
Wear (2004)
we live here (2004)
Whisper Moon (1981)
Whole in the Head (2010)
Woolf Phrase (2001)
workwithinwork (1998)
Woundwork 1 (1999)
woundwork II (2005)
Yes We Can't (2008, 2010)

Installations

Additive Inverse (2007)
Antipodes I / II (2007)
Behaupten ist anders als Glauben (2009)
Bookmaking (2008)
Book N(7): Dance/Mechanics/3pm/Streets/Red Flame/Erato (1989)
City of Abstracts (2000)
Collide-oscope (2009)
Flandona Gagnole (2007)
From a Classical Position (1997)
Gamelan/Schleife (2008)
Hausführung (2003)
Hinderhold (2007)
*Hommage to Steina and Woody Vasulka*n (2010)
Human Writes (2005)
I don't believe in outer space (2008)

Instructions (2003)
KNOTUNKNOT (2011)
Monster Partitur (2006)
Nowhere and Everywhere at the Same Time (2005)
Scattered Crowd (2002)
Solo (1997)
Suspense (2008)
Theatrical Arsenal (2007)
The Defenders Part 2 (2008)
The Defenders Part 3 (2009)
The Fact of Matter (2009)
Thematic Variations on One Flat Thing, reproduced (2007)
White Bouncy Castle (originally *Tight Roaring Circle*) (1997)
You made me a monster (2005)

Exhibitions

Equivalence (2007)
Proliferation and Perfect Disorder (2006)
Suspense (2008)
Transfigurations (2009)

Chronological list of works

All premieres from 1994–2004 are by the Ballett Frankfurt at the Opera House in Frankfurt unless otherwise noted. From 2005 all premieres are by The Forsythe Company unless otherwise noted.

Choreographies

1976

Urlicht (pas de deux)
Music: Gustav Mahler, Symphony No. 2, 4th Movement
Premiere: 18 November 1976, Noverre Society, Stuttgart

1977

Daphne (one-act ballet)
Music: Antonin Dvořák, Symphony No. 7 in D minor, 2nd and 3rd movements
Stage design and costumes: William Forsythe
Premiere: 26 March 1977, Stuttgart Ballet, Stuttgart

Bach Violin Concerto in A Minor (pas de deux)
Music: Johann Sebastian Bach, Violin Concerto in A minor
Premiere: Basel Ballet, Basel

Flore Subsimplici (one-act ballet)
Music: George Frideric Handel, Concerti Grossi, op.6
Stage design and costumes: William Forsythe
Premiere: 8 November 1977, Stuttgart Ballet, Stuttgart

1978

From the Most Distant Time

Music: György Ligeti, Double Concerto for Flute and Oboe
Stage design and lighting: William Forsythe
Costumes: Arthur Brady
Speaker: Gisela Pfeil
Texts: Tang dynasty poems
Premiere: 23 February 1978, Stuttgart Ballet, Stuttgart

Dream of Galilei/Traum des Galilei (one-act ballet)

Music: Krzysztof Penderecki, Symphony No. 1
Stage design and costumes: William Forsythe
Premiere: 21 May 1978, Stuttgart Ballet, Stuttgart

Aria de la Folía Española (pas de deux)

Music: Hans Werner Henze, *Aria de la Folia Espagñola*
Premiere: July 1978, Montepulciano, Italy

1979

Orpheus (two-act ballet)

Music: Hans Werner Henze
Stage design: Axel Manthey
Costumes: Joachim Herzog
Premiere: 17 March 1979, Stuttgart Ballet, Stuttgart

Love Songs (one-act ballet)

Music: Pop songs sung by Aretha Franklin and Dionne Warwick
Stage design and lighting: William Forsythe
Costumes: Eileen Brady
Premiere: 5 May 1979, Stuttgart Ballet, Munich

Time Cycle (one-act ballet)

Music: Lukas Foss, *Time Cycle* (song cycle for soprano and orchestra)
Stage design: Axel Manthey
Stage design, lighting, and costumes: Axel Manthey
Text: W. H. Auden, A. E. Housman, Franz Kafka, and Friedrich Nietzsche
Premiere: 22 December 1979, Stuttgart Ballet, Stuttgart

1980

Joyleen Gets Up, Gets Down, Goes Out (one-act ballet)
Music: Boris Blacher, 'Blues, Espagnola und Rumba Philharmonica für 12
Solo Cellos'
Stage design: William Forsythe
Costumes: Eileen Brady
Premiere: 22 May 1980, Bavarian State Opera Ballet, Munich

Say Bye Bye (one-act ballet)
Music: Terry Riley and Stan Kenton's arrangement of 'The Peanut Vendor'
Sound Collage: William Forsythe
Stage design: Axel Manthey
Lighting: Joop Caboort
Costumes: Axel Manthey
Premiere: 26 November 1980, Nederlands Dans Theater, The Hague, The
Netherlands

'Tis A Pity She's A Whore (full-length ballet) after John Ford's play
of the same name (1633)
Music: Thomas Jahn
Stage design: William Forsythe and Randi Bubat
Lighting: Hans-Joachim Haas
Costumes: Eileen Brady and Randi Bubat
Premiere: Montepulciano, Italy

Famous Mother's Club (solo for Lynn Seymour)
Music: David Cunningham, 'I Want Money'
Premiere: London

1981

Whisper Moon (one-act ballet)
Choreography: William Forsythe and Axel Manthey
Music: William Bolcom, *Whisper Moon*, *Dream Music* No.3, and Quintet for
Violin, Violoncello, Flute, Clarinet and Piano
Stage design: Axel Manthey and William Forsythe
Lighting: Hans-Joachim Haas
Premiere: 12 April 1981, Stuttgart Ballet, Stuttgart

Tancred und Clorinda (one-act ballet)
Music: Claudio Monteverdi, *Il combattimento di Tancredi e Clorinda*
Musical Arrangement: Luciano Berio

Lighting: Hans-Joachim Haas
Costumes: William Forsythe
Text: Torquato Tasso
Premiere: 5 May 1981, Stuttgart Ballet, Stuttgart

Die Nacht aus Blei (full-length ballet)
Music: Hans-Jürgen von Bose
Stage design: Axel Manthey
Costumes: Axel Manthey
Text: Hans Henny Jahnn
Premiere: 1 November 1981, Ballet Deutsche Oper, Berlin

Event 1, 2, 3 (full-length ballet)
Choreography: William Forsythe and Ron Thornhill
Music Collage: William Forsythe and Ron Thornhill
Costumes: Rundi Bubat
Premiere: 1981, Wagenburg Tunnel, Stuttgarter Internationaler Kunst Kongress

1982

Gänge, ein Stück über Ballett (Part 1)
Music: William Forsythe, Dick Heuff, and Michael Simon
Stage design: Michael Simon
Lighting: Michael Simon
Costumes: Tom Schenk
Visual Direction: William Forsythe and Michael Simon
Premiere: 25 February 1982, Nederlands Dans Theater, The Hague, The Netherlands

1983

Gänge (full-length version)
Music: Thomas Jahn
Stage design: Michael Simon
Costumes: Randi Bubat, Igolf Thiel, and Tom Schenk
Premiere: 27 February 1983, Ballett Frankfurt, Frankfurt

Mental Model (one-act ballet)
Music: Igor Stravinsky, *Quatre Études pour Orchestre, Four Norwegian Moods, Scherzo à la Russe*
Stage design: William Forsythe
Lighting: William Forsythe and Joop Caboort

Costumes: Stephen Meaha
Premiere: 16 June 1983, Nederlands Dans Theater, The Hague, The Netherlands

Square Deal (one-act ballet)
Music: William Forsythe, Thomas Jahn, and Michael Simon
Arrangement for tempered piano and trombone: Thomas Jahn
Composition and visual effects: William Forsythe
Stage design: William Forsythe
Lighting: William Forsythe and Jennifer Tipton
Costumes: Douglas Ferguson
Slides: Arthur Brady
Premiere: 2 November 1983, Joffrey Ballet, New York

France/Dance (one-act ballet)
Music: Johann Sebastian Bach, *The Art of the Fugue*
Music collage: William Forsythe and Thom Willems
Stage design, lighting and costumes: William Forsythe
Objects and images: Cara Perlman
Premiere: 14 December 1983, Ballet de l'Opéra de Paris, Paris

1984

Artifact (full-length ballet)
Music Parts I and IV: Eva Crossman-Hecht; Part II: Johann Sebastian Bach, Chaconne from Partita No. 2 in D minor for solo violin (Nathan Milstein); Part III: sound collage by William Forsythe
Stage design, lighting, costumes, and text: William Forsythe
Premiere: 5 December 1984, Frankfurt

Berg Ab (a motion picture)
Project: Gerhard Benz, Alida Chase, William Forsythe, Cara Perlman, Marcus Spies, Ron Thornhill
Music: Alban Berg, *Three Pieces for Orchestra*, Op. 6
Premiere: 23 May 1984, Vienna

1985

Steptext (one-act ballet)
Music: Johann Sebastian Bach, Chaconne from Partita No. 2 in D minor
Stage design, lighting, and costumes: William Forsythe
Premiere: 11 January 1985, Aterballetto, Reggio Emilia, Italy

LDC (full-length ballet)

Music: Thom Willems
Stage design: Michael Simon
Lighting: Michael Simon and William Forsythe
Costumes: Benedikt Ramm
Premiere: 1 May 1985, Frankfurt

How To Recognize Greek Art I and II (pas de deux)

Music collage: William Forsythe
Premiere: 31 December 1985, Frankfurt

1986

Isabelle's Dance (full-length musical)

Music: Eva Crossman-Hecht
Lyrics: Eva Crossman-Hecht, William Forsythe, Sara Neece, and Stephen
Saugey
Stage design and lighting: Michael Simon
Costumes: Férial Simon
Premiere: 3 February 1986, Frankfurt

Pizza Girl (Ninety One-Minute Ballets)

Choreography: Alida Chase, William Forsythe, Stephen Galloway, Timothy
Gordon, Dieter Heitkamp, Evan Jones, Amanda Miller, Vivienne Newport,
Cara Perlman, Antony Rizzi, Ana Catalina Roman, Iris Tenge, Ron Thornhill
and Berna Uithof
Music: Thom Willems
Stage design: William Forsythe and Cara Perlman
Lighting: William Forsythe
Costumes: William Forsythe and Benedikt Ramm
Painting: Cara Perlman, 'Pizza Girl'
Premiere: 27 February 1986, Frankfurt

Skinny (one-act ballet)

Choreography: William Forsythe and Amanda Miller
Music: William Forsythe and Thom Willems
Stage design and lighting: William Forsythe
Costumes: William Forsythe and Amanda Miller
Text: William Forsythe
Premiere: 17 April 1986, Frankfurt

Baby Sam (one-act ballet)

Music: Thom Willems
Music Collage: William Forsythe
Stage design, lighting, and costumes: William Forsythe
Text: William Forsythe
Premiere: 21 May 1986, Bari, Italy

Die Befragung des Robert Scott (one-act ballet)

Music: Thom Willems
Stage design, lighting and costumes: William Forsythe
Text: William Forsythe
Premiere: 29 October 1986, Frankfurt

Big White Baby Dog (one-act ballet)

Music: Thom Willems
Stage design, lighting, and costumes: William Forsythe
Premiere: 10 November 1986, Frankfurt

1987

New Sleep (one-act ballet)

Music: Thom Willems
Stage design, lighting, and costumes: William Forsythe
Premiere: 1 February 1987, San Francisco Ballet, San Francisco

The Loss of Small Detail (version 1) (full-length ballet)

Music: Thom Willems
Stage design and lighting: William Forsythe
Costumes: Benedikt Ramm
Text: William Forsythe, David Levin, and Patrick Primavesi
Digital gloves: Michel Waisvisz
Premiere: 4 April 1987, Frankfurt

In The Middle, Somewhat Elevated (one-act ballet)

Music: Thom Willems in collaboration with Leslie Stuck
Stage design, lighting, and costumes: William Forsythe
Premiere: 30 May 1987, Ballet de l'Opéra de Paris, Paris

Same Old Story (one act ballet)

Music: Thom Willems
Stage design, lighting, and costumes: William Forsythe
Text: Nicholas Champion, Kathleen Fitzgerald, and William Forsythe

Premiere: 5 June 1987, Ballett Frankfurt, Hamburg

1988

Impressing The Czar (full-length ballet)
(Part I: *Potemkins Unterschrift;* Part II: *In the Middle, Somewhat Elevated;* Part III: *La Maison de Mezzo-Prezzo;* Part IV: *Bongo Bongo Nageela* and *Mr. Pnut Goes to the Big Top)*
Music: Ludwig van Beethoven, Leslie Stuck, Thom Willems, and Eva Crossman-Hecht
Stage design: Michael Simon and William Forsythe
Lighting: William Forsythe and Michael Simon
Costumes: Férial Simon
Text: William Forsythe, Richard Fein, and Kathleen Fitzgerald
Premiere: 10 January 1988, Frankfurt

Behind the China Dogs (one-act ballet)
Music: Leslie Stuck
Lighting: William Forsythe
Costumes: William Forsythe and Barbara Matera
China dogs: Cara Perlman
Premiere: 7 May 1988, New York City Ballet, New York

The Vile Parody of Address (one-act ballet)
Stage design, lighting, and costumes: William Forsythe
Text: William Forsythe
Premiere: 26 November 1988, Frankfurt

1989

Enemy in the Figure (one-act ballet)
Music: Thom Willems
Stage design, lighting, and costumes: William Forsythe
Premiere: 13 May 1989, Frankfurt

Slingerland (Part I)
Music: Gavin Bryars, *Three Viennese Dancers* and String Quartet No.1
Stage design and film: Cara Perlman
Lighting and costumes: William Forsythe
Premiere: 25 November 1989, Frankfurt

1990

Limb's Theorem (contains *Enemy in the Figure*) (full-length ballet)

Music: Thom Willems
Stage design: Michael Simon (Parts I and III) and William Forsythe (Part II)
Lighting: William Forsythe and Michael Simon
Costumes: Férial Simon (Parts I and III) and William Forsythe (Part II)
Premiere: 17 March 1990, Frankfurt

Slingerland (Parts I–III) (full-length ballet in three acts)

Music: Thom Willems, Gavin Bryars
Stage design, lighting, and costumes: William Forsythe
Objects and images: Cara Perlman
Premiere: 25 June 1990, Amsterdam

Slingerland (Parts I–IV) (full-length ballet in four acts)

Music: Thom Willems, Gavin Bryars
Stage design, lighting, costumes: William Forsythe
Objects and images: Cara Perlman
Premiere: 20 October 1990, Paris

1991

The Second Detail (one-act ballet)

Music: Thom Willems
Stage design and lighting: William Forsythe
Costumes: William Forsythe; 'Colombe' white dress by Issey Miyake
Premiere: 20 February 1991, National Ballet of Canada, Toronto

Snap. Woven Effort (one-act ballet)

Music: Thom Willems
Stage design and lighting: William Forsythe
Costumes: Gianni Versace
Text: William Forsythe
Premiere: 26 October 1991, Frankfurt

Marion/Marion (duet)

Music: Bernard Herman, *Temptation No. 5* (music from Hitchcock's *Psycho*)
Stage design and lighting: William Forsythe
Costumes: Gianni Versace
Premiere: 8 November 1991, Nederlands Dans Theater III, The Hague, The
Netherlands

The Loss of Small Detail (full-length ballet in two acts)
(incorporates *The Second Detail*)

Music: Thom Willems
Stage design and lighting: William Forsythe
Costumes: Issey Miyake
Text: William Forsythe, Yukio Mishima *(Runaway Horses)*, and Jérôme Rothenberg *(Technicians of the Sacred)*
Film: Helga Funderl *(Hund im Schnee)* and Fiona Léus *(Between Mediums)*
Premiere: 21 December 1991, Frankfurt

1992

Herman Schmerman (pas de cinq)

Music: Thom Willems *Just Ducky*
Stage design: William Forsythe
Lighting: Marc Stanley
Costumes: Gianni Versace
Premiere: 28 May 1992, New York City Ballet, New York

Herman Schmerman (pas de deux)

Music: Thom Willems
Stage design and lighting: William Forsythe
Costumes: Gianni Versace
Premiere: 26 September 1992, Frankfurt

As a Garden in This Setting (one-act ballet)

Music: Thom Willems
Stage design and lighting: William Forsythe
Costumes: Issey Miyake and Naoki Takizawa
Video: Sean Toren
Premiere: 13 June 1992, Frankfurt

Alien/a(c)tion (full-length ballet)

Music: Arnold Schönberg and Thom Willems
Stage design: William Forsythe
Lighting: William Forsythe
Costumes: Steven Galloway
Video: Sean Toren
Computer programming: David Kern
Premiere: 19 December 1992, Frankfurt; new version 5 November 1993, Frankfurt

1993

Quintett (one-act ballet)
Choreography: William Forsythe in collaboration with Dana Caspersen,
Stephen Galloway, Jacopo Godani, Thomas McManus, and Jone San Martin
Music: Gavin Bryars, *Jesus's Blood Never Failed Me Yet*
Stage design and lighting: William Forsythe
Costumes: Stephen Galloway
Premiere: 9 October 1993, Frankfurt

As a Garden in This Setting (full-length version)
Music: Thom Willems
Stage design and lighting: William Forsythe
Costumes: Issey Miyake and Naoki Takizawa
Dramaturgical assistance: Steven Valk
Premiere: 18 December 1993, Frankfurt

1994

Self Meant To Govern (one-act ballet)
Music: Thom Willems in collaboration with Maxim Franke
Stage design and lighting: William Forsythe
Costumes: Stephen Galloway
Violin: Maxim Franke
Premiere: 2 July 1994, Frankfurt

Pivot House (one-act ballet)
Music: Kraton Surakarta, *Sirimpi* (Provisions for Death)
Stage design and lighting: William Forsythe
Costumes: Stephen Galloway
Video: Richard Caon
Premiere: 13 December 1994, Reggio Emilia, Italy

1995

Eidos : Telos (full-length ballet in three acts)
(contains *Self Meant to Govern*)
Choreography: William Forsythe in collaboration with the ensemble
Music and processing: Thom Willems in collaboration with Maxim Franke
(Part I); Thom Willems in collaboration with Joel Ryan (Parts II and III)
Assistant: Dirk Haubrich
Stage design and lighting: William Forsythe
Costumes: Stephen Galloway (Part II) and Naoki Takizawa (Miyake Design
Studio)

Text: Monologue, Part II, Dana Caspersen; additional texts Part II, William Forsythe
Premiere: 28 January 1995, Frankfurt

Firstext (one-act ballet)

Choreography: Dana Caspersen, William Forsythe, and Antony Rizzi
Music: Thom Willems
Stage design and lighting: William Forsythe
Costumes: Naoki Takizawa and Raymond Dragon Design Inc.
Premiere: 27 April 1995, The Royal Ballet, London

Invisible Film (one-act ballet)

Music: Johann Sebastian Bach, *Goldberg Variations;* George Frideric Handel, Concerti Grossi, Op. 6; Henry Purcell, *Fantazias, In Nomines*
Stage design and lighting: William Forsythe
Costumes: Stephen Galloway
Text: William Forsythe and pop music texts
Speaker: David Morrow
Premiere: 27 May 1995, Frankfurt

Of Any If And (one-act ballet)

Music: Thom Willems
Stage design and lighting: William Forsythe
Costumes: Stephen Galloway
Text: Dana Caspersen and William Forsythe
Premiere: 27 May 1995, Frankfurt

The The (duet)

Choreography: Dana Caspersen and William Forsythe
Stage design and lighting: William Forsythe
Costumes: Stephen Galloway
Premiere: 8 October 1995, The Hague, The Netherlands

Four Point Counter (one-act ballet)

Music: Thom Willems
Stage design and lighting: William Forsythe
Costumes: Stephen Galloway
Premiere: 16 November 1995, Nederlands Dans Theater, The Hague, The Netherlands

1996

Duo

Music: Thom Willems
Stage design, lighting, and costumes: William Forsythe
Premiere: 20 January 1996, Frankfurt

Trio

Music: Ludwig van Beethoven, String Quartet No. 15 in A minor, op. 132, and Alban Berg, String Quartet, op 3.
Stage design and lighting: William Forsythe
Costumes: Stephen Galloway
Premiere: 20 January 1996, Frankfurt

Approximate Sonata (one-act ballet)

Music: Thom Willems and Tricky
Stage design and lighting: William Forsythe
Costumes: Stephen Galloway
Premiere: 20 January 1996, Frankfurt

The Vertiginous Thrill of Exactitude (one-act ballet)

Music: Franz Schubert, Symphony No. 9 in C major, 3rd movement
Stage design and lighting: William Forsythe
Costumes: Stephen Galloway
Premiere: 20 January 1996, Frankfurt

Sleepers Guts (full-length ballet in three acts)

Choreography: William Forsythe in collaboration with the ensemble (Part I); William Forsythe (Part II); Jacopo Godani (Part III)
Music: Thom Willems and Joel Ryan
Digital music composition: Joel Ryan and Dirk Haubrich
Music assistant: Chris Salter
Stage design and lighting: William Forsythe
Costumes: Stephen Galloway
Video: Nik Haffner and Bill Seaman
Projection graphics: Mark Goulthorpe
Premiere: 25 October 1996, Frankfurt

1997

Hypothetical Stream II (one-act ballet)

Choreography: William Forsythe, Regina van Berkel, Christine Bürkle, Ana Catalina Roman, Jone San Martin, Timothy Couchman, Noah Gelber, Jacopo Godani, Antony Rizzi, and Richard Siegal
Music: Stuart Dempster, *Standing Waves* and Ingram Marshall, *Fog Tropes*
Stage design and lighting: William Forsythe
Costumes: Stephen Galloway
Premiere: 14 September 1997, Frankfurt

1998

Small Void (one-act ballet)

Choreography: William Forsythe in collaboration with Stefanie Arndt, Alan Barnes, Dana Caspersen, Noah Gelber, Anders Hellström, Fabrice Mazliah, Tamas Moritz, Crystal Pite, Jone San Martin, Richard Siegal, Pascal Touzeau, and Sjoerd Vreudghenhil
Music: Thom Willems
Stage design and lighting: William Forsythe
Costumes: Stephen Galloway
Premiere: 30 January 1998, Frankfurt

Opus 31 (one-act ballet)

Music: Arnold Schönberg, Variations for Orchestra, op. 31
Stage design and lighting: William Forsythe
Costumes: Stephen Galloway
Premiere: 30 January 1998, Frankfurt

Quartetto (one-act ballet)

Music: Thom Willems
Stage design and lighting: William Forsythe
Costumes: Stephen Galloway
Premiere: 8 September 1998, Balletto del Teatro alla Scala di Milano, Milan

workwithinwork (one-act ballet)

Music: Luciano Berio, *Duetti* for two violins (1983)
Stage design and lighting: William Forsythe
Costumes: Stephen Galloway
Premiere: 16 October 1998, Frankfurt

Quartette (one-act ballet)

Music: Thom Willems

Stage design and lighting: William Forsythe
Costumes: Stephen Galloway
Premiere: 16 October 1998, Frankfurt

1999

Woundwork 1 (one-act ballet)
Music: Thom Willems
Stage design and lighting: William Forsythe
Costumes: Stephen Galloway
Premiere: 31 March 1999, Ballet de l'Opéra de Paris, Paris

Pas./parts (one-act ballet)
Music: Thom Willems
Stage design and lighting: William Forsythe
Costumes: Stephen Galloway
Premiere: 31 March 1999, Ballet de l'Opéra de Paris, Paris

Endless House (full-length work in two parts)
Part I
Directed by: Dana Caspersen
Music: Kraton Surakarta, *Sirimpi* (Provisions for Death)
Stage design and lighting: William Forsythe
Text: Charles Manson
Premiere: 15 October 1999, Opera House, Frankfurt

Part II
Choreography: William Forsythe
Music: *Autopoiesis*, Ekkehard Ehlers, Sebastian Meissner, and Thom Willems
Stage design and lighting: William Forsythe
Costumes: Stephen Galloway
Direction: William Forsythe
Sound design: Bernhard Klein, Dietrich Krüger, and Niels Lanz
Text: Emily Brontë, Dana Caspersen, William Forsythe, and Charles Manson
Dramaturgical assistance: Dana Caspersen and Steven Valk
Premiere: 15 October 1999, Bockenheimer Depot, Frankfurt

2000

Die Befragung des Robert Scott (new evening-length version)
(contains *One Flat Thing, reproduced*)
Music: Thom Willems
Stage design and lighting: William Forsythe
Costumes: Stephen Galloway

Premiere: 2 February 2000, Frankfurt

One Flat Thing, reproduced (one-act ballet)
Music: Thom Willems
Stage design and lighting: William Forsythe
Costumes: Stephen Galloway
Premiere: 2 February 2000, Bockenheimer Depot, Frankfurt

7 to 10 Passages (one-act ballet)
Music: Thom Willems
Stage design and lighting: William Forsythe
Text: William Forsythe and Edgar Allen Poe
Premiere: 23 February 2000, Frankfurt

Kammer/Kammer (full-length work)
Directed by: William Forsythe
Music: Johann Sebastian Bach, Heinrich von Bieber, Georg Philipp Telemann, Johann Sebastian Bach/Ferruccio Busoni, Thom Willems, and Lynn Anderson, *Cry*
Stage design, lighting, and costumes: William Forsythe
Film: Martin Schwember, *First Touch*
Video software 'Image/ine': Tom Demeyer/S.T.E.I.M.
Video design: Philip Bussmann
Live video coordination: Agnieszka Trojak
Camera: Ursula Maurer
Sound design: Joel Ryan
Piano: David Morrow
Text: Anne Carson, 'Irony is not enough: Essay on My Life as Catherine Deneuve' (2nd draft) and Douglas A. Martin, *Outline of My Lover*
Premiere: 8 December 2000, Bockenheimer Depot, Frankfurt

2001

Woolf Phrase (one-act ballet)
Music: Ekkehard Ehlers, Thom Willems
Stage design, lighting, and costumes: William Forsythe
Sound design: Bernhard Klein
Text: William Forsythe and Virginia Woolf, *Mrs Dalloway*
Premiere: 15 March 2001, Frankfurt

Woolf Phrase (evening-length version)
Music: Part 1: Thom Willems; Part 2: William Forsythe and David Morrow

Stage design, lighting, and costumes: William Forsythe
Piano: David Morrow
Sound design: Bernhard Klein, Dietrich Krüger, and Niels Lanz
Text: William Forsythe and Virginia Woolf, *Mrs Dalloway*
Premiere: 21 September 2001, Frankfurt

2002

The Room As it Was (one-act ballet)

Music: Thom Willems
Stage design and lighting: William Forsythe
Costumes: Stephen Galloway
Premiere: 14 February 2002, Frankfurt

Double/Single (one-act ballet)

Music: Johann Sebastian Bach
Stage design, lighting, and costumes: William Forsythe
Violin: Nathan Milstein
Premiere: 14 April 2002, Amsterdam

33/3 (one-act ballet)

Music: Thom Willems in collaboration with Olivier Sliepen
Stage design, lighting, and costumes: William Forsythe
Tap consultant: Holly Brubach
Saxophone: Olivier Sliepen
Premiere: 11 September 2002, Frankfurt

N.N.N.N. (one-act ballet)

Music: Thom Willems
Stage design, lighting, and costumes: William Forsythe
Premiere: 21 November 2002, Opera House, Frankfurt

2003

Decreation (full-length ballet)

Music: David Morrow
Stage design: William Forsythe
Lighting: Jan Walther and William Forsythe
Costumes: Claudia Hill
Video design: Philip Bußmann
Sound design: Niels Lanz and Bernhard Klein
Dramaturgy: Rebecca Groves
Premiere: 27 April 2003, Frankfurt

Ricercar (one-act ballet)

Music: David Morrow, variations of Johann Sebastian Bach, 'Ricercar a 6' from *The Musical Offering*
Stage design, lighting, and costumes: William Forsythe
Piano: David Morrow
Premiere: 13 November 2003, Frankfurt

2004

Wear (one-act ballet)

Music: Ryoji Ikeda, Op. 1 performed live by Ensemble Modern
Stage design and lighting: William Forsythe
Costumes: Yasco Otomo
Premiere: 22 January 2004, Bockenheimer Depot, Frankfurt

we live here (one-act ballet)

By and with: Yoko Ando, Cyril Baldy, Francesca Caroti, Dana Caspersen, Mauricio de Oliveira, William Forsythe, Stephen Galloway, Amancio Gonzalez, Rebecca Groves, Thierry Guiderdoni, Ayman Harper, Sang Jijia, David Kern, Dietrich Krüger, Marthe Krummenacher, Brock Labrenz, Vanessa le Mat, Jone San Martin, Fabrice Mazliah, Georg Reischl, Heidi Vierthaler, Jan Walther, Thom Willems, and Ander Zabala
Premiere: 19 April 2004, Frankfurt

2005

woundwork II (one-act ballet)

Music: Thom Willems
Stage design and lighting: William Forsythe
Costumes: Issey Miyake
Premiere: 16 June 2005, Staatsschauspiel Dresden, Dresden

Clouds after Cranach (full-length ballet in two acts)

Music: David Morrow
Stage design, lighting, and costumes: William Forsythe
Sound design: Dietrich Krüger and Niels Lanz
Voice treatment, DSP programming: Andreas Breitscheid and Manuel Poletti in collaboration with the Forum Neues Musiktheater Staatsoper Stuttgart
Speakers: Amancio Gonzalez, David Kern, and Jone San Martin
Text: William Forsythe
Premiere: 26 November 2005, Bockenheimer Depot, Frankfurt

2006

Three Atmospheric Studies (full-length ballet in three acts) *Parts I and II: Clouds after Cranach; Part III: Study III*

Music, Part II: David Morrow; Part III: Thom Willems
Stage design and lighting: William Forsythe
Costumes: Satoru Choko and Dorothee Merg
Sound design and synthesis: Dietrich Krüger and Niels Lanz
Voice treatment, DSP programming: Andreas Breitscheid, Oliver Pasquet, and Manuel Poletti in collaboration with the Forum Neues Musiktheater Staatsoper Stuttgart
Speakers, Part II: Amancio Gonzalez, David Kern, and Jone San Martin; Part III: Dana Caspersen, David Kern, and Ander Zabala
Text, Part III: Dana Caspersen, William Forsythe, and David Kern
Premiere: 2 February 2006, *spielzeiteuropa,* Haus der Berliner Festspiele, Berlin

Heterotopia (full-length ballet in one act)

Music: Thom Willems
Costumes: Dorothee Merg
Sound design: Dietrich Krüger and Niels Lanz
Dramaturgy: Freya Vass-Rhee
Premiere: 25 October 2006, Schauspielhaus Zürich, Zurich

Rong (one-act ballet)

Music: Silkk the Shocker featuring Mystikal, Prince
Stage design and lighting: William Forsythe
Costumes: Dorothee Merg and Gianni Versace
Premiere: 22 November 2006, Bockenheimer Depot, Frankfurt

2007

Fivefold (one-act ballet)

Music composed and performed by: David Morrow
Costumes: Dorothee Merg
Premiere: 1 February 2007, Festspielhaus Hellerau, Dresden

Angoloscuro/Camerascura (full-length ballet in two parts)

Music: Thom Willems
Stage design and lighting: William Forsythe
Costumes: William Forsythe, Dorothee Merg, and Issey Miyake
Software design: Andeas Breitscheid
Sound design: Niels Lanz
Glass harp music: Anna Tenta and David Kern

Video direction: Philip Bußmann
Video design: Philip Bußmann, William Forsythe, and Dietrich Krüger
Assistant, camera programming: Hubert Machnik
Assistant, stage design Part 1: Susanne Brenner
Fabric design: Mina Perhonen
Dramaturgy: Freya Vass-Rhee
Premiere: 3 May 2007, Bockenheimer Depot, Frankfurt

The Defenders (full-length ballet in one act)

Music: Dietrich Krüger and Thom Willems
Stage design: William Forsythe
Lighting: Tanja Rühl
Costumes: Dorothee Merg
Technical realisation: Max Schubert
Sound: Dietrich Krüger
Dramaturgy: Imanuel Schipper and Freya Vass-Rhee
Premiere: 4 November 2007, Schiffbau Halle I, Zurich

Nowhere and Everywhere at the Same Time (new full-length version)
Premiere: 16 November 2007, Bockenheimer Depot, Frankfurt

2008

Yes We Can't (full-length ballet in one act)

Music: Dietrich Krüger, Niels Lanz, and David Morrow
Lighting: Ulf Naumann and Tanja Rühl,
Costumes: Dorothee Merg
Production assistance: Thierry Guiderdoni and Freya Vass-Rhee
Production scoring software: David Kern
Premiere: 5 March 2008, Festspielhaus Hellerau, Dresden

I don't believe in outer space (full-length ballet in one act)

Music: Thom Willems
Stage design: William Forsythe
Lighting: Tanja Rühl and Ulf Naumann
Costumes: Dorothee Merg
Sound design: Niels Lanz
Graphics: Dietrich Krüger
Dramaturgical assistance: Freya Vass-Rhee
Additional Text: Dana Caspersen, Tilman O'Donnell, and William Forsythe
Premiere: 20 November 2008, Bockenheimer Depot, Frankfurt

2009

Angoloscuro (full-length ballet in one act) (new version)

Music: Thom Willems
Stage design and lighting: William Forsythe
Costumes: William Forsythe, Dorothee Merg, and Issey Miyake
Sound design: Niels Lanz
Assistant, stage design: Susanne Brenner
Dramaturgical assistance: Freya Vass-Rhee
Premiere: 12 February 2009, Bockenheimer Depot, Frankfurt

The Returns

Music: Dietrich Krüger, Sebastian Rietz, Thom Willems, and Ricky Lee Jones
Stage design: William Forsythe
Lighting: Ulf Naumann and Tanja Rühl
Costumes: William Forsythe, Stephen Galloway, and Dorothee Merg
Piano: David Morrow
Graphic design: Dietrich Krüger
Dramaturgical assistance: Freya Vass-Rhee
Premiere: 24 June 2009, Festspielhaus Hellerau, Dresden

Theatrical Arsenal II (full-length ballet in two acts)

Music: Thom Willems
Lighting: Tanja Rühl and Ulf Naumann
Costumes: Stephan Galloway
Sound design: Niels Lanz
Video: Dietrich Krüger
Texts: William Forsythe
Premiere: 20 November 2009, Bockenheimer Depot, Frankfurt

2010

Yes We Can't (full-length ballet in one act) (new version)

Music: David Morrow
Lighting: Ulf Naumann and Tanja Rühl,
Costumes: Dorothee Merg
Production assistance: Thierry Guiderdoni and Freya Vass-Rhee
Premiere: 16 April 2010, Mercat de Flors, Barcelona

Two Part Invention (solo)

Music: Thom Willems
Dancer: Noah P. Gelber
Premiere: 10 April 2009, Dance Salad Festival, Houston, Texas

Whole in the Head

Music: Thom Willems
Lighting: Tanja Rühl and Ulf Naumann
Costumes: Dorothee Merg
Premiere: 18 November 2010, Bockenheimer Depot, Frankfurt

Installations

1989

Book N(7): Dance/Mechanics/3pm/Streets/Red Flame/Erato
Choreographic object for Daniel Libeskind's *The Books of Groningen*, 1989

1997

White Bouncy Castle (originally *Tight Roaring Circle*)
Installation by Dana Caspersen, William Forsythe, and Joel Ryan
Co-production with Group.ie
Originally commissioned by Artangel, London
Premiere: 26 March 1997, The Roundhouse, London

Solo (film)
Choreography and performance: William Forsythe
Music: Thom Willems, in collaboration with Maxime Franke
Director: Thomas Lovell Balogh
Camera: Jess Hall
Production: RD-Studio Productions, France 2, and BBC TV 1997

From a Classical Position (film)
Choreography, performance and direction: Dana Caspersen and William Forsythe
Music: Thom Willems
Produced by Deborah Hauer for Euphoria Films, 1997
Editor: Jo Ann Kaplan

First broadcast 13 April 1998 as part of 'Dance on Four' in the UK

2000

City of Abstracts (choreographic object)
Video software development: Philip Bußmann
Premiere: 24 November 2000, Opernplatz/Hauptwache, Frankfurt

2002

Scattered Crowd (installation)
Music: Ekkehard Ehlers
Production manager: Julian Gabriel Richter
Premiere: 15 March 2002, Messe Frankfurt, Hall 7, Frankfurt

2003

Instructions (public choreography)
Premiere: 4 October 2003, Nuit Blanche, Paris

2005

Hausführung
Performer: William Forsythe
Premiere: 18 January, 2005, Bockenheimer Depot, Frankfurt

You made me a monster (performance installation)
A production by The Forsythe Company in co-production with la Biennale di Venezia and Tanz im August 2005 – Internationales Tanzfest Berlin
Supported by Siemens Arts Program
Directed by: William Forsythe
Video: Philip Bußmann
Sound: Dietrich Krüger, Niels Lanz, and Hubert Machnik
Technical and lighting: Michael JIV Wagner
Stage design management: Marion Rossi
Voice treatment, DSP programming: Andreas Breitscheid and Manuel Poletti in collaboration with the Forum Neues Musiktheater Staatsoper Stuttgart
Performers: David Kern, Roberta Mosca, Nicole Peisl, and Christopher Roman
Premiere: 28 May 2005, Teatro Piccolo Arsenale, Venice, Italy

Nowhere and Everywhere at the Same Time (installation performance)
Music: Thom Willems
Performer: Brock Labrenz
Premiere: 14 October 2005, Creative Time, The Plain of Heaven, New York

Human Writes (choreographic installation)
Concept: William Forsythe and Kendall Thomas
Music: Thom Willems
Design: William Forsythe

Sound design: Dietrich Krüger, Niels Lanz, and Thom Willems
Premiere: 23 October 2005, Schauspielhaus Zürich, Schiffbauhalle 1, Zurich

2006

Monster Partitur (choregraphic object)

Sound: Dietrich Krüger, Niels Lanz, and Hubert Machnik
Construction supervision: Marion Rossi
Voice treatment, DSP programming: Andreas Breitscheid and Manuel Poletti
in collaboration with the Forum Neues Musiktheater Staatsoper Stuttgart
Premiere: 26 April 2006, Pinakothek der Moderne, Munich

2007

Additive Inverse (choregraphic object)

Music: Thom Willems
Production: The Forsythe Company and 21_21 Design Sight, Tokyo
Premiere: 7 April 2007, 21_21 Design Sight, Tokyo

Antipodes I / II (video)

Music: Ryoji Ikeda
Camera: Holger Detmering
Premiere: 16 May 2006, Pinakothek der Moderne, Munich

Flandona Gagnole (choregraphic installation)

Music: Thom Willems
Premiere: 19 October 2007, Festspielhaus Hellerau, Dresden

Hinderhold (choregraphic installation)

Music: Thom Willems
Performers: Students of Dance Apprenticeship Network aCross Europe
(D.A.N.C.E.)
Premiere: 19th October 2007, Festspielhaus Hellerau, Dresden

Thematic Variations on One Flat Thing, reproduced (film)

Directed by: Thierry de Mey
Premiere: 19 October 2007, Festspielhaus Hellerau, Dresden

Theatrical Arsenal (performance installation)

Premiere: 19 October 2007, Festspielhaus Hellerau, Dresden

2008

Gamelan/Schleife (choreographic object)
In collaboration with Dietrich Krüger
Premiere: 17 May 2008, Ursula Blickle Foundation, Kraichtal

I don't believe in outer space (choreographic object)
Premiere: 17 May 2008, Ursula Blickle Foundation, Kraichtal

Suspense (film)
Camera: Dietrich Krüger
Premiere: 17 May 2008, Ursula Blickle Foundation, Kraichtal

The Defenders Part 2 (choreographic object)
Sound: Thom Willems and Dietrich Krüger
Premiere: 17 May 2008, Ursula Blickle Foundation, Kraichtal

Bookmaking (video)
Camera: Dietrich Krüger
Premiere: 17 May 2008, Ursula Blickle Foundation, Kraichtal

2009

Behaupten ist anders als Glauben (choreographic object)
In collaboration with Dietrich Krüger
Premiere: 16 April 2009, Springdance Festival, Centraalmuseum, Utrecht

The Defenders Part 3 (choreographic object)
Premiere: 16 April 2009, Springdance Festival, Centraalmuseum, Utrecht

The Fact of Matter (choreographic object)
By The Forsythe Company with the Venice Art Biennale, and the Ursula Blickle Stiftung
Premiere: 6 June 2009, 53rd Art Exhibition, Fare Mondi, Venice

Collide-oscope (choreographic object)
Video software design: Philip Bußmann
Premiere: 9 December 2009, Grimaldi Forum, Monaco

2010

Hommage to Steina and Woody Vasulka (video)
Video software development: Philip Bußmann
Premiere: 22 June 2010, Musée Fabre, Montpelier

2011

KNOTUNKNOT
Dana Caspersen and William Forsythe
The Forsythe Company in cooperation with Frankfurter Positionen
Premiere: 21 January 2011, Frankfurt

Exhibitions

2006

Proliferation and Perfect Disorder

A project by the Pinakothek der Moderne in coproduction with the Bavarian
State Ballet and The Forsythe Company.
Curators: Dr. Bernhart Schwenk and Bettina Wagner-Bergelt
26 April–4 June 2006, Pinakothek der Moderne, Munich

2007

Equivalence
Spatial, and video installations by William Forsythe
19–21, and 24–28 October 2007, Festspielhaus Hellerau, Dresden

2008

Suspense
William Forsythe in collaboration with Markus Weisbeck
Catalogue: JRP Ringier Kunstverlag
18 May–29 June 2008, Ursula Blickle Stiftung, Kraichtal

2009

Transfigurations
Curated by Charles Helms
2 April–26 July 2009, Wexner Center for the Arts, Columbus

Index